SADSAWU demonstration at the gates of Parliament; Cape Town, March 2001. Photograph by author.

Endorsements

If our democracy acknowledges and promotes human rights, there is no way to sideline women's rights. Through the powerful voices of South African women, this book captures the struggle for domestic workers to gain social, economic and political equality. Fish's research reveals how domestic labour remains one of the greatest challenges to gender transformation in South Africa.

—Pumla Mncayi, Director, Gender Advocacy Programme, South Africa

Nowhere is the contradiction of race relations in post-apartheid South Africa more apparent then in the "gendered institution of paid domestic labor." In *Domestic Democracy*, Jennifer Fish explores how black women's invisible labor reproduces white South Africans' daily lives and examines the significance of black South African women's absence within discussions of post-apartheid reconstruction. Her in-depth exploration of the gender, race, and class politics of paid domestic labor demonstrates how the experiences of black South African women are shaped by and, in turn, contour the larger political context. While Fish analyzes how this form of labor remains the "last bastion of apartheid," she also highlights how domestic workers are organizing to challenge the structural inequalities and to insert their demands for social change into the democratization process. Drawing on ten years of ethnographic observation, archival research, and interviews with 85 respondents, Fish convincingly argues for policy changes as well as the need for more central attention to patterns of class inequality and patterns of gender and racialized differences.

—Nancy A. Naples, author of *Grassroots Warriors: Activist Mothering, Community Work, and the War on Poverty* and *Feminism and Method: Ethnography, Discourse Analysis, and Activist Research*

Domestic Democracy is a stunningly brilliant example of how the intimate everyday interaction of maids and madams measures the maintenance, transformation, and elimination of apartheid. Jennifer Fish's insightful analysis captures all the nuances of changing hierarchies of race, class and religion in South Africa's post-apartheid reconstruction. The voices of women as workers, labor organizers, and activists present us with both the challenges and the promise for the new South Africa.

—Mary Romero, Arizona State University, author of *Maid in the USA*

NEW APPROACHES IN SOCIOLOGY
STUDIES IN SOCIAL INEQUALITY, SOCIAL CHANGE, AND SOCIAL JUSTICE

Edited by

Nancy A. Naples
University of Connecticut

A ROUTLEDGE SERIES

New Approaches in Sociology
Studies in Social Inequality, Social Change, and Social Justice

Nancy A. Naples, *General Editor*

DOMESTIC DEMOCRACY
At Home in South Africa

Jennifer Natalie Fish

Routledge
New York & London

Published in 2006 by
Routledge
Taylor & Francis Group
711 Third Avenue
New York, NY 10017

Published in Great Britain by
Routledge
Taylor & Francis Group
2 Park Square
Milton Park, Abingdon
Oxon OX14 4RN

First issued in paperback 2013

International Standard Book Number-10: 0-415-97513-1 (Hardcover)
International Standard Book Number-13: 978-0-415-97513-1 (Hardcover)
International Standard Book Number-13: 978-0-415-64908-7 (Paperback)
Library of Congress Card Number 2005020588

Library of Congress Cataloging-in-Publication Data

Fish, Jennifer Natalie.
    Domestic democracy : at home in South Africa / Jennifer Natalie Fish.-- 1st ed.
        p. cm. -- (New approaches in sociology)
    Includes bibliographical references and index.
    ISBN: 978-0-415-97513-1
    1. Women domestics--South Africa. 2. Democratization--South Africa. 3. Social change--South Africa. I. Title. II. Series.

HD6072.2.S6F57 2005
331.4'8164046'0968--dc22
                                                      2005020588

informa
Taylor & Francis Group
is the Academic Division of Informa plc.

Visit the Taylor & Francis Web site at
http://www.taylorandfrancis.com

and the Routledge Web site at
http://www.routledge-ny.com

In dedication to the memory of
Judith Mae McFarland Fish (1937–2005)

Contents

List of Figures and Tables

FIGURES

TABLES

List of Abbreviations

ANC	African National Congress
BCEA	Basic Conditions of Employment Act
CEDAW	Convention on the Elimination of All Forms of Discrimination Against Women
CGE	Commission on Gender Equality
COSATU	Congress of South African Trade Unions
DA	Democratic Alliance
DWA	Domestic Workers Association
DWEP	Domestic Workers Education Project
GEAR	Growth, Employment and Redistribution
GMAC	Gender Monitoring and Advocacy Coalition
GMAC-UIF	Gender Monitoring and Advocacy Coalition on the Unemployment Insurance Fund
MP	Member of Parliament
NP	National Party
R	South African Rand (currency)
RDP	Reconstruction and Development Programme
SADSAWU	South African Domestic Service and Allied Workers Union
SADWA	South African Domestic Workers Association
SADWU	South African Domestic Workers Union
TRC	Truth and Reconciliation Commission
UIF	Unemployment Insurance Fund

Acknowledgments

I wish to thank a number of individuals who have supported this book throughout my intellectual journey. For their academic mentoring, guidance and early belief in this work, I am grateful to Bette J. Dickerson and Gay Young. Their scholarship and commitments remain a source of great inspiration. Wendy Bokhorst-Heng was pivotal to the completion of this project through her insightful feedback and unwavering emotional support. I thank a number of individuals who offered invaluable reflections on earlier versions of this work: Linda Carty, Beverley Mullings, Lily Ling and Andrea Brenner. Hannah Britton's consistent support, intellectual companionship and poignant insights take form throughout this book. I am profoundly thankful to Lauren Eastwood for her continual encouragement, academic enthusiasm and impeccable review of every page of this book.

I would like to express my deep appreciation to Mary Romero for mentoring this book through invaluable reflections on its development. Her pioneering scholarship has provided an intellectual role model throughout this entire process. My sincere gratitude extends to Nancy Naples for her visionary work on this series, as well as her commitment to merging scholarship and activism. I thank Benjamin Holtzman at Routledge for his support in the completion of this book.

In South Africa, I am appreciative of the academic community at the Centre for African Studies and the African Gender Institute at the University of Cape Town. I thank Elaine Salo, Amina Mama and Helen Moffett for their valuable input on this project. I wish to also thank a number of individuals in South Africa who provided rich insights about the broader context of my study over the past ten years: Vuyo Sontashe, Bill Blunt, Anita and Justice Majola, Elize Kock, Ndidi Violent Zandi, Pumla Mncayi, Ashleigh Murphy and Catherine Clark.

My greatest appreciation is extended to the participants in this study—who trusted me with their life stories, and the deeply personal apartheid legacies within them. In particular, I thank Myrtle Witbooi, Hester Stephens, Ntombizanele Felicia Msila, Nontsikelelo Adelaide Buso, Sabina Stephens and Johanna Gouws, who so valuably facilitated the collection of these interviews.

I would also like to recognize those individuals who have supported me throughout this journey: Chadwick Fleck, Betsy Kummer, Tiffany Montavon, Elizabeth Powley, Eric Tammes, Jeff Romanoski, Amy LeJeune, and Vicki Nesper. Jennifer Rothchild provided immeasurable encouragement, profound *reflections* and partnership throughout this entire project. The realization of this book is a result of her central investment in *every* phase. I am especially grateful to Karin Dekker, who shared my earliest travel to South Africa. *Ik zal je daar altijd dankbaar voor zijn.*

I am grateful to my parents, James and Judith Fish, for their continual encouragement to realize this life goal. Most of all, I thank Daniel O'Leary. His understanding, unwavering support and continual belief nourished me throughout this *entire* project.

Chronology of South Africa's Significant Historical Events

This chronology contextualizes the events in South Africa's history most relevant to this study. The creation of the apartheid state, acts of resistance and mobilization, and the process of democratization are outlined to provide a socio-historical framework that situates the complexities of the life narratives presented throughout this book.

1652: First Dutch settlement on the Western Cape.
1652–1795: The Dutch "Afrikaaners" conquer the Khoisan indigenous group of the Western Cape. Slaves are imported from Indonesia, India, Ceylon, Madagascar (Malagasy) and Mozambique, which eventually form a large proportion of the Coloured population.
1795: The British take control of Cape Colony from the Afrikaaners.
1803: The Dutch regain control of Cape Colony.
1806–1898: Britain reconquers the Cape Colony, followed by a series of regional disputes and eventually annexes specific areas such as Lesotho.
1899–1902: The "War between the Whites" (Thompson 1990), ending with Britain's victory over the Dutch Afrikaaners.
1910: The Union of South Africa is established, granting voting rights only to white men.
1912: Founding of South African Native National Congress, which would later become the African National Congress (ANC).
1913: **The Land Act** is passed, restricting Africans (75 percent of the population) to only 13 percent of the land and marking the beginning of a series of segregation laws.
1930: White women are granted voting power.
1944: The African National Party Youth League is formed.

1948: The Afrikaaner National Party (NP) comes to power and institutes policies of **"separate development"** under **"apartheid."**

1949: **Prohibition of Mixed Marriages Act** is passed, banning interracial marriage.

1950: A pivotal year that initiates strategic state policies of separateness among the races.

The **Population Registration Act** classifies South Africans by race and begins a process of granting specific privileges based completely on racial status as either African, "Coloured," Indian or White.

The **Immorality Act** is passed this same year, banning sexual relations across the races.

The **Group Areas Act** forces people to reside in racially zoned areas.

1951: **The Bantu Authorities Act** is promulgated, dividing South Africa into white areas and **"homelands"** for the indigenous portion of the population.

1952: **The Pass Laws** are implemented, channeling black women's labor specifically into domestic work.

1953: **The Bantu Education Bill** is passed, limiting African educational opportunities to preparation specifically for work as servants. Severe disparities in educational system resources and quality, based upon racial school categorization, sustain the apartheid era.

1955: **The Congress of South African Trade Unions (COSATU)** is established.

1956: Women protest Pass Laws, specifically for domestic workers.

1960: The government bans African political organizations.

1962: Nelson Mandela is sentenced to life imprisonment for political organizing during the Rivonia Treason Trial.

1964: Black women are forced to carry passes. Nelson Mandela goes to Robben Island where he remains for the next 27 years.

1973: Trade union strikes begin as a powerful venue for political resistance organizing.

1976: The Soweto student uprising marks a critical moment of state violence against youth.

1980: Domestic workers begin organizing around education and improved working conditions in Cape Town.

1983: The United Democratic Front (UDF) is formed to oppose the state practices of separate government while violence escalates throughout South Africa.

1985: A State of Emergency is declared after anti-apartheid demonstrators in Langa (Cape Town) are killed.

1986: **SADWU, the South African Domestic Workers Union** is formed and begins more progressive efforts to unionize domestic workers and protest apartheid.

1990: This early decade marks the beginning of a process of disbanding apartheid and preparing for democracy negotiations. Nelson Mandela and other political prisoners are released from Robben Island. An overall recognition of South Africa's trajectory toward majority governance forms the topic of negotiations between the ANC and the NP.

1991: **The Land Acts, Group Areas Act and Population Registration Act of 1950 are repealed.** Convention for the Democratic South Africa begins. The first conference on Women and Gender in Southern Africa is held.

1992: The Women's National Coalition is launched to mandate gender representation in the upcoming process of democratic negotiations.

1993: An interim democratic constitution is adopted. The Basic Conditions of Employment Act is promulgated, which protects domestic workers for the first time in formal labor legislation.

1994: April 16: The first national democratic elections are peacefully conducted after 46 years of apartheid governance. **Nelson Mandela of the ANC is voted President by the vast majority of the population.**

1995: **The Truth and Reconciliation Commission,** led by Desmond Tutu, begins national hearings as a critical component of "healing the nation" from the countless human rights violations and acts of state-led violence in the apartheid era.

1996: The new Constitution is adopted with a comprehensive Bill of Rights and an ANC-led Reconstruction and Development Programme (RDP). The Labour Relations Act is passed to legalize the unionization of domestic workers. SADWU disbands as a result of substantial organizational challenges. No domestic worker unions exist for the next four years.

1997: The Basic Conditions of Employment Act is revised to include domestic workers for the first time. The same year, the Growth Employment and Redistribution Strategy (GEAR) replaces the RDP. Overall job losses total half a million by 1999.

1999: June 2: The second democratic elections take place. **Thabo Mbeki is elected national President.**

2000: SADSAWU, the South African Domestic Service and Allied Workers' Union, is launched. The Truth and Reconciliation Commission ends its work after hearing 21,000 testimonies of apartheid era human rights violations.

2001: Domestic workers are included in unemployment insurance for the first time.

Sources: Farr (2002); Thompson (1990); Sparks (1990); Walker (1982).

OVERVIEW OF SOUTH AFRICA

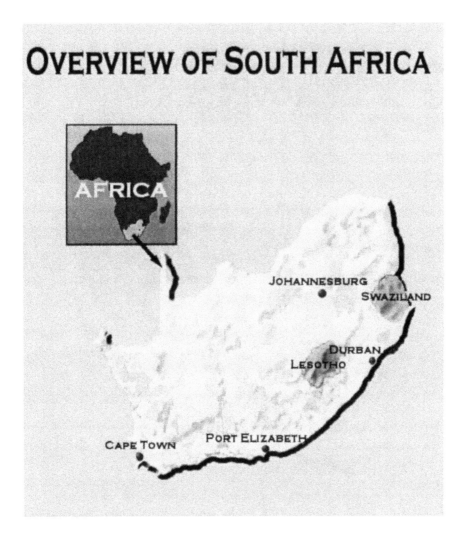

Figure A1: Overview of South Africa
All maps were designed for this study by Joseph Abbate. © All Rights Reserved

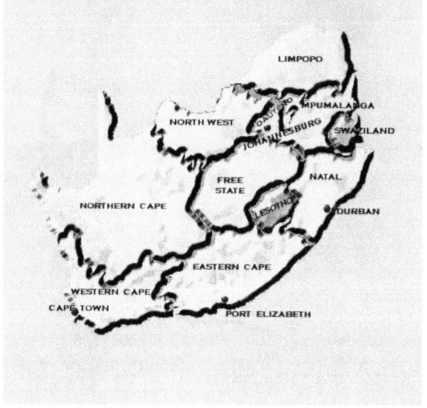

Figure A2: South African Provinces

Chapter One
South Africa in Transition

South Africa embodies paradox. Tourists flock to the nation to see international landmarks such as Table Mountain, Kruger National Park and even Nelson Mandela's prison cell on Robben Island. Yet, these destinations remain inaccessible for the majority of the population. The natural beauty throughout the nation paints breathtaking backdrops, always countered by the social landscape of severe inequality and inescapable poverty. The Truth and Reconciliation Commission (TRC)[1] sets a world precedent for reconstructing society in the aftermath of apartheid, while thousands wait for reparations that will determine the "value of a lost limb."[2] The nation prioritizes gender rights as central to democracy; meanwhile women refuse to ride city trains for fear of rape. Living in South Africa means confronting these paradoxes hundreds of times each day. The severe economic inequalities appear through hawkers, car guards and street children—a daily presence so universal they are almost transparent. Flying into Cape Town necessitates facing South Africa's most severe contradiction—the massively impoverished townships that practically line the runway. These are spaces where whites still will not go, exemplifying the residue of apartheid's geography of separation.

THE TOPIC

Within these paradoxical daily realities, what most powerfully encapsulates the contradiction between democracy and severe social inequality is the *normalcy* by which South Africa is maintained and almost unquestionably reproduced by the black women[3] domestic workers who collectively denote what I assert to be the strongest vestige of the apartheid era. A morning walk through Cape Town's affluent Sea Point neighborhood reveals the embedded familiarity of paid household labor in South Africa. At 7:00

A.M., women pour off city buses and taxis to work as day laborers in gated, high-level luxury homes facing the striking Atlantic seaside. They have traveled two hours by now. Those workers who "live-in" these homes to work as full-time "maids" are easily identified throughout the neighborhood. They are walking the dogs, hanging the laundry, pushing (white) children in prams along gated avenues, shaking rugs from the balconies, cleaning the windows from the daily saltwater residue, and even shopping in stores they could not begin to afford for their employers' daily groceries—from which their own meal will be rationed if they work for a "nice madam." Their occupation is easily identified to even the most unfamiliar visitor; they are the only black women in this residential community.

Inside the homes of white South Africans—as well as the small group of "newly elite" employers—domestic workers literally reproduce the household on a *daily* basis. They iron every garment, prepare and serve most meals, care for children of all ages, and maintain an astonishing level of cleanliness that relieves employers of any responsibility for picking up after themselves.[4] These standards extend to South Africa's public spaces as well—where black women are employed on a full-time basis in almost all private and public institutions. Their daily presence—serving tea, washing the office dishes, and tidying up—reinforces the privilege of leaving the "dirty work" to black women.

This extreme level of service performed by domestic workers is rarely questioned in the nation's dialogue on post-apartheid reconstruction. The impact of these cumulative acts on maintaining South Africa's institutionalized strict racial order, severe class inequality and gender-based discrimination is multi-faceted and understudied. I assert that domestic work[5] plays a critical role in South Africa's transition because the institution manifests the enormous contradictions between a new democracy and the last vestige of apartheid.

Public and Private Transitions

After nearly 50 years of the most systematic institutionalization of racist governance in the twentieth century, South Africa's democracy was celebrated as a defining victory for social struggle. Those most severely oppressed sectors of the population waited in lines for hours to elect the African National Congress (ANC) as the first black majority party to govern South Africa.

> April 27, 1994—the day for which we had waited all these many long
> years, the day for which the struggle against apartheid had been waged,
> for which so many of our people had been tear gassed, bitten by police

dogs, struck with quirts and batons, for which many more had been detained, tortured, and banned, for which others had been imprisoned, sentenced to death, for which others had gone into exile—the day had finally dawned when we would vote, when we could vote for the first time in a democratic election in the land of our birth (Tutu 1999:3).

Since the "rainbow nation"[6] emerged under the charismatic leadership of Nelson Mandela, South Africa embodied hopeful possibilities for forgiveness, reconciliation and transformation. The emergent public documents crafted soon after the 1994 elections, such as one of the world's most progressive Constitutions,[7] symbolized the new nation's commitment to social reconstruction in alignment with political change. In post-1994 South Africa, *democracy* incorporates both an intentional societal transfiguration from the dominant apartheid regime and the incorporation of critical equality-based human rights in the process of nation building.[8] In particular, "non-racialism" and "non-sexism" maintain central positions in the construction of democracy in South Africa (Constitution of South Africa 1996). To redress gender inequality, a national *Gender Machinery*[9] was established in alignment with the revolutionary 26 percent women's representation in national parliament—one of the highest levels of governmental leadership in the world.[10] These monumental transformations created an euphoric national 'spirit' as South Africa celebrated the end of apartheid and the construction of a "new nation." Yet, in 2001, Nomonde—a longstanding ANC leader who was publicly tortured by apartheid police force for organizing women activists—told me, "*This* is not the freedom I fought for."

This book examines the striking contrast between South Africa's democratic ideology and the lived experiences of the majority of its population in the first decade after the 1994 political change. By focusing on the prevailing colonial institution of domestic work, the overlapping complexities of actualizing human rights emerge as daily contradictions between the public level of change and the inequalities embedded in everyday social relations. Julia, a prominent human rights leader and employer of a domestic worker, vividly depicted her experience of this journey through South Africa's transition:

Nelson Mandela's period was a very necessary one because we were coming out of a violent conflict and it was an astonishing period, but the reality is that we've had 350 years of skewed resources and you can't just say, "OK guys, that's the end of the game now let's just carry on as normal" and I think that is where *a lot* of whites are . . . But anyway I think we've done a lot of incredibly good things . . . I just have this sense that some of the stuff is somewhat imposed even though it was, a lot of it was really negotiated, and negotiated in a very open and inclusive way. I mean our Constitution—our Constitution is an absolutely astonishing document, so I mean those are the things that South Africans forget. So I think that a lot of the legacies are now coming forefront. The euphoria of the bloodless revolution could only last so long. Now we've got to deal with the nuts and bolts and the thing I find about being back in South Africa is that there is *nowhere* to hide from issues. You know the race and the class issues are just there *all* the time and while in the beginning, yes, we were really fine, everybody had the votes, and everybody could have a say and hopefully equal access to resources, but we weren't naïve about it . . . this is the real world, '94 was amazingly euphoric, it was astonishing . . . [yet now] people are having to actually confront the reality instead of this sort of brothers and sisters kissing and making up, having to do something about it now—which all makes having a domestic worker *fraught as all hell!*

I suggest that, more than any other social institution, paid domestic labor embodies the complexities of engendering democracy in South Africa. Because of the severe race, gender and class-based inequalities encapsulated within it, participants in this research continually referred to domestic work as the "last bastion of apartheid." By examining the extent to which domestic work has changed in accordance with national processes of transformation, this research captures the challenge of implementing the nation's commitment to gender equality at the most intimate level of social relations.

"The Struggle Continues"

At the ten-year anniversary of democracy, South Africa continues to confront its legacy—the social psychological residue of severe inequality, the massive disparity still defined by race, and a history that has proven to be extremely difficult to transform even after a revolutionary Truth and Reconciliation Commission process. As South Africa emerges from this deeply embedded apartheid history, new obstacles prolong the transition: a growing internal disillusionment about the "failed promises" of democracy; 40 percent unemployment sharply defined by race; extreme levels of internal violence, gang wars and crime that seriously call into question the nation's status as a "post-conflict" society; sprawling "townships" where residents struggle to access safe water and sanitation; and the highest figures of violence against women in the world.[11]

With the remarkable steps toward democracy in place, the stratification processes that continue to dominate South Africa reveal what many participants in this study described as an ongoing *"social apartheid."* The apartheid regime's racial categorization practices still shape social relations and divide groups based upon skin color and strong associations of identity within four distinctly defined groups. The most severely marginalized group, the highly diverse indigenous black population with nine official languages, was homogenized as "African" under apartheid. This group now composes 78 percent of the population and lives in the most severe poverty in comparison to the other three racial groups. The mixed race "coloured"[12] group—crafted by the apartheid era to assure slightly higher privilege than the black majority of the population and concentrated in the Cape Town area—now totals 9 percent of the national population. Asian or Indian sectors remain in the smallest minority with only 3 percent, concentrated in mainly the Durban area (see Figure 1.2). Apartheid's dominant group, the white population derived from colonial Dutch (Afrikaans) and English settlers[13] composes 10 percent of the population (Statistics South Africa 2000). In the post-apartheid context, social privilege remains centered in this group as a result of the negotiated transition that assured whites the maintenance of economic power, even though their political power was renounced in the shift to democracy. As a result, the privileges of everyday life remain virtually unchanged for whites because social status continues to be defined by economic power and the former system of racial hierarchy entrenched throughout apartheid.

The "Last Bastion of Apartheid"

"If you want to see apartheid *today,* just look at domestic work." So I was told on a number of occasions throughout this research. Collectively, domestic workers and farm workers form the largest sector of working women in the nation. The 1999 Household Survey[14] estimated that of the total 4,353,000 working women in South Africa, 763,000 are employed in domestic work and 835,000 work in "elementary occupations" (Statistics South Africa 2000). Yet, as the government admits, accurate records of domestic workers are difficult to obtain due to their placement in private homes. Also importantly, the term "elementary occupations" encompasses women who work as farm laborers where domestic work is also very often mandated through either their marriage to male farm workers or the surplus labor they provide through residence on farm locations. Therefore, of the total women's working population, 17 percent are employed as domestic workers and the combined domestic worker/elementary occupation category yields 37 percent of working women.[15] More general estimates, as well as the Minister of Labour's public address in June 2001, however, indi-cated over "a million domestic workers" in the country—23 percent of all women workers. Critical to this study, these workers are also composed *completely* of black women, either African (88 percent) or coloured (12 percent). Also telling in relation to the feminized nature of this sector, 95.5 percent of those working in domestic service are women.[16] These figures demonstrate the interlocking nature of gender, race, and class-based oppression and its particular operation in the South African context where apartheid structures prevail throughout the social fabric.

Domestic work completely encapsulates the proliferation of the ongo-ing "social apartheid" described by participants in this study. Severe race and class inequalities continue to dominate the relationship between work-ers and employers, while reinforcing the power structures established in the apartheid era. Employers are therefore freed from acknowledging the extent to which their private lives reinforce the hierarchies of the "old regime." Similarly, they do not have to account for the ongoing exploita-tion of domestic workers because the 40 percent unemployment rate invokes a sense of benevolence among employers who "take care of the dis-enfranchised" through salaries that fall far below living wage standards.

This rationale relieves employers of responsibility for partaking in South Africa's ongoing social apartheid and seriously limits the extent to which democracy extends to the private household. The employment of domestic workers in modern South Africa virtually mirrors its practice in the apartheid era. Even though the demographics of a *few* employers have changed, the institution reinforces the limited nature of structural change within the highly racialized and gendered labor sector. Thus, the ongoing colonial nature of domestic work poses serious questions about the extent of South Africa's actual transition.

Thandi Modise, South Africa's first female Minister of Defence, espoused, "As long as there is inequality and un-education, democracy will not be realized."[17] I assert that domestic labor both institutionalizes inequality and poses the most serious obstacle to the realization of democ-racy in South Africa. This book situates the household as a political space where power is defined by race, class, gender and inequalities that are con-stantly negotiated—particularly when the micro private sphere is also a public labor site for domestic workers. It is the social space where apartheid relations are reproduced on a *daily* basis. Therefore, in order to realize a new South Africa, an imperative need to democratize the private household illustrates the ongoing work of transformation. As women par-liamentarians similarly indicated, in order to actualize the nation's public gender rights victories, the real work of transformation remains centered in the private sphere (Britton 1999). The study of domestic work provides a lens into South Africa's transition to democracy through an examination of these private spaces where apartheid history continues to dominate power relations—embodying the nation's enormous challenge to realize democracy at all levels.

AN OVERVIEW OF THE STUDY

How has the institution of domestic work changed in South Africa's democracy? By exploring this central research question, this book establishes an inquiry about the mutuality of the public and the private spheres (Ling 2002), particularly within the framework of national democratic transition. It affords an opportunity to examine democracy's greatest challenge—the breakdown of power structures, racial stratification, gender oppression, and an ongoing class struggle. Thope, a black member of parliament (MP) and domestic work employer,[18] shared the following with me when asked how she envisioned change in the institution of domestic work:

> I can tell you since 1994, people have seen no change, but parliament wise, there have been many changes. But I think the problem is how do we enforce those changes onto people so that people understand that times have changed and things have changed and the law has changed, so they must abide by the laws, they don't.

This study claims the institutionalized nature of domestic work as the most deeply embedded and complex endurance of apartheid's legacy. In this regard, by maintaining daily life for privileged portions of the population, a great deal goes *unchanged* in South Africa's new democracy. Furthermore, I suggest that the expected conflict from massive social change is assuaged to a great extent through the daily and familiar comforts provided by domestic workers. Their presence allows the white population to maintain its privileged lifestyle, regardless of the 1994 loss of political strength.

While this institution remains deeply embedded in apartheid structural dominance, domestic workers are actively engaging to change the working conditions of this sector through mobilization and unionization. Capturing these collective acts of resistance affords valuable insights about the central position of gender in the national process of social change. Unless domestic work is progressively transformed, I assert that South Africa's realization of democracy remains seriously jeopardized. Therefore, embracing the interlocking nature of the private household and the public sphere contained within the institution of domestic work, my research reveals the complexities of gendered power relations in South Africa at the crossroads of a deeply entrenched apartheid legacy and ongoing work of democratization.

This book captures South Africa in a dynamic process of social change. The narratives of participants from a variety of social locations speak to the delicacy of national change and the pressing limitations of South Africa's ongoing transition. As one employer assessed, "It's a tender time for us because the race issue is there, it's open, it's a wound and it's being exploited as well as being a reality." This depiction of the current phase captures South Africa's transition, as well as the value of conducting social research at this pivotal moment. Domestic work, while situated within the protected private location of the household, provides an important lens into this public transition because of the interwoven nature of the household and the state.

Situating this study in Cape Town affords a particular analysis because its regional dynamics are unlike any other area of South Africa. Race issues are magnified in the Western Cape[19] because of the prevalence of the coloured population. While 9 percent of the total South African population, the coloured population reaches 56 percent in the Western Cape, by far the highest concentration throughout the country (Statistics South Africa 2000). This demography defines social relations and the political nature of the region. The Western Cape is the only national province that continues to support the "Democratic Alliance" (repackaged National Party of the apartheid era) through the vote of the coloured population. Because of this entrenched racial order of the former regime—which afforded higher privileges to coloureds over blacks—there is a particular tension in the Western Cape surrounding the democratic transition and black governance.

Participants in this research continually pointed to heightened prejudices within the coloured community as an encapsulation of former racial hierarchies. As one domestic worker in this study portrayed, "The Western Cape is full of apartheid now." This regional dynamic inverts the traditional "maids and madams" (Cock 1980) dichotomy in the institution of domestic work because in the Western Cape, it is coloured women who are both workers and employers, divided by economic status, religion and rural/urban location. This study is the first to capture these nuances by looking at within-group marginalization in this particular South African location.

Guiding Frameworks

This book engages with a growing body of literature on domestic work as a *global* institution that particularly marginalizes women in this sector through a number of interconnected power asymmetries. Because women of color[20] perform domestic work worldwide, I draw upon theories of intersectionality and postcolonial feminism to illustrate the interlocking nature of workers' oppression as a result of marginalized race, class, gender and geographic location divides (Hill Collins 1990; Mohanty 1991). These theoretical underpinnings are central to understanding women's distinct experiences based upon their social position as either worker or employer. Building upon these tenets, this book provides another empirical case that seriously challenges the extent to which 'sisterhood is global.' Furthermore, my research extends Cock's (1980; 1989) study of domestic work in the apartheid context because it examines the relationship between this institution and the overarching gender rights at the public level that have been pivotal to the first decade of democracy. In addition, I explore women's activism to transform the institution of domestic work as a central component of this study in order to provide further empirical evidence that contributes to the growing body of literature on collective acts of resistance.

This project builds upon my ten-year study of South Africa and its post-apartheid transition. Using a qualitative, triangulated approach, I rely heavily upon interview data with 85 participants, in collaboration with case study analysis, participant observations and archival research. The range of data collected—among workers, employers, union members, parliamentarians, nongovernmental organization (NGO) leaders and human rights activists—provides the most varied and comprehensive data on domestic work in post-apartheid South Africa. Linking this study to a theoretical assumption about the value of knowledge to engender social change (hooks 1989; Mohanty 1991; Dickerson 1995), I embrace feminist "liberating methods" (DeVault 1999) and self-reflexive practices about the acquisition of data and my own position as a social researcher. Therefore, this research works in alignment with local communities to contribute to South Africa's ongoing transition. The feminist, community-based methodology I employed has particular salience in a developing nation like South Africa, where the social differentials between researcher and informants are even further heightened. I weave this complexity into both the methodological discussion and the data analysis throughout this book.

Concluding Comments

Notwithstanding the growing skepticism about the implementation of democracy in the everyday lives of the nation's most severely marginalized citizens, South Africa's public victories remain laudable and worthy of their transformational claims. The process of complete social change in the aftermath of apartheid is a complex and long-term endeavor. The revolutionary processes in place to realize democracy—after nearly 50 years of the most racialized apartheid governance throughout the twentieth century—continues to embody optimistic notions of humanity and the potential for peaceful social change. The ideologies central to South Africa's democratic transition motivated my long-term interest in this country and serve as a foundation for this research. For these reasons, I refer at times to the "new South Africa" and its "transformation" throughout this book to distinguish the current national context from its apartheid history and to engage the discourse that emerged from participants in this study. I acknowledge, however, that in many ways these terms connote an *ongoing* aspiration more than a definitive victory, particularly for those who continue to live with the daily impact of apartheid's inequalities.

As a commitment to the vision of a democratic South Africa, I offer constructive criticism of the national transition throughout this book. The particular challenges facing South Africa to overcome massive social inequality, redress the lived experiences of its most marginalized citizens and actualize democracy are taken up in the case of domestic labor. Through this lens, the portrait of transformation in the everyday lives of the majority of South Africa's population remains grim. Yet understanding this space—where lived realities challenge the revolutionary national ideology—is critical to furthering the process of democratization. The data revealed in the following chapters capture this chasm. Although many of the narratives are discomforting, placing them in the broader context of social change affords a valuable understanding of the places where democracy is inaccessible. By documenting this particular phase in South Africa's development and offering an analytically constructive conversation about its shortcomings, this research aspires to contribute to the democratic, equality-based, human rights ideology at the center of South Africa's democracy.

Overview of the Chapters

In the following six chapters, I emphasize those aspects of this research that are most salient to elucidating the relationship between democracy and domestic work. To begin, Chapter Two situates the household as a political space that is integral to the State, as well as international relations. I draw upon the literature on domestic labor in other locations to illustrate the structural dynamics that define this institution. This chapter then establishes critical components of South Africa's history to contextualize the analytic chapters that follow. Chapter Three discusses the methodological framework by detailing the research design and integrating a discussion of relevant complexities in the application of these methods in the South African case. Chapter Four begins the analysis by telling the story of domestic work in South Africa, at the crossroads of apartheid and democracy. Next, Chapter Five inverts the traditional colonial "maid and madam" (Cock 1980) construction by closely examining South Africa's "newly elite" employers and the meaning of domestic work *within* marginalized groups—an institutional dynamic that suggests new patterns of social hierarchy in the democratic context. I explore the dialectic of structural domination and agency in Chapter Six through an analysis of domestic workers' unionization and collective participation in the broader gender rights movement in South Africa. Chapter Seven closes with a summary discussion of those contributions most salient to the situating domestic labor within South Africa's *ongoing* transition.

Notes to the Reader

Throughout this book, I draw heavily upon interview data that I collected in South Africa from 2000–2001 among domestic workers, employers of domestic workers, parliamentarians, and "experts" in a variety of settings—six years after South Africa's transition to democracy. Since the collection of these data, however, I have returned to South Africa twice and continue to research its ongoing transformation through longitudinal work with the participants in this study. Therefore, my analyses, when appropriate, suggest a reflection on ten years of democracy in South Africa to illustrate the span of my ongoing research in this context, which began in 1995.

I present these narratives as evidence of the context of change in South Africa from the direct experiences of participants, each of whom lived through the transition from apartheid to democracy. Throughout the process of re-presenting the voices of South Africans in the form of the written word, I intervened in only *minimal* occasions to offer the reader the fullest possible immersion in the lives of these participants. Therefore, the narrative excerpts in this book appear in a manner that is as close as possible to my interview conversations. My choices to divert from the literal transcripts[21] were made only in cases where the word-for-word account distracts significantly from the readability of the narrative. I make these interventions minimally and with extensive caution because of my overarching ideological commitment to present the voices of South Africans in their own words. By doing so, I hope to give the reader a full appreciation for the complexity of the life stories contained within the narrative excerpts throughout this book.

Chapter Two
The Household as a Political Space

That is, what pertains within the individual/household/nation contributes to the community/state/world, just as what happens in the world/state/community affects us as a nation/household/individual.

—L.H.M. Ling

The household provides a critical site to observe the dialectic relationship between micro-and macro levels of society. Historically critiqued for its encapsulation of the devalued nature of women's contribution to society, this social space is integrally connected to the feminized construction of household labor to reproduce daily life. Central to this study, when the *private* household becomes a *public* labor site, severe race, class, and global location divides manifest in addition to the reinforcement of traditional assumptions about "women's work." Furthermore, this private space encapsulates the systematic dependency on women's labor central to the emerging patterns of globalization, thereby becoming a microcosm of international relations (Chin 1998). As Ling (2002) contends, micro social relations in the household are directly connected to world relations, just as global processes continually reshape the most private interactions. This chapter begins by mapping these dialectic processes that inform our investigation of the institution of paid domestic labor as a critical social space that encapsulates race, class, gender and national divides within the private sphere. The particular salience of paid household labor in the South African context is then discussed at length to situate this study and illustrate its complex meaning in a society transitioning from apartheid to democracy.

TRANSGRESSING THE PUBLIC/PRIVATE DIVIDE

Feminist scholars problematize the household as a strategic site in the binary construction of gender divides that value the public/paid sphere over the private/unpaid realm central to women's labor (Oakley 1974; Hochschild 1983; Pateman 1989; Enloe 1990). Social constructionists point to the household as a critical space within which men and women learn to "do gender" (West and Zimmerman 1987) through deeply engrained processes central to daily existence. In particular, the association between women's biological reproductive capacities and the highly gendered construction of care work in the household/family domain relegates women to marginalized positions through a created dependency upon men's (public) labor for economic survival. Further critiques of this entrenched public/private divide illustrate how the wide range of household labor—such as emotional work (Hochschild 1983), "feeding the family" (DeVault 1991), "housework" (Oakley 1974) and caregiving (Romero 1992)—affords men extensive daily benefits while enhancing their position in the public sector. Moreover, the construction of these gendered labor binaries shapes the participation of women who do enter the public sphere through a pervasive "sex-ordered division of labor" (Hartmann 1976) that relegates public work that is deemed feminine to the lowest material and ideological stratum.

Feminist international relations theorists[1] problematize this traditional paralleling of the "public" with state processes that confine political engagement as that which occurs *outside* of the household domain. By inverting this traditional dichotomy between the state's dominant influence on the private household, a reframing of this dialectic relation asserts that the "personal is political" and the "personal is international" (Chow and Berheide 1994:23). Lily Ling (2002) engages this dialogue by drawing upon Confucian logic of *interrelationality* to deconstruct this public/private binary:

> Agents and structures do not function as pre-existing entities that happen to interact with one another to produce 'social life.' Rather, they emerge from compounds of mutually generating rules and rule, institutions and practices, materialities and subjectivities (P. 174).

Ling posits an inherent "mutuality" of domains that traditional Western thinking keeps separate. Namely, she notes the central linkages between the "public ('political') and private ('sex'), domestic ('household') and international ('war')" heightened in the context of globalization (2002:34).

The institution of paid domestic labor disrupts this public/private duality by situating paid labor in the household domain. This site therefore encapsulates the interconnectedness of the private/public spheres. Ling's notion of dialectic "compounds" is evident as privileged women are both marginalized by the gendered nature of domestic labor and participate in its perpetuation through the hiring of "other" women to reproduce the household. Similarly, as the institution of domestic labor contributes substantial portions to developing nations' "export revenue" (Chin 1998), women are both invisible and central to the creation of global "rules" of trade. This private institution therefore becomes a political space, integrally shaped by state policy and bound by structural determinants of everyday life. The institutionalized practices in the private household enact and reproduce severe asymmetries of power based in race, class and national divides. Paid household labor therefore magnifies deeply instilled gendered divisions of labor, while encapsulating interconnected social inequalities. For these reasons, the institution of domestic work provides a central site to explore both the socio-political nature of the household as well as its integral connection to state and global process that reinforce essentialized gender differences, thereby relegating women to the private sphere as a *paid* sector of labor.

The Nature of Paid Domestic Work

This study is built upon the pioneering work of a wealth of feminist scholars who analyzed domestic labor as a microcosm of broad societal structures of race, class and gender inequality in a number of locations.[2] Here, I offer a broad overview that draws upon the most salient aspects of these studies and situates the institution within a much broader global context that sees a rapid growth in this particular sector of highly gendered labor. Three questions guide my inquiry within the literature on domestic labor: What are the common linkages central to the nature of domestic work regardless of geographic location? How does domestic labor advance the feminist conversation through the analysis of relations *among* women? In what ways is the institution of domestic work operating within the global economy?

Studies across a wide variety of theoretical and regional perspectives repeatedly point to common features that define the paid institution of domestic work as one of the most vulnerable sectors of women's labor.[3] Women employed as domestic workers are deemed "unskilled labor" for three predominant reasons. First, their employment is seen as an extension of what is considered innately "women's work." Second, their labor takes place in the private household, which has traditionally been associated with unpaid labor. Third, because the sector is comprised almost completely of women in marginalized race and class positions, predominant macro structures of inequality shape the further devaluation of this particular sector.

Women employed in the household, however, are expected to perform a wide array of competencies and draw upon a variety of skill sets to meet the shifting demands of their daily employment contexts. Task and time management are also central to the job, which generally comes with minimal training in an isolated environment. In addition to the commonly associated responsibilities of cooking, cleaning, childcare and laundry, domestic workers provide *emotional* labor—as caregivers, nurses, counselors, educators, mediators and security agents. Importantly, even though substantial geographic divides separate domestic workers from their own families, this emotional caretaking labor is expected to fulfill the job. The work itself is characterized by low salaries, long hours and a lack of legislative protection, leaving no room for upward mobility. These latter working conditions create substantial barriers to women's organizing and unionization, coupled by the challenges of multiple employment sites and the private nature of the work context. Furthermore, such conditions point to a critical feature of this job—the nature of the work environment is directly connected to the nature of the *relationship* with the employer. Judith Rollins' (1985) classic *Between Women* analyzed the particular construct of domestic work in the U.S. by centrally examining "how race and class inform this female-female relationship" within the structural conditions of domination (p. 7).[4] Two important analytical conversations emerged in the dialogue generated from Rollins' work: 1) contradictions in women's experiences based upon race and class differentials, and 2) feminism's inability to transform the private sphere. Across three regions including the U.S. (Rollins 1985; Nakano Glenn 1987; Romero 1992; Thornton Dill 1994), South America (Bunster and Chaney 1989; Chaney and Castro 1989; Gill 1994), and the Caribbean (Chaney and Castro 1989), theorists illustrate how paid household labor divides women based upon their variant access to race and class status. Through use of poignant contradictions in the voices of workers and employers, these studies illustrate how "domestic service must be studied because it raises a challenge to any feminist notion of 'sisterhood'" (Romero 1992:15).

The complex relationship between workers and employers is characterized by a pervasive shifting of household "dirty work" from privileged to less privileged women through the institutionalized nature of paid household labor. Mary Romero (1992) links overarching capitalist structural conditions to this institution by illustrating the extent to which women enrolled in the paid labor market are also expected to maintain full responsibility for the household—creating a "housework dilemma" that continues to free men from the burden of domestic responsibility. Therefore, ". . . if women are to avoid the double day, those who can afford it have little recourse but to purchase the labor and services of others" (1992:164). The extent to which this process engrains traditional gendered assumptions about women's work, however, remains completely unchallenged. Therefore, these grounded analyses of the work relationship point to feminism's inability to actualize real change in both the gendered division of household labor and within the lives of those most severely marginalized women employed in paid domestic work. Furthermore, placing class domination at the center of analysis, we see a mutual dependency between employers and workers. The outward construction of domestic labor is one that positions workers as dependent upon employers because of the multiple levels of inequality and economic need. Yet employers are similarly dependant upon workers to uphold their own class positions through the daily processes of household reproduction (Romero 1992).

This relationship of mutual dependency exemplifies the pervasive contradictions contained within the institution of domestic work. Similarly, the manner by which domestic workers are both marginalized and actively transforming the conditions of their employment points to a striking structure-agency dialectic. These spaces where workers access some sense of power, albeit limited, illustrate important shifts from analyses of workers' vulnerability to an emphasis on the social agency of women in this sector (Rollins 1985; Cock 1989; Romero 1992). How do domestic workers reconcile their roles in this extremely isolated work context? Essential coping mechanisms identified include women's ability to balance the demanded emotional labor of "maternalism" with a "mask of deference" (Rollins 1985), which protects workers from the pervasive affective demands of the job by psychologically distancing themselves from the employer. Workers similarly pronounced the dependency of their employers by enacting mockery, cajolery, or confrontation (Cock 1989; Romero 1992; Thornton Dill 1994). In many cases, domestic workers gained a sense of self-dignity through realizing that their own mothering skills far exceeded those of their employers (Cock 1989; Romero 1992; Thornton Dill 1994).

At the institutional change level, the ability to build alliances and provide support networks has been instrumental to overcoming oppressive work situations (Thornton Dill 1994). Some domestic workers transformed their work conditions by shifting to contract labor, which affords employment by task rather than by time (Romero 1992). Moving out of live-in situations is also seen as particularly valuable to the empowerment of domestic workers (Romero 1992; Thornton Dill 1994). Yet these acts—while exhibiting powerful agency—do not change the inherent power dynamics among women who are positioned in distinctly asymmetrical relations to one another through class and race privilege. Furthermore, the transition to a broader collective recognition of the value of domestic labor has yet to be realized. Therefore, men continue to be relieved of the burden of household labor by women who are most severely marginalized as a result of race, class, gender and nation inequalities that structure this institutionalized labor sector.

This brings us to a third focal explanation for the encapsulation of severe inequality within the institution of paid household labor. Beyond the public/private divide central to the gendered construction of labor, paid domestic work can also be centrally defined as a racialized institution that places particular burdens on women of color. Refuting notions of a "universal sisterhood," the institution of domestic labor allows us to see how gender is relational, historically situated, and not separate from race, class and nationality (Mohanty 1991; Young and Dickerson 1994). Therefore, rather than assuming women share a common oppression, examining the multiple layers of social position and marginalization illustrates distinctly different experiences of patriarchal domination based upon women's race, class, sexuality, nationality, religion, language, citizenship and geographic locations. In this regard, examining the *intersections* of social position is critical to situating the complex and overlapping inequalities in women's lives.

Patricia Hill Collins (1990) contends that a "matrix of domination" relegates black women to the lowest stratum of society based upon the simultaneous, mutually reinforcing oppressions of race, class and gender. These interlocking oppressions manifest as particularly derogatory images of black womanhood, including the "maid" and the over-sexualized exotic "other." Hill Collins describes the construction of black womanhood as a process of "othering," whereby dichotomous categorizations of social groups are based upon a perceived opposite difference from each other. In this regard, "one part is not simply different from its counterparts—it is inherently opposed to its 'other'" (1990:69). Racially, black becomes the "other" to white as women and men are perceived as binary opposites. This practice constructs hierarchies of power that ultimately objectify, manipulate and control the "other." Hill Collins applies this concept of "othering" in this U.S. to portray the severe objectification of black women employed in private households:

> The treatment afforded black women domestic workers exemplifies the many forms that objectification can take. Making black women work as if they were animals or "mules uh de world" represents one form of objectification. Deference rituals such as calling Black domestic workers "girls" and by their first names enable employers to treat their employees like children, as less capable human beings. Objectification can be so severe that the Other simply disappears, as was the case when Judith Rollins's employer treated her as if she were invisible by conducting a conversation while ignoring Rollins's presence in the room (P. 69–70).

These acts of othering therefore connect to intersectional notions of inequality that position women in distinctly separate spheres based upon binary constructions of 'black/white,' 'rich/poor.' In the case of domestic labor, I suggest that employers "other" workers to distance themselves from the conditions of their own oppression in the private sphere. By reinforcing the intersectional difference in gender experiences through these processes of othering workers, employers are able to avoid the inherent contradiction of displacing housework on women with less social privilege.

Building upon these theories of intersectionality, postcolonial feminists pay particular attention to how geographic locations situate women in distinct and often binary/oppositional manners (Mohanty 1991; Mama 1995; Pettman 1996). The monolithic construction of "Third World Women" and their comparison to women in "the West" enacts a severe dichotomy and oversimplification of status between two presumed monolithic groups. This practice of constructing the universal "Third World Woman" (predominantly among scholars in the Global North) reinforces the hegemonic privileging of Western perspectives by creating an "other" that is continually defined in relation to the dominant power group (Mohanty 1991). Western scholars therefore construct a "third world difference" that ultimately renders non-Western women to ascribed ethnocentric assumptions and lower power positions, as Chandra Mohanty (1991) argues:

> The average third world woman leads an essentially truncated life based on her feminine gender (read: sexually constrained) and her being "third world" (read: ignorant, poor, uneducated, tradition-bound, domestic, family-oriented, victimized, etc.) This, I suggest, is in contrast to the (implicit) self-representation of Western women as educated, as modern, as having control over their own bodies and sexualities, and the freedom to make their own decisions (P. 56).

This monolithic analysis of the "average third world woman" fails to recognize social agency and the multiple complexities of women's lives. The notion that "sisterhood is global" is therefore strongly refuted by postcolonialists who critique the ascribed universal commonality of struggle among women. Mohanty (2003) posits both an ideology and methodology that considers the historical and material conditions of women's highly contextual lived experiences as central to the production of knowledge.

The institution of domestic labor epitomizes this binary construction of women's positions in relation to geographic location. In the South African case particularly, white women—while living in a Global South location—maintain stronger ties to white/Northern (often British) power structures while domestic workers are monolithically constructed as "African" women and consequently perceived as "less civilized." Therefore, the specific context of this study demonstrates how the First World/Third World divide exists among women who share the same nation status. This divide is even further exaggerated with the significant distances between workers' countries of origin and employment contexts through the growing global trade of domestic workers. To illustrate the relevance between postcolonial feminism and the case of domestic labor, this chapter now turns to a discussion of the scholarship that links the institution to broader patterns of migration and globalization.

Globalized Intimate Labor

The current studies of domestic labor are situated within the context of global restructuring/globalization[5] to illustrate how women's labor is central to the transforming world order (Sassen 1998; Chin 1998; Hondagneu-Sotelo 2001; Parreñas 2001; Chang and Ling 2002; Marchand and Runyan 2002). Drawing upon the public/private framework to problematize the severe marginalization of women in the *global* capitalist system, Maria Mies (1994) critiques the enormous contradiction between the vital nature of women's labor and its overwhelmingly devalued status:

. . . no economy can function without women, women as procreators and women as workers. But capitalism is the first social formation which has created the notion that women are not part of the economy, not part of the public sphere, of politics, culture, science, technology and progress, but that they belong to the private, the family, the household and . . . the realm of nature (P. 110).

Saskia Sassen (1998) asserts that this global capitalist system exists only through the inherent reliance upon a vast *service* sector that is both racialized and gendered. Therefore, these processes of global restructuring are specifically dependent upon the institution of paid household labor to support the inflated wealth of developed nations (Chin 1998; Parreñas 2001; Hondagneu-Sotelo 2001). As analysts examine the intersection of globalization with gender, the excessive reliance upon an exploited women's informal labor pool can be sharply juxtaposed with globalization's progress (Ward 1990; Staudt 1998).

Chang and Ling (2002) illustrate two parallel forms of globalization: the high-tech, glossy, masculinized system governed by the dominance of "techno-muscular capitalism" and a less acknowledged "regime of labor intimacy" (domestic work) that is "in every sense the intimate other of techno-muscular capitalism" (p. 27). This "labor intimacy" is built upon distinct *racial* constructions of women who perform service labor, particularly in private households. Because domestic work is performed almost completely by economically disadvantaged women of color, we see how intersectionality plays out on a global scale.[6] Throughout the world, poor countries are most often those with high populations of people of color. In the context of globalization, the mutual dependency we see within the institution of domestic work reflects larger systems of hierarchical dependency between developed and underdeveloped nations. Therefore, global restructuring is heavily reliant upon flows of labor to serve the interests of elite nations while providing economic resources for developing nations. These exchanges, however, are specifically gendered and largely built upon the labor women perform in private households throughout the world.

Domestic Labor and Migration

In the context of globalization, poor countries have become not only production sites but also unlimited labor pools for rich countries to import particular services through processes that are less often formalized (Sassen 1998; Chang 2000; Chang and Ling 2000; Hondagneu-Sotelo 2001). In order to meet the growing demands of capitalist-based globalization, the employment of women in private households is central to the critical service labor provided to developed nations. Global restructuring requires more women in wealthy countries to enter public labor sectors. Even though their labor in the public sphere remains devalued in comparison to that of men, economic conditions increasingly mandate dual incomes in order to access the 'goods' of the globalized world. As a result, capitalism further reinforces the hiring of less privileged women by women with higher levels of economic (and most often race/geographical location) power because the system exists through the exploitation of cheap labor and the dominance of patriarchy.[7] Women's household labor therefore becomes a valuable traded commodity— the sale of which provides enormous resources to developing countries (Sassen 1998). For example, the highest source of export revenue in the Philippines is generated from the salary remittances of domestic workers (Chin 1998). The export-based nature of transnational domestic labor is consequently a bi-product of the gross economic disparities between countries that send and receive women workers (Lycklama 1994).

Pierrette Hondagneu-Sotelo (2001) illustrates the heavy dependency of the U.S. on domestic workers from Mexico and Latin America to eluci-date this global trade at a highly personal level:

> Today, many of these [Latina] domestic workers care for the homes and children of American families while their children remain "back home" in their societies of origin. This latter arrangement, which I call transnational motherhood, signals new international inequalities of social reproduction (P. 24).

This "transnational motherhood" is based upon *required* migration—a central component of the added vulnerability of this labor sector. In most cases, formal citizenship is forsaken when workers travel across the globe to seek employment. Furthermore the extensive distances between domestic workers and their regions of origin inflate the emotional demands of this work, particularly when women leave their own families to care for the children of more privileged sectors of society. This transnational trade of workers therefore deeply entrenches global patterns of social inequality within the micro labor context. In a parallel fashion, these power asymme-tries between workers and employers enact and reproduce the disparate global positions of sending and receiving nations.

The following map (Figure 2.1) provides a visual representation of these global migratory patterns.

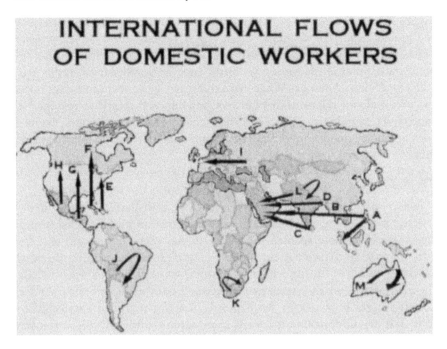

Figure 2.1: International Flows of Domestic Workers

A Workers from the Philippines to Singapore and Malaysia
B Workers from the Philippines and Thailand exported to the
  Middle East
  (primary receiving countries include Saudi Arabia, United Arab
  Emirates and Qatar)
C Workers from Sri Lanka to the Middle East
D Workers from Bangladesh to the Middle East
E Workers from the Caribbean to USA
F Workers from the Caribbean to Canada
G Workers from Central America to USA
H Workers from Mexico to USA
I Broad movement from Eastern Europe to Western Europe
J Internal migration patterns in South America, defined by rural/urban
  divides
K Internal migration in South Africa
L Internal migration in India by caste and export of workers to the
  Middle East
M Slight internal migration in Australia with the aboriginal population

Figure 2.1 illustrates the most predominant regional migration patterns in the global export of domestic labor. As it reveals, the flow of workers extends primarily from the Global South to the Global North, with a few contexts of internal migration patterns, such as South Africa, India, Australia and South America. While not exhaustive, patterns in this map reflect the predominant relationships between sending and receiving regions.[8] To more fully examine the processes that facilitate these exchanges, we now turn to an examination of state participation in transnational domestic labor.

The Role of the State

The State performs a central function in these transnational trades in two specific ways. First, it constructs *formal* migration and citizenship policies that define how women in this particular sector enter and exit specific countries. More often, however, governments render domestic workers invisible through *informal* processes that fail to acknowledge the central role of this sector in developed nations' economies. As rich countries rely on workers from poor countries to fulfill service sector jobs that are undesirable for local populations, informal migration patterns emerge among countries with these strategic relations of dependency (Sassen 1998; Lycklama 1994). In these contexts, reliance upon the transnational trade of domestic workers remains virtually obsolete from foreign policy, political platforms or national development plans. And because predominantly men remain in power positions, the extent to which women are relegated to the least valued, lowest paid stratum of labor is rarely problematized by state agents. Also central to this process, globalization's shaping of a new world system of interdependence is often characterized by the decreased power of states as the private/capitalist-based sector gains further control over transnational processes. Yet the state operates in alliances with these private capitalist structures. Therefore, both benefit from the widespread trade of domestic workers while the nature of globalization takes the form of patriarchal capitalism—built upon essentialized notions of women's labor (both paid and unpaid) in the private sphere.

State policies that define legitimate forms of migration and citizenship point to sharp divides between formal and informal practices. For example, while most states require a formal visa and extensive documentation to attain citizenship, in the case of domestic labor, these policies often become very fluid or are virtually ignored. As Romero (1992) illustrates, the borders between Texas and Mexico are extremely porous on "Maid's Day" because of the widespread assumption that women crossing the border do so for private household labor jobs. Therefore, border officials operate under a collusive assumption that formal labor and migration policies need not be applied to the domestic work sector. This fissure between policy and practice is likely a result of overarching ideologies that position domestic labor as an insignificant sector because it is informal, performed in the private household, and composed of women of color.

Elite state officials also contribute to the devaluation of domestic workers through a substantial reliance upon household labor without formal protection mechanisms. The diplomatic community provides an interesting case study because the private household is also a public space. In elite circles, composed predominantly of men, the State demands an extremely high frequency of social functions and the maintenance of elevated levels of cleanliness in diplomatic homes, which represent the State (Enloe 1989). Domestic labor is therefore required to enable both formal decision-making and informal social interactions to take place in the homes of diplomats, where elite state functions commonly occur. Even though state processes provide formal documentation for domestic workers who accompany diplomatic families, household labor is certainly not recognized as central to state functions or international relations. Therefore, domestic workers employed within the diplomatic community are not provided avenues for upward mobility, thus further exaggerating the power differentials and entrapment within this highly gendered and devalued sector. Furthermore, if domestic workers are released from service, their state visas are often immediately withdrawn, leaving workers with no citizenship protection within the countries where they reside. In addition, a latent class function is also at play as (female) "trailing spouses" are relieved of hands-on household labor demands in order to serve in other highly gendered diplomatic functions such as social entertainment and philanthropy.[9] As these cases convey, both state ideologies and officials who enforce state policy at a variety of levels fail to recognize domestic labor as a valuable sector that contributes to the global economy.

Interestingly, the Philippines provides an alternative case where state policy is both formal and strategic in its acknowledgement of the central role played by migrant domestic workers to promote foreign trade as well as *Filipina* culture (Chin 1998). Workers who are "exported" from the Philippines to predominantly Malaysia and Singapore are given strong messages from the State that their roles in domestic service are critical to the promotion of positive Filipina values throughout the receiving countries. In this way, state officials manifest a sense of duty among women to 'serve the country' by taking part in highly structured processes that contribute the largest source of export revenue to the Philippines (Chin 1998). The processes by which these transnational exchanges are manifested also serve to reinforce dominant state ideologies of gender and class divisions through messages about appropriate 'family life.' Therefore, in the case of the Philippines, recognition of this sector is built upon a rhetoric of women's obligation to export cultural values, rather than an overt acknowledgement that the nation's overall economic livelihood is dependant upon the salary remittances of domestic workers.[10]

As these examples illuminate, the role of the State is integral to the central processes by which domestic work operates in the global economy. Through migration and citizenship policies—as well as the pervasive disregard for such policies in practice—states support the ongoing devaluation of labor in the private sphere. Even though household labor has shifted to migrant women workers, systems of capitalism that dominate both the private and public spheres entrench an even deeper dependency on this institution. Therefore, while performed in the private micro household sphere, paid domestic labor is structured by the most macro levels of transnational interaction that determine state policies and international terms of trade through the interdependent relationship between women's exported intimate labor and the economic development of both sending and receiving countries.

These macro-structural forces pose serious barriers to the extent of transformation within the domestic work sector. As globalization increases in its dominance, women in this sector remain severely marginalized and often *invisible* in the context of global restructuring. Yet domestic workers throughout the world are actively engaging in processes of change to reshape this institution and resist the dominant forces of globalization. Through collective organization at the regional, national and global levels, domestic workers are shifting state processes, engaging in global politics and mandating the integration of this sector into broader global gender justice campaigns (Karides 2002). This structure-agency dialectic is central to Chapter Six, which presents an extensive case of South African domestic workers' collective organization to engage directly with the State and transform critical labor policy in the context of the national transition to democracy.

Summary of the Literature on Domestic Labor

Three vantage points guided our discussion of the research to date on the institution of domestic labor: 1) the public/private dialectic that defines the nature of household labor; 2) asymmetrical relationships among women based in social location divides; and 3) the vital role that the institution of domestic work plays in the context of global restructuring. By drawing upon those most salient aspects of research from a variety of contexts, I wish to engage this study in a broader conversation that positions domestic labor and the household space as a central socio-political site that is integrally connected to macro-level state and global structures. From this body of knowledge, I want to emphasize key discussion points that are most relevant to the study at hand. First, regardless of the contextual location, domestic labor institutionalizes the severe race, class, gender and national divides that position women in extremely asymmetrical relations as workers and employers. As the literature on intersectionality and postcolonial feminism posits, these extreme social location differentials seriously challenge the notion of a collective women's experience. Therefore, women with heightened social location power participate in the ongoing marginalization of "other" women with less privilege through enacting race and class inequalities in the private sphere. Consequentially, this shifting of household labor among women with variant social positions fails to transcend the public/private essentialist divide in ways that foster men's responsibility for household reproduction.

The global collection of studies on domestic labor grounds this research through detailed analyses of central features that connect the institution across each context. Regardless of geographic location, the nature of the work itself is virtually parallel—defined by extreme exploitation, required migration, emotional labor, severe isolation and substantial challenges to organization.

This broader global lens facilitates an understanding of the South African case, where my findings repeatedly illustrate these same defining features in the nature of this particular sector of labor. Analysis of the broader structures that shape the institution of domestic work, however, points to a very distinct case in the context of South Africa. Notably, the colonial, apartheid history and the recent national democratic transition position this institution as a pivotal case to illuminate the complexities of social change and the multiple layers of South Africa's transition. As my data portray, changes at the state level have not yet transformed the private household—where the colonial nature of paid domestic labor prevails among the privileged sectors of South African society. The rapid pace of South Africa's national transition therefore provides a rich site of analysis to examine the interconnected nature of the public and private realms. Moreover, the shifting nature of race and class relations in South Africa's ongoing process of social change provides a rich context to investigate how domestic work is central to the active reconstruction of particular patterns of social stratification. Drawing upon the situated knowledge base provided through the literature on domestic labor, as well as the theoretical bases of intersectionality and interrelationality, let us now engage with the highly particular regional context of South Africa to guide the methodological and analytic conversations that follow.

THE SOUTH AFRICAN CASE OF DOMESTIC WORK

The institution of domestic work holds a particular resonance in South African society. I contend that beyond any other social space, the household most strikingly reflects the tension between apartheid South Africa and its new democracy. As one domestic worker in this study described, "When I leave my work, I leave the First World and return to the Third World." The extreme disparities in wealth, social position and access to the new South Africa are vividly contained within this institution—which remains one of the few spaces where members of different racial groups encounter one another at a personal level. Jacklyn Cock's (1980; 1989) pivotal *Maids and Madams* vividly captured South Africa's apartheid inequality by positioning the institution of domestic work as a "microcosm" of race relations. This research revisits some of the central questions in Cock's work. My focus, however, is the relationship between the institution of domestic work and South Africa's democratization *since 1994*. By focusing on the first ten years of democracy, the relationship between the private sphere and the State converge in ways that reveal the critical juncture between significant change and the ongoing vestiges of apartheid in everyday social relations.

To appreciate both the deeply engrained nature of paid household labor in South African society and the literature that has emerged on this particular case, we must first establish a grounded historical context. Just as global restructuring is dependent upon the migrant labor of women with the least access to social power, the success of the apartheid regime was centrally linked to the strategic construction of the institution of domestic work. By reproducing daily life for white South Africans, domestic labor actualized the dominant political order of severe race, class and gender inequalities. To contextualize the discussion of the literature in this local context—as well as the analytical chapters to follow—I now turn to a broad overview of those aspects of apartheid history most salient to the case of domestic labor.

The Legacy of Apartheid and the New Democracy

The apartheid regime was arguably the most intentional, overt and strategically racist governance of the twentieth century. With its policies enacted through state-led violence and extreme oppression, an ethos of racial purity motivated the government's systematic oppression of the majority of South Africa's population for nearly 50 years. Recounting these acts of dominance—including massive military rape, public killings, torture and extreme systematic denigration of all "non-white" members of the nation—necessitates fundamental questions about the core nature of humanity and power. Coupled with these most egregious enactments of apartheid rule, the ubiquitous structural violence that divided South African society and apportioned social privilege in accordance with skin tone created pervasive *daily* barriers for the majority population. These memories of "everyday apartheid" surfaced most frequently in my interviews:

> Oh, in that apartheid years, it was that "baas"[11] and "madam" call . . . and you can't go to places. Most of the places was white or non-white. Even in the buses, when you go in the bus, you have to go right at the back because it's only for whites. And when you go to the shops, you have to—you can't go *into* the shop—you have to stand outside and buy your bioscopes [cinema tickets], you can't go in where the white is—they got separate. And you go to a separate bioscope, cinema, places like that. That was not nice.

As this domestic worker recalled, daily life required confronting the ideology of apartheid—literally meaning "apartness" in Afrikaans.

The complex social-political history of South Africa merits volumes of analysis beyond the scope of this book.[12] While my intention is not to oversimplify this rich history, I suggest that three critical events from the apartheid era are most worthy of in-depth discussion to situate the study of domestic labor: 1) the geographical separation enacted through the creation of "homelands;" 2) the subsequent "pass laws" required for women to work in urban centers; and 3) women's collective acts of resistance.

"Homeland" Strategies

Based on an underlying ideology of racial purity, the apartheid government structured "homelands" to privilege colonial settlers and establish formal separation from the majority indigenous African population. In 1950, the Group Areas Act dispersed South Africa's land in accordance with the apartheid ideology of privilege. Accordingly, "13 percent of the land for 75 percent of the population means that each white person gets twenty times more land than each black person, with a huge disparity in resources besides" (Sparks 1990:211). Geographic separation remained critical to the success and dominance of apartheid. As such, the policies enacted paralleled the racial thinking of the era. Coloured populations in Cape Town, for instance, were forcibly removed from central urban areas such as District Six because of a belief that residence in the city metropolis was a privilege reserved only for the white population. This vibrant music and cultural center was bulldozed in a matter of days, with no warning to its residents because of a perceived threat of coloureds living too close to the designated white city centers. Coloured residents of District Six were placed in established "townships" substantially beyond (approximately 20 kilometers) Cape Town's city limits.[13] At the same time, "Africans" were assigned to townships even further outside the city—*if* they attained the appropriate "passes" granting rights to live near the metropolitan centers. Without government's stamp of approval to reside in urban centers, Africans were relegated to "homeland" locations, reflective of the apartheid government's longer-term vision to establish separate nation states. Coloured and African populations were therefore strategically divided and stratified based upon privilege, with slightly higher status afforded to coloured members. These racialized policies materialized through the relative geographical proximity to urban areas afforded to black and coloured sectors of the population.

Africans who did not acquire passes to live in cities were consigned to one of the eight "homelands" designed specifically for the indigenous population. As Figure 2.2 illustrates, apartheid's ideology of separation was blatantly materialized through the establishment of separate geographic homelands. The regions denoted identify the homelands established during apartheid—with separate governance structures and absolute minimal public services such as education and infrastructure support. Not coincidentally, these regions were also the least desirable lands from an agricultural production perspective. Outside of the separate Lesotho and Swaziland nation states, the remaining 76 percent of the land was reserved for the white population under apartheid governance. The black majority was then forced to attain "passes" in order to leave their homeland locations.

APARTHEID'S GEOGRAPHY OF SEPARATION

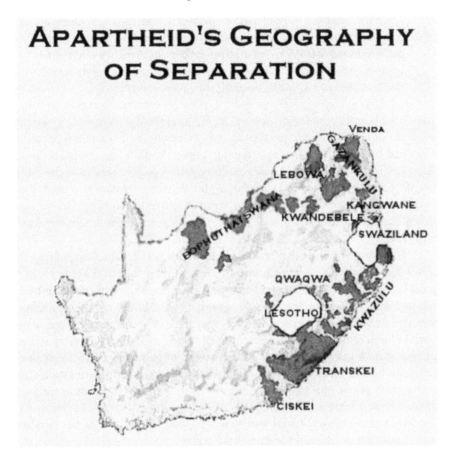

Figure 2.2: Apartheid's Geography of Separation

Pass Laws

South Africa's apartheid governance instituted pass laws throughout its history to control the labor of the majority population by legislating their access to certain regions through bound relationships of *servitude* (Wells 1993). Pass laws were required of black (and at times coloured) workers in order to monitor migration, placement of racially appropriate workers in certain sectors, and the availability of large wage labor pools as demanded in various fields (such as mining or farming). Initiated in Cape Town, passes were mandatory for all "servants" to assure their employers' approval of their residence in urban areas. As Julia Wells (1993) describes in relation to this sector:

The most common type of pass confirmed a written labour contract detailing the period of work expected of the labourer, the identity of the employer and the terms of compensation. Workers who left jobs because of low pay, unreasonable employer demands or unsafe conditions committed a crime by breaking their contracts (P. 5).

Pass laws later become instrumental to the apartheid government's extreme control over migration, available labor pools and racial separation. Checked by security police as a regular aspect of daily life for black South Africans under apartheid, passes were required of workers in order to be permitted to reside in certain geographical areas. Notably, passes were issued to black workers *only* if they were employed in appropriate sectors. Being "caught without a pass" meant immediate imprisonment for black workers.[14]

In alignment with the Urban Areas Act of 1952, which stipulated the terms for Africans' residence in urban centers, the scope and application of pass laws assured the apartheid regime's enormous control over the black labor force. Furthermore, the geographic separation of the homeland strategies mirrored the intended racial "apartness" central to government's social engineering. With the tightening of control mechanisms as apartheid governance developed, African women were *only* permitted to cross these homeland boundaries if they attained work in domestic or farm labor. Critical to this study, the private homes of white employers became the only space where whites encountered the black majority (Cock 1980) because of this strict geographical racial structure now considered one of the harshest and damaging policies of the apartheid regime.

Domestic labor also illustrates how the education and labor structures reinforced one another through school curricula for black women focused specifically on improving "servant skills." Furthermore, these processes systematically feminized and racialized women's labor by constructing domestic work as the primary approved sector for *black women*—thus bartering access to urban centers and waged labor for long-term servitude through employment in white families.

Women's Collective Resistance

The instrumental enforcement of such oppressive policies was certainly not passively received among women throughout apartheid's history. Efforts to mobilize collectively spanned communities, trade unions and political organizations in resistance to apartheid's structural violence. The history of these acts of resistance repeatedly provides examples of women's organizing across the ubiquitous racial divides central to apartheid rule (Meer

1998). Collective writing, for example, emerged as a powerful venue of resistance that asserted the importance of women's voices within the freedom struggle (Farr 2002). The women's agenda, however, continuously fell second in priority to the liberation struggle to end apartheid (Walker 1991; Meer 1998; Britton 1999). Therefore, a sharp contradiction persisted between the widely associated historical perception of women as the "backbone of the struggle" for liberation and the lower priority of gender issues within the anti-apartheid movement.[15]

A central historical moment in relation to women's resistance and domestic work is significant to the study at hand. The Johannesburg Anti-Pass Demonstrations of 1956 were motivated by a mandate from government requiring employers to send their "Native female servants" to be registered and issued a pass as part of the "Native Population Register." Because passes at that time were not yet legally required of domestic workers, this particular mandate represented a strategic effort to heighten levels of government intervention in private life and dominate the "native population." As Cherryl Walker (1991) describes:

> The government had chosen its target well. Domestic workers were in a vulnerable position, their bargaining powers weak. Few had the resources with which to resist their own employers, even if they were aware of the implications of reference books, which many were not (P. 216).

Rather than blanket acceptance, however, this mandate resulted in an historical group action. Even with the deeply entrenched unequal power relations in the institution of domestic work, women aligned across racial divides to resist this strategic government act. Their collective mobilization resulted in the "Sophiatown March" of 1956—the largest women's resistance campaign focused on the exploitation of domestic workers. The demonstration led to the eventual arrest of over 2400 women for holding an "illegal procession." Women's commitment to collective action was intended to subvert the apartheid government's attempt to issue the "badge of slavery" to thousands of domestic workers without their consent and outside of legal boundaries (Walker 1991).

In relation to the current study, a critical component of this historical event was the way in which the government later successfully appealed to employers by promoting the threat to their own personal lives, should their "maids" collectively organize. This demonstrates that even in this early era of apartheid, paid domestic labor became a powerful and divisive institution to assure government compliance because of its placement in the most private context of employers' personal households.

Situating Domestic Work in the Historical South African Context

From these three critical points in South African history—the creation of homelands, the mandated pass laws, and women's collective resistance—the following interlocking ways in which each shaped domestic work as it is structured in the current post-apartheid context are most relevant. First, the migration patterns established in South Africa were characterized by a rapid flow of women from rural "homelands" to urban centers where domestic work remained the primary occupation for black women throughout the apartheid regime's dominance. Notably, this migration demanded of workers for employment in urban centers still continues to dominate the nature of the job, as my research consistently illustrated. Constructing domestic labor as a profession specifically for "African" women served the apartheid ideologies in distinctive ways. Second, the relegation of black women to the private sphere—without access to alternative sectors of labor—reinforced the capitalist/racist state policy and the colonial ideologies about privilege through the wide availability of and justification for domestic "servants." Third, this institution was further embedded by state structures that afforded only limited education for black women, which functioned to train them specifically to fulfill domestic work roles. Fourth, separating black families through women's migration as domestic workers substantially weakened a critical institution in the majority African population. Therefore, control over black women's labor became a powerful familial and community destabilization mechanism of state control that continued to grow throughout the apartheid regime.

The institution of domestic labor impacted the white minority in strikingly dissimilar ways. Because household labor was widely available and reinforced by the apartheid regime, the white population experienced a level of comfort and luxury in their daily lives that was rarely called into question—thereby ascribing distinct privilege at the expense of black women's indentured service. This created an apartheid context whereby the most personal daily existence central to the private nature of the household reinforced the extremely asymmetrical racial power relations at the core of the ideology of separation. At the same time, the State strategically utilized the household and the family in order to maintain a collective ownership of entitlement among the white population that was consistent with apartheid governance. As a result, the institution of domestic labor remained central to reinforcing the mutuality of state/public policy within the private sphere throughout apartheid.

The extreme privilege afforded to whites—reinforced by the normalcy of domestic labor—nourished and reproduced a dominant social psyche about the importance of racial separation. Allister Sparks (1990) captures the inherent contradictions of separation, intimacy and power between whites and blacks that remained vital to apartheid ideology:

> White South Africans are not evil, as much as the world believes. But they are blind—blinded by the illusion they have created for themselves that they live in a white country in Africa, that it belongs to them by right and to no others, and by the self-centeredness this has induced. From the beginning they have regarded the people of Africa as "aliens," foreigners from beyond the hedge or beyond the frontier or beyond the city limits, people whose real home was somewhere else, in a "homeland" far away, out of sight. The notion of a border, behind which white civilization must protect itself against the coming of the black barbarians is fundamental to white South African psyche. On the other side of the hedge, the blacks know more about the white world than whites know of theirs, for most spend their working days in it and even live there as domestic servants in white homes (P. xvii).

Domestic work, therefore, inverted this notion of border separation by creating the one social space where highly personalized labor permeated the dominant ideology of physical distance between the races. It is critical to note this ironic contradiction in the way that black women were both othered within the system of apartheid and hired to perform *intimate,* emotional labor that reproduced the households of white employers on a daily basis. Furthermore, this intimate knowledge that blacks contained about the dominant white population afforded some level of social power. As my interviews also suggest, such knowledge incited agency among workers that was enacted at both the individual and collective levels of transformation.

The research on domestic labor in South Africa is relatively limited in comparison to the long-standing and central role the institution played throughout the apartheid years. However, this is not surprising given the dominance of state control in all realms of social life—including the production of knowledge. I draw from an exhaustive collection[16] of the research to date on the case of South African domestic labor during the apartheid years to conclude this discussion of the historical foundation. The central analytic references I borrow from these sources provide a striking backdrop to later analysis of the extent of change within this deeply engrained social institution.

The earliest examples of local writing on domestic work embodied the apartheid ideology of servitude. Written generally as governmental guidebooks for employers rather than theoretical works, these pieces sought to facilitate amiable relations between employer and employee—encapsulating the paternal culture of domestic labor at this time. Guides such as the 1962 "Your *Bantu*[17] Servant and You" produced by the "Non-European Affairs Department" advocated harmony in the household to foster broader social stability:

> Generally it can be said that where there is courtesy and mutual respect between people of different groups, this permeates into the groups as a whole. As an employer of Bantu, you can therefore help tremendously in establishing a harmonious relationship between the European and the Bantu in this country (P. 8).

This government document illustrates how state discourse promoted the interrelationality of the public/private spheres by holding employers accountable for the "harmonious" race relations of the country through their creation of "mutual respect" in the private household. This example provides an interesting contrast to Chin's (1998) analysis of the role of the state in promoting a sense of "duty" among migrant domestic workers. Under the apartheid regime, this sense of obligation to the state was directed at employers to maintain orderly race relations for the betterment of the nation.

Whisson and Weil (1971) similarly engaged this public/private interdependence in their report, "Domestic Servants: A Microcosm of 'the Race Problem.'" While much more analytical through its detailed depiction of race, class and gender stratification within the institution, the authors ultimately draw upon the intersectional inequality central to apartheid ideology to suggest that domestic service is fitting for black women's "inferiority:"

> Domestic service is thus both the obvious resort of the woman who feels herself to be an inferior person and the context in which the sense of inferiority is institutionalised into the formal relationship of total dependence (1971:39).

Furthermore, although Whisson and Weil value the merit of expanding labor protection measures for this particularly vulnerable sector, they ultimately warn against rapid transformation of this institution from a structural level and place the responsibility for improved working conditions on the "Christian consciousness" of employers.

In a slightly more critical approach, Eleanor Preston-Whyte (1976) addressed the mutual reinforcement of apartheid's racial order through the institutionalization of unquestioned hierarchy within domestic service during the apartheid era:

> In South Africa, the etiquette of domestic service may be, and indeed is, indicative of an acceptance of racial inequality, as well as inequality stemming from the contractual relationship of employer and employee. It is this *double* pattern of inequality which leaves no ambiguity in the interpretation of the ranking of individuals. Whatever the degree of informality operating between master and servant, there is no question in the minds of the former, at least, who is in the dominant position. Familiarity may indeed, be encouraged by White employers within this framework of accepted and uncontested inequality (P. 87).

Preston-Whyte therefore suggests that while the relationship between worker and employer may be personal in nature, it is undoubtedly structured by non-negotiable, deeply entrenched stratification processes that reflect an overarching ideology of racial superiority.

During the height of apartheid's most violent decade of the 1980s, we see the emergence of a critical and theoretical discourse on domestic labor that challenges these institutionalized processes and their severe impact upon black women. Drawing upon social and historical conditions of apartheid, Deborah Gaitskell (1982; 1984; 1986) offers an original analysis of both the role of men in the institution and the various shifts in employment demographics from white women to black and coloured women.[18] Using what is now considered an intersectional approach, Gaitskell, et al. (1984) illustrate that:

> The relegation of large numbers of African women workers to this sector of wage labour in South Africa is a product of the complex operation of class, race and gender divisions over time (P. 107).

Gaitskell's work further depicts the importance of advocacy for the organization and unionization of domestic workers to change the structural conditions of their lives. Her research documents both the barriers to change and the realized successes that resulted from workers' mobilization. In contrast to Whisson and Weil, Gaitskell contends that collective organization remains one of the only viable options for institutional change—a progressive standpoint given the overarching social conditions at the time of her writing.

All other pre-democracy academic literature on domestic labor in South Africa is either predominantly historical[19] or highly specific in addressing certain related factors within the institution such as language (Von Kotze 1991), regional studies (Makosan 1989), violence (Kedijang 1990) or legal policy analyses of workers' rights (Brown 1994; Delport 1992). The most comprehensive work on the individual life stories of domestic workers, *A Talent for Tomorrow* by Suzanne Gordon (1985), documents the lives of 23 workers from the 1970s to the 1980s based upon her own interviews and direct involvement with workers' unionization. Building upon Gaitskell's work, this piece was pivotal to its time period because it provided a collection that both humanized domestic workers and challenged the complexity of relations *among* women during apartheid South Africa. Gordon also provided an important methodological contribution through her work within her own shared race and class group to advocate for equitable working conditions and an improvement in the overall "attitude" of employers. At the same time, Gordon developed non-formal educational organizations for domestic workers—representing a model of scholar-activism throughout her research.[20]

Maids & Madams

Most notable for her theoretical analysis of domestic work in apartheid South Africa, Jacklyn Cock's (1980; 1989) *Maids and Madams* provides the most comprehensive analysis of the socio-political relations embedded in this institution.[21] From a feminist Marxist perspective, Cock situates domestic labor as a site of class struggle central to the prevailing conditions of apartheid. Cock's interview data among workers and employers reveal the dichotomous nature of women's social position as "maids" and "madams." Similar to Hill Collins' (1990) "matrix of domination," Cock described South African domestic workers during the height of apartheid as trapped by a "triple oppression" through the systems of racial and sexual domination within an overarching capitalist system of production (1980:5–9). Drawing upon data at the micro-social interactional level of household work experiences—including employment relationships, self imagery of workers, and the mindset of employers—Cock continually situates her findings within broader social structures of race, gender and class-based discrimination molded in the apartheid era. To illustrate the significance of paid household labor in relation to broader social structures, Cock asserts the following:

> The institution is a microcosm of the existing pattern of racial inequal-
> ity in South Africa. But it is also more than this. Domestic workers play
> an important role in the reproduction of labour power, the capacity to
> work. This includes not only the physical maintenance (through the

preparing of meals and the laundering of clothes), but also ideological maintenance. The role of the domestic worker is important in socialisation into the dominant ideological order. Often it is the only significant interracial contact whites experience, and they experience this relationship in extremely asymmetrical terms. Many white South African children learn the attitudes of racial domination from domestic relationships with servants and "nannies." The converse is also equally true in that many blacks presumably learn the attitudes of submission (or at least the semblance thereof) that apartheid requires, and also the resentment it generates, through some experience of domestic service (1980:8–9).

Cock's emphasis on the central role of domestic work in racializing the socialization process illustrates how deeply embedded this institution remained throughout apartheid. By examining the impact of learned racism within the private household (for domestic workers, employers and children), Cock provides a social psychological analysis that poignantly illustrates the multiple layers of connectedness between the private and public spheres.[22] Even though at the time of her study predominant perceptions among employers were that "talking about domestic work is like talking about what goes on in the bedroom,"[23] Cock's work publicly uncovered domestic labor as a critical component of the racialized apartheid era. Additionally, through her analysis of the intersections of social position central to women's lived experiences, Cock's work ultimately challenged the extent to which 'sisterhood is global' through the severe asymmetry of power relations located within the institution of domestic work.

Throughout my time in the field, as I explained the topic of my research I was continually asked, "A modern *Maids and Madams* is it?" In many regards, yes. Cock's work certainly motivated this research and initially grounded my theoretical insight about the institution in the South African context. And as the data reveal, many of the findings from this research parallel those of Cock's study—particularly in the context of the work environment itself which tellingly reveals little change in microprocesses over the last 20 years. Similarly, reflective of Cock's work, these data demonstrate that work relationships changed very minimally in only a few cases of benevolent employers. Therefore, Cock's contribution provides a primary foundation for this research, which is centrally seeking to explore social change within the institution of domestic work.

This investigation of domestic labor, 20 years after *Maids & Madams*, also extends Cock's work in three critical ways. First, my research examines the *range* of intersectional relationships among women who can no longer

be universally defined as white/colonial madam and black/African maid—
as was the focus of Cock's research. By exploring the role of South Africa's
"newly elite" employers as well as Cape Town's coloured domestic workers, this study captures the institution of domestic work in ways that reveal
the multiple complexities of social positionality in the new democracy. To
date, this is the only extensive study that examines the multiplicity of racial
relationships within the institution of domestic work at a critical juncture
in the nation's transformation from apartheid to democracy.

Cock's work examined how the structural conditions of apartheid
were embodied and reinforced through the micro relationships between
women workers and employers in the institution of domestic work. This
study also captures the institution as a microcosm of prevailing structural
conditions. In the existing South African context, however, these conditions
are much different than Cock's 1980 data. The nation has since realized ten
years of democracy, innovative social policies, 32 percent women's representation in parliament, a revolutionary Truth and Reconciliation Commission process, and subsequently a growing collection of "newly elite"
employers who severely complicate the colonial race dynamics of domestic
work. Even though a portion of the findings in this current research are certainly discouraging because they are virtually parallel to Cock's study during the height of apartheid, they also afford further understanding of the
process of social change by examining the disjuncture between public victories and women's lived realities. In South Africa's current transformation
process, my data suggest that within the institution of domestic labor,
democracy has least been realized.

From this theoretical underpinning established through the discussion
of the bodies of knowledge that guide this research, I take the literature on
domestic labor and the South African case as a point of departure for the
remainder of this book. Let us now turn to establishing the specific framework for this study by examining South Africa's democratic transition and
the overarching context of change in the institution of domestic labor since
1994.

MAPPING THE "NEW SOUTH AFRICA"

The 1994 realization of democracy dramatically transformed both South
African society and its relation to the broader global community. South
Africa's emergence as the most economically developed country within Sub-
Saharan Africa afforded the nation much greater possibility for active par-
ticipation in the global arena. Johannesburg developed as a second-tier
international city and a strong economic center within Africa. Similarly,

ANC governance included visions of continental leadership intended to move the entire African continent to a more central position within the globalized world.[24] With this widely lauded transition, expectations about a rapid recovery remained high, particularly internally among those most severely disenfranchised by the apartheid era.

Since the 1994 transformation, however, the realities of a massive national debt carried over from the apartheid governance—combined with the ongoing severe socio-economic divides—lessened the optimistic accounts about South Africa's democratization within the international community. Rather, local analyses on the status of the nation's transition most often question the extent to which South Africa is realistically able to redress the massive inequality remaining now a decade after the end of apartheid. The Reconstruction and Development Programme (RDP), implemented by the ANC in 1994, prioritized social development and the redress of past racial/gender inequalities equally with economic progress (African National Congress 1994). In 2000, this plan was replaced by a Growth Employment and Redistribution (GEAR) scheme, a neo-liberal, economic-centered development approach which required a focus on debt relief through export production and a movement away from social development at the core of the RDP. Local experts in this study continually pointed to the ineffectiveness of both development models in dealing with the enormous economic and social/racial disparities of modern South Africa—ultimately suggesting that the nation maintains two parallel yet very unequal societies: the ongoing (still predominantly white) power group and the (predominantly black) "formerly disadvantaged."[25] These disparate social realities are essentially constructed by race, yet somewhat altered by new class structures in the post-apartheid context. Severely asymmetrical power relations, particularly with this new class component, continue to dominate South African society as one of the most impervious obstacles to realizing transformation.

Also central to this unhinging of transformation, perceptions of the new ANC governance are far less optimistic than the 1994 vision. Although Mandela's early leadership was widely celebrated (even among many whites) and certainly afforded substantial leeway given its tall order,[26] the post-euphoric Thabo Mbeki phase of democratic leadership has been widely criticized—particularly *within* South Africa, across all sectors of society. The data in this study pointed to the following perceptions as central criticisms of South Africa's new government: 1) inability to deliver services; 2) focus on economic rather than social issues; 3) under-prepared leadership;[27] 4) over-investment in defense; and 5) internal corruption. The international community similarly decreased its support for South Africa by redirecting funding to other conflict regions after the perceived public success of democratization.[28] These realities illustrate the daunting task of transformation and the massive challenge remaining to redress nearly 50 years of apartheid dominance. Rather than a revolutionary emergence as a new nation, the existing socio-economic conditions in South Africa reveal the necessity for *long-term* processes of change in order to realize congruence between a human rights-based democratic ideology and the severe social inequalities that continue to dominate the nation's landscape.

Bringing Democracy to the Household

How do these post-apartheid realities impact the institution of paid domestic labor in South Africa, particularly after the end of the honeymoon of new democracy? The structural conditions that permeate South Africa's transition shape the institution of paid domestic labor through four predominant connections. First, barriers of severe poverty and a 40 percent[29] unemployment rate most harshly impact women, leaving domestic labor a primary means for family survival. In this study, for example, 16 of the 20 domestic workers interviewed in-depth earned the only income within their immediate family structures. Because power groups are able to easily purchase the domestic labor of disempowered, typically black, women at extremely low wages, domestic work remains a deeply embedded, normalized institution that allows class privilege to be maintained in ways the parallel the apartheid era. And while the demographics of privilege may have shifted slightly such that elite black and coloured populations can also purchase domestic labor at very low rates, the power asymmetries of the traditional "maids and madams" (Cock 1980) relationship predominate the social fabric of South Africa—thus revealing how the institution remains virtually unchanged in the post-apartheid context.

Because of this heavily embedded normalcy that surrounds domestic labor in South Africa, affording fair living wages and labor rights to domestic workers as a *formal* sector represents an enormous cultural shift. This challenge speaks to the second important relationship between structural conditions and domestic work that encapsulates the current context of the institution: the policy/lived experience disjuncture. Although South Africa's structural labor policy changes are quite impressive, they remain unable to substantially shift the severe class and race-based inequalities rooted in the apartheid era. Therefore, even though the law mandates protection, domestic workers realize few benefits in their actual work contexts. For example, the 1997 Basic Conditions of Employment Act (BCEA) required that employers issue a contract of employment for all labor in private homes. Although this initiative was specifically designed to protect domestic workers through a formalization of the sector, of the 40 employment contexts studied in this research, only three actually utilized a contract, four years after the promulgation of such legislation.

This disconnect between South Africa's democratic policies and the ability to *access* protection is the central topic of local writing on the institution of domestic work since democracy. The existing conversation within South Africa on the case of domestic labor is widely policy-driven and found predominantly in the feminist AGENDA journal and within the NGO discourse. These issue-focused reports examine failed implementation of legislation in the areas of maternity benefits (Kehler 2000), unionization (Nyman 1996; 1997), legal rights (Delport 1992; Brown and Reynolds 1994), "occupational engagement" and work hazards (Galvan 2000), and wages (Bhorat 2000). The most recent in-country documents about domestic work therefore indicate an emphasis on applied issues of citizenship and democracy-building within the sector through the realization of rights, rather than a comprehensive analysis of the extent to which domestic work disrupts the overall structure of transformation in the post-apartheid era.

This limited ability to access rights among domestic workers can be directly linked to a third critical structural condition in the new democracy. The movement to the GEAR model of economic recovery severely diminishes women's access to rights because of its economic rather than social development core ideology. As evident in other national contexts (Staudt 1998), with this focus on economic reconstruction, women bear the most severe burden of structural redress. In the South African case, because domestic workers are the largest sector of working women, they incur a particular structural disadvantage with the movement to neo-liberal adjustment plans. Since democracy, for example, the institution of domestic work in South Africa is now characterized by an increase in the number of part-time workers, known as "chars." This pattern parallels the global movement toward more informal, unprotected, part-time labor, particularly among women (Sassen 1998). Domestic workers employed on a "part-time" basis, however, do so in several households, usually constituting a minimal 60-hour workweek. Yet these women remain unprotected from labor legislation because each job is considered part-time or "casual labor." This process re-instills severe class inequality as employers are freed from instituting mandated legislation in the household while workers report that each part-time work setting demands extraordinary outputs of labor because of increased expectations to perform what entails a week's work in a few days, *without* any formal protective benefits.

Lastly, these structural conditions limit workers' ability to collectively organize, as we see in the global context of paid household labor. Eva Lazar

(2000) examined "consciousness, resistance and identity" among domestic workers in the Johannesburg area using a neo-Gramscian approach to analyze the possibility of "transformative politics."[30] Consistent with my own research with the national domestic workers' union, the predominance of these social structures seriously challenges women's collective resistance. At the same time, these rapidly shifting structural conditions in South Africa's ongoing democratization provide new avenues for change. Through the mobilization of those most severely disenfranchised, South Africa embodies persistent social tension as well as the possibility for ongoing transformation in both the macro-structural and micro-relational realms. I wish to also suggest that the institution of domestic work provides a critical lens to examine resistance to change because of the inherently intertwined public/private nature of this labor. Domestic worker unions mediate this divide through organizational efforts to influence change. Therefore, in this case, we see how the mutuality of the public/private intersects with the persistent structure-agency dialectic as women actively engage in transformation of this institution—even in the face of these severe and interconnected obstacles.

CONCLUSIONS

This chapter mapped the multiple foundations of established knowledge that inform this research. My hope is to transcend notions of the household as private and disconnected from macro structures of power. In the South African case, the state's accelerated transformation offers a rare opportunity to explore the mutuality of change in both the private and public spheres—as well as the spaces where such transitions are most pervasively delayed. Drawing upon these complementary vantage points provides a solid foundation to explore how the deeply entrenched colonial institution of paid household labor remains virtually unchanged in the new South Africa.

I offer explanations for resistance to change in this last vestige of apartheid through the voices of South African women—positioned as domestic workers, employers and parliamentarians who are crafting the State's relation to this institutionalized labor sector. To do so, I draw upon the theoretical frameworks established in the literature that examine the public/private mutuality—with particular attention to how paid household labor complicates assumptions about the perceived duality of these spheres. The notion of intersectionality is particularly applicable to elucidate the overlapping social inequalities embedded in this institution. By positioning domestic labor as the central space in South African society where ongoing race, class and gender power asymmetries persist, we see how social institutions fail to actualize the ideology of equality and gender rights central to South Africa's public transformation. Moreover, the particular dynamics of South Africa's history and its existing racial diversity construct a "First World/Third World" (Mohanty 1991) divide that makes the literature on postcolonial feminism particularly insightful in the analysis of the relationships among women positioned as both employers and workers. Lastly, the existing research on paid domestic labor across a variety of regions and temporal conditions is critical to positioning this study within a global context where this private institution continues to reify severe structural inequality. I draw upon these studies to both illustrate that the South African case does not exist in a vacuum and draw particular insights about the local relationship between domestic labor and democratization. In doing so, the research on paid domestic work generated during apartheid South Africa (Cock 1980; Gaitskell 1984) is most directly applicable to the comparative component of this study that measures the extent of change in this institution.

My findings suggest that the residue of systematic oppression settles in the private household where domestic workers realize few benefits of the national transformation to democracy. The notable public transfigurations—such as the election of a democratic black majority party, the completion of a national Truth and Reconciliation Commission process, the leap toward 32 percent women's representation in parliament, several critical social and labor policy changes, and the assurance of "human dignity, the achievement of equality and the advancement of human rights" (South African Constitution 1996)—have not yet translated to the private household where domestic workers remain the largest and most severely marginalized sector of working women in South Africa. Capturing these multiple contradictions, that particularly disadvantage women, and analyzing their meaning in the newly democratic nation is the underlying tenet of this research.

With the local case of domestic labor grounded in these larger bodies of scholarship, we are now equipped to join this theoretical foundation with the methodological approach to this study. I conceptualize these two components as interconnected and mutually complementary to both the collection of data and the broader analytical contribution of this study. In this regard, I am reminded of Chandra Mohanty's (1991) assertion that "there can, of course, be no apolitical scholarship" (p. 53). My contention is that the *acquisition* of knowledge is also an inherently political endeavor. Let us now turn to the methodological processes—with this continual reminder of their integral connection to the bodies of knowledge that complementarily inform this study.

Chapter Three

Weaving Content, Context, and Self: The Methodological Journey

> *Having rejected women's historical status as the object of the male sub-*
> *ject's defining gaze, feminism demands that those who have been objec-*
> *tified now be able to define themselves, to tell their own stories. This is*
> *essentially a claim that each human being occupies a legitimate position*
> *from which to experience, interpret, and constitute the world.*
>
> —Camilla Stivers

> *Here I refer to those qualitative research projects in which researchers*
> *self-consciously translate 'for' Others in order to promote social justice.*
> *Sometimes explicitly trading on race/class privilege, in these instances*
> *researchers understand the [Self-Other] hyphen all too well. Bartering*
> *privilege for justice, we re-present stories told by subjugated Others,*
> *stories that would otherwise be discarded. And we get a hearing.*
>
> —Michelle Fine

My methodological approach to this study is grounded in a belief that the acquisition of knowledge cannot be separated from either the methods from which we gather data (Fonow and Cook 1991; Gottfried 1996) or our own social identities as central instruments throughout the research process (Wolf 1996). This chapter recounts the collection of knowledge that informs my study on domestic labor in South Africa's new democracy. Part of this story details the multiple methodological techniques I employed to acquire the data at the center of this study. Yet each step of that process was shaped by the constantly shifting dynamics of the field, the complexities of my case study of *private* households and my own identity, assumptions, emotions and intellectual development throughout this project. Therefore, I see these two parts of the research story as integrally connected to the content and analytic findings throughout this book. This chapter introduces three central parts of that story: the methodological 'directions' for this study, the complexities of applying these methods in a dynamically shifting field context and the meaningful components of my own research identity as the lens through which these data were acquired.

FEMINIST METHODOLOGIES

I engaged a qualitative, feminist, triangulated methodological design in an attempt to gather the most comprehensive portrait of the institution of domestic work in South Africa's new democracy. Feminist methodologists assert that connecting ideologies of gender equality with applied fieldwork practices requires a much broader restructuring than simply the shifting of data gathering processes (DeVault 1999). Rather, feminist methodologies call for a transfiguration of the perspectives from which we analyze the social world through the *centering* of analyses on women's lived experiences. Because historical knowledge bases have been grounded in men's experiences, the absence of women's voices seriously challenges the validity of prior scientific inquiry. As Dorothy Smith (1987) established, feminist methodology calls for a restructuring of research such that women's "standpoints" are valued and utilized as vital frameworks from which to understand the social world while redressing past biases in representation. Therefore, feminist methodology becomes a counter-hegemonic practice that transgresses traditional epistemological assumptions that lay claim to power through the production of scientific knowledge.

As researchers challenged traditional positivist approaches to social inquiry, diverse perceptions emerged about what constitutes "feminist methodology." From the wide spectrum of definitions established over the past 20 years,[1] the meaning I associate with feminist methods in the social sciences embraces the following tenets. First, feminist research attempts to shape the social world in ways that positively impact women by challenging patriarchal norms and redressing the gender imbalance. At its core, feminist research is committed to action and social change. Grounded in a notion of struggle and solidarity with women's movements throughout the world, feminist methodologies resist the elitist power structures traditionally associated with research that serve to maintain divisions between those leading studies and those being studied. Therefore, feminist research is essentially driven by the mutual prospect of social activism in alignment with scholarship.

These epistemological underpinnings are now more widely acknowledged as the central components of feminist methodologies in contrast to the initial emphasis on the data collection practices they employ.[2] Marjorie

DeVault (1999) describes this development and her own approach to defining feminist methods:

> When I am pushed to define feminist methodology simply and completely in the terms of mainstream social science, I risk distorting what feminist methodologists do. Instead of rushing to answer, it may be more useful to notice that the question comes from a discourse that is not eager to make room for us. Feminist scholars insist that the answers to questions should fit with the contours of women's lives, including our own. Thus, the researchers doing feminist work, and using feminist methods, are the starting point and the anchor for my answer, rather than some established notion of what a "methodology" should look like (P. 23).

As DeVault illustrates, feminist methods remain 'at the margins' of mainstream social science inquiry. Therefore, not only their practice, but also the underlying aspirations of social change inherent to feminist methods have certainly not yet infused the wider social science discourse.

Recognizing the intersecting junctures between ideology and methodology, the applied practices associated with feminist research most commonly embrace a highly qualitative nature, utilizing in-depth interviews, participant observation, ethnography and triangulated approaches that value a contextual depth of acquired data over quantity of responses gathered. Therefore, an emphasis on induction over deduction and process over structure is evident throughout feminist research (Reinharz 1983). Furthermore, moving away from assumptions about the 'objective' nature of social science inquiries, feminist methods value the *relationship* between the researcher and those researched as a core component of the quality of the data acquired. In general, this methodological approach abandons notions of 'value-free' science and builds upon the inherent subjectivity of all social research as a means of generating understanding. Therefore, the *relationship* between participants (vs. subjects) and researchers (vs. experts) becomes central to analysis in a way that is not possible in traditional methods of data gathering.

This project was designed to integrate these central components of feminist methodology with a particular attention to "giving back"[3] to the local communities in order to attempt to reciprocate the value of the knowledge provided for this study. In this way, I also engaged aspects of action research methodologies that advocate collaborative, participatory and inclusive projects in which the benefits of social research are shared by *both* the researcher and those communities researched (Reason 1994).[4] Both of these approaches demand the establishment of solid relationships among participants in order to contribute to local priorities throughout the research process. Building relationships became the most integral component of this research for two reasons. First, in order to work with communities as an "outsider," it was essential that I establish trust among a variety of communities. Second, because my topic of paid domestic work is considered one of the most private aspects of daily life in South Africa, I could only acquire honest reflective narratives through the establishment of close relationships with the participants in this study. To further examine this notion of building relationships in the field, let us now turn to the specific components of the overarching research design and fieldwork, with particular attention to how the conceptual foundations of feminist methodologies were taken up throughout this research.

THE RESEARCH DESIGN

My research questions, design and analysis cannot be separated from the path by which I embarked on the study of the household as a political space with particular meaning in the South African context. From 1995–1996, I conducted research at the University of Port Elizabeth[5] that explored the transformation of higher education in the first year after the democratic transition. While my initial work in South Africa focused on formal education, I was struck by the extent to which the country (as well as my own university apartment) was maintained by the labor of domestic workers with a normalcy that seemed unquestioned in the context of daily life. As I embarked upon a doctoral program, the questions I held about domestic workers in South Africa remained central to my studies on international development, social stratification, gender theory, formal and informal education, race relations and research methodology. The study of domestic labor as a central institution in South African society encapsulated my core questions about social change within the context of ongoing race, class and gender inequalities. In 1999, I returned to South Africa to conduct a one-month pilot research project in order to explore the feasibility of this study and establish initial field relationships. From these foundational experiences, I developed the perspective of utilizing the institution of domestic labor as a lens from which to assess the extent of social change in South Africa's ongoing transition to a human rights-based democracy.

Centrally, I framed this research with the following guiding question:

> *How has the institution of domestic work changed in South Africa's democracy?*

By situating domestic labor as a central social institution, I developed the following sub-questions to guide the fieldwork and establish thematic linkages between social relations at the household level and the broader context of democratic transition.

- *To what extent does the nature of the household reflect structural changes?*
- *How does domestic work inform our understanding of the relationships among women based upon differences in social location?*
- *How have women mobilized to transform domestic labor in accordance with the national democratic transition?*

In order to answer these research questions in the context of South Africa's democratization, I utilized multiple qualitative methods throughout nine focused months of fieldwork from November 2000-August 2001. Primary data collection included in-depth, semi-structured interviews; case studies; participant observation and archival research methods—each of which informed this project in specific and complementary ways. My goal throughout this research was to gain a comprehensive, multi-faceted integrated picture of the institution of domestic work through diverse interactions with 'slices' of South African society at multiple levels. Because I wanted to capture the many complexities and subtle nuances of my topic, a triangulated qualitative approach was most appropriate to this project.

"Getting in"

Domestic work in South Africa remains a highly normalized yet rarely discussed aspect of daily life (Cock 1989). With a growing emphasis on labor legislation to include domestic workers as a formal sector in the new democracy, I found an increased protectiveness about disclosing information surrounding the details of employment in private household spaces. This overarching context necessitated the establishment of relationships in the field that reflected heightened levels of trust in order to ask both domestic workers and employers to discuss the most personal aspects of their lives. To form these relationships, the National Office of the South African Domestic Service and Allied Workers' Union (SADSAWU) became an integral component of this research. I worked closely with leaders of this union for six months in a variety of capacities in order to gain trust and establish a reciprocal relationship that would contribute to local needs while I was collecting data from the field. Through these relationships, I was afforded exposure to multiple contexts otherwise inaccessible, which ultimately provided some of the richest sources of analysis. My relationship with SADSAWU fostered both critical access to domestic workers' daily realities and the opportunity to work with several other organizations that shared goals highly complementary to this research—such as a coalition of NGOs that devised a labor policy reform initiative during the time of this research (see Chapter Six). Furthermore, my relationship with SADSAWU created a context whereby my interpretation of acquired data was continually evaluated by women "on the ground" in the "real world." In this way, through merging scholarship and activism, I was forced to consider the extent to which my research had meaning and value in the local context.

Selecting Interview Participants

To maintain the regional focus of this project, all data were drawn from the Western Cape. I selected both domestic worker and employer participants for in-depth interviews in a similar manner utilizing a purposive snowball sampling approach facilitated by a wide range of social relationships. From this sample, I attained 40 in-depth individual interviews, 20 with employers and 20 with workers. Initial access to domestic workers emerged through the primary relationships built with key informants in the domestic workers' union. I established further worker contacts through references offered by early interview participants. The process of trying to attain interviews *without* previous relationships or solid references continually reflected the delicate and extremely politicized nature of this topic in South Africa. I initially attempted to approach women working in affluent neighborhoods and in public spaces such as city parks. All of these "cold contacts" however resulted in the perception among workers that I was seeking to *hire* rather than interview them—a reality that illuminates the rigidly embedded norms about women's relations across racial groups. Thus, in gaining access to workers, some prior experience, personal connection or organizational affiliation was critical to establishing informants' trust and willingness to participate in this research.

I became purposive in my sampling early in the process of selecting participants. Because of the highly particular nature of race in Cape Town, I wanted to assure that I attained equal representation of both coloured and black domestic workers. The life experiences of these two groups remains integrally shaped by the history and relative privilege granted in the apartheid era. Therefore the associated experiences of domestic workers from these particular groups vary in many respects. The representation of both black (N=10) and coloured (N=10) domestic workers situates the research in accordance with the highly particular nature of the regional Cape Town context.

Union membership was also central to my purposive sampling among workers. Currently in South Africa, estimates suggest that only 3 percent of domestic workers are enrolled in the national union.[6] The motivations, personal attributes and experiences of union members, I believe, are much different from domestic workers who do not join unions. Because of my interest in these attributes and the collective resistance of workers, I intentionally oversampled for union membership. Accordingly, I attained an equal representation of union and non-union members in the workers' sample (N=10 in each group). This 50 percent representation far exceeds the 3 percent national enrollment rate; however, because the union's work as an agent of social change and women's rights in South Africa was so central to this project, I wanted to be able to capture the range of perspectives among union members as well as their attitudes about the reform of domestic labor.

In sampling workers, I also selected equally between those who "live-in" the work context and those who live in their own homes and commute to work each day. The experiences of domestic work are much different depending upon whether workers also live at employers' residences. For example, power differentials are extremely magnified when workers' everyday existence outside of the hours of their labor is controlled within the living environment of employers (see Chapter Four). Because of the central nature of this condition specific to household labor, I attained an equal sample (N=10) of both "live-in" and "live-out" workers. While estimates of this distinction are not available to describe the overall population of domestic workers in South Africa, identifying varying perspectives based upon living conditions was central to this research because other theorists on domestic work (Romero 1992; Thornton Dill 1994) and women within South Africa asserted that moving "out of the backyard"[7] of employers remained critical to reforming the institution in a more equitable fashion.

The living situation of domestic workers added a complicated dimension to accessing this population and securing a safe and comfortable space to hold interviews. My primary focus was assuring that workers would feel free to discuss the nature of their work situations in an open environment. This was much easier for women who lived outside of their place of work because I could meet them in their own homes. For women who lived-in, not only was access to them filtered by employers who served as powerful gatekeepers, but the numerous obstacles to meeting such workers and conducting confidential interviews distinguishes one of the most challenging aspects of research with this particular sector. Because of the highly privatized nature of the work context itself and the power dynamics at play with employers, my methods of accessing workers necessitated creativity. In a few contexts, I met women downtown and brought them to my home to conduct the interview, although this process also embodied social location complexities and vulnerabilities on the part of workers. Very often, the process was facilitated through shared networks. For instance, when I knew one worker who recommended me to another, we could sometimes meet in the private space of the mutual connection. Although each instance was particular, it is central to note that overall access to workers provided one of the most complex applications of methodology throughout the fieldwork. The highly protected, private location of this topic and the power-laden differentials between workers and employers created severe (sometimes impermeable) barriers to assuring confidential spaces to initially build relationships or eventually conduct interviews.

Because the dynamic of the "new employers" from black and coloured groups has not yet been captured in the literature, I specifically sought out workers with employers different than the traditional (white) "madam." This proved in some cases to be challenging because the overall ratio of black and coloured employers is relatively low. Also, as many "newly elite" employers are now in powerful positions, particularly in parliament, access to their domestic workers remained quite guarded. In the formal interviews, of the 20 workers, four worked for "new employers" at some point throughout their career. In other situations, such as in one focus group, I conducted interviews with five other workers who were employed in coloured households and recruited by "agencies" from rural areas (see Chapter Five).

The last aspect of sampling among workers integrated in the study was age. I wanted to capture the experiences of older women workers to provide the full context of both apartheid history and democratic transitions in the data. The age range for workers was 21–64, however, only four of the workers were younger than 40. Therefore, to supplement the age range in my data, I conducted focus group interviews (N=10) in rural areas in the outlying areas of the Western Cape with workers under the age of 25.

In terms of marital and parental status, I did not specifically consider these constructs when selecting workers. Interestingly, of the 20 workers in the sample, only three were married and four were widowed. Thus, 13 had never married, a strong descriptor of the nature of the work and its demanded costs to workers' personal and intimate lives. What is also important is that *all* of the workers were mothers themselves, with a range of number of children from one to four. Of the 20 workers who were mothers, only two had *not* been separated from their own children in order to attain work in domestic service.

The following table (Table 3.1) provides a summary of these important descriptors within the domestic worker in-depth interview sample. It also illustrates relevant intersections of particular dynamics (such as race, live-in status and motherhood) that centrally defined workers' experiences in this sample. These descriptors are provided to more specifically portray this group of participants and establish a detailed context for the later analytical chapters that draw heavily upon narratives from this particular collection of worker interviews.

Table 3.1: Description of Domestic Worker Sample

Descriptor	Number of Workers (Total N=20)		Comments
Race of Worker	Coloured N=10		Purposively sampled to capture Cape Town racial dynamics
	African N=10		
Employers' Race	White N= 19	White N= 19	3 workers who worked for white families at the time of this study previously worked for coloured and African families (thus N>20).
	Coloured N=2	Live-in N=0	
	African N=2	Live-in N=1	
Union Membership	Union N=10	6 coloured; 4 black union members	Union members were purposively over-sampled to capture women's collective acts of resistance through unionization.
	Non-Union N=10	4 coloured; 6 black non-union members	
"Live-in" vs. "Live-out" Employment	Live-in N=10	Only 1 was satisfied with her accommodations.	Purposively sampled to capture diversity of experience
	Live-out N=10	* 7 lived in informal township locations and three lived in new housing development projects.	
Educational Range	Standard 1–Standard 10 (=U.S. Grade 3–12)		Mean education =Standard 6 (=U.S. Grade 8); only one worker completed high school
Age Range	21–64		Mean age=50
Marital Status	Single never married N=13		Predominance of single women indicates the *costs* to workers' personal lives in this sector.
	Married N=3		
	Divorced N=0		
	Widowed N=4		
Motherhood	N=20		All workers were mothers, (ranging from 1–4 children) who cared for the children of their employers at some point in their employment.

Accessing Employers

The highly personalized nature of the institution itself mirrored the techniques employed in order to access the topic at hand—highly personalized social networks. I sampled employers in a non-representative fashion similar to the process employed for union workers.[8] Critical to the ethics and confidentiality of this project, however, I did *not* interview any employers of workers, or workers of employers in my sample. Because I specifically wanted to document the emerging "newly elite" coloured and black women employers, I intentionally over-sampled these groups. This emphasis emerged from data collected in the field prior to employer interviews. As I discovered a predominant discourse about the "new madam," I realized the importance of capturing this emergent group of employers. Therefore, I purposively interviewed eight coloured, two Indian, three black and seven white employers. Of the seven white employers, I identify four as "non-traditional" because of their role in key human rights groups or their identity as strong feminists.[9] Also, within the coloured, Indian and black group of employers, (N=13) eight were either identified feminists or highly professional women, or both. Therefore, while my employer sample is certainly not representative of employers as a whole in South Africa, the data gathered from these particular groups became a central component to understanding the complexities of the institution of domestic work in the newly democratic nation. The following table (Table 3.2) summarizes the descriptive characteristics of employers important to this study, along with intersections of particular constructs that are central to the analytical discussions to follow.

Selecting employers added another interwoven aspect of identity and social location. Unlike domestic workers, where a central organizational body facilitated access, attaining interviews with employers occurred only through the relationships I formed in other social networks. Therefore, I had a limited ability to select various attributes, particularly because of the social power/access barriers to talking with employers about the highly personalized nature of the institution of domestic work.

Black employers in the Cape Town area are primarily parliamentary women. In order to access this group, I employed Britton's (1999) method of "squatting" outside of government offices and seeking references through administrative staff members. Several hours of squatting and a few other key informants eventually assured three interviews with parliamentary employers. Given these barriers to access laced in social power, however, my ability to sample employers on multiple attributes beyond race remained highly limited.

Table 3.2: Description of Employer Sample

Descriptor	Number of Employers (Total N=20)		Comments
Race	Black N=3	All parliamentarians; 2 identified as feminists	Race was a critical factor in the purposive sampling of employer groups in order to capture the class shifts in the new democracy through "newly elite" categories of employers.
	Coloured N=8	2 Muslim; 4 identified as feminists	
	Indian N=2	1 Muslim; 1 Hindu; 1 identified feminist	
	White N=7	3 worked in human rights NGOs; 3 identified as feminist	
Occupation	Paid Professional	N=5 (3 coloured, 1 white & 1 Indian)	The occupations of employers were considered in the purposive sampling.
	Human Rights/ NGO work	N=4 (2 white, 1 coloured & 1 Indian)	
	Academic	N=4 (1 white & 3 coloured)	
	Government	N=3 (3 black)	
	Not Employed	N=4 (3 white & 1 coloured)	
Employment Conditions	Live-in	N=11 (2 black, 3 coloured, 1 Indian, 5 white)	Live-in status intersected with class and race for employer groups (see Chapter Five).
	Live-out	N=9 (1 black, 5 coloured, 1 Indian, 2 whites)	
Feminist Identity	Identified Feminist N=10	2 black, 4 coloured, 1 Indian, 3 white	This category includes employers that either self-identified as "feminist" or who espoused gender rights in their narratives. Purposively over-sampled to gain perspectives on the new employer and social change oriented employers.

Because of the extremely high levels of consciousness about security in South Africa, simply "getting in" to the home environments where I conducted employer interviews required a great deal of trust. This dynamic was heightened substantially in the homes of wealthy employers, living in gated wall-enclosed communities. To break through these barriers with employers, I established trust through social network references. With workers, trust was assumed when I shared either my union affiliation or my willingness to travel to their home, particularly as a white woman. Similarly, in contrast to workers who almost always ended the interview with eager references to other workers, only three of the 20 employers offered references to other women like themselves.[10]

Interview Methods

I adopted a semi-structured approach to each interview with both workers and employers, utilizing a standard set of questions while providing ample space for discussion of specific areas relevant to each participant. Many of the conversations transitioned from semi-structured to open-ended narratives several times within the interview. I attempted to model Ann Oakley's (1981) interview method such that each contained "all the warmth and personal exchange of conversation with the clarity and guidelines of scientific research" (p. 33).

In each interview, I utilized a guide from which specific questions were asked of all participants in five major thematic areas. Depending upon the relevance of each woman's life experience, in some cases other questions were posed to particular informants (e.g., union leaders, parliamentary employers). For domestic workers, I utilized a 54-question guide of which 20 key questions were asked of every participant. The relevant use of the remaining 34 questions varied on an individual interview basis. For the employers, a total of 25 questions guided the interview, of which 20 were asked consistently of each participant.[11] The interviews varied from 45 minutes–4 hours with workers' interviews tending to be substantially longer. Each of the interviews with domestic workers was taped and later transcribed. Of the 20 interviews with employers, 16 were taped and transcribed.

In light of the substantial power differentials between employers and employees and the *highly* politicized nature of domestic work in modern South Africa, I found many employers reluctant to share their experiences in a formal interview context. Therefore, the remaining four interviews were acquired only through the assurance that responses would not be taped because of the high vulnerability of particular participants in very public roles. In these cases, copious notes were taken and immediately transcribed. I believe that the attitudes, perceptions and experiences attained in these non-recorded interviews allowed for access to the worldviews of highly privileged sectors of South African society in a way that would otherwise not be available in formal, taped interview processes. This reality, however, is deeply entangled in power differentials, which lead to a definite protectiveness among employers regarding their experiences with employing domestic workers in their private homes, and therefore a resistance to being tape-recorded. Of these four non-taped interviewees, all were fully aware of the nature of the research project and my eventual publication of the work. Each of the interviewees (both employers and workers) was assured that their identity would be protected through the use of a pseudonym and provided a consent form that fully described the project. In the case of non-literate informants, the consent form was fully described and authorized through verbal consent.

English was the primary language of communication in each of the individual interviews. Because English is the most commonly shared (often second) language of communication in South Africa, its use in this research was relatively free of complications. Language has historically been integrally linked to political structures of the apartheid era. Therefore, the black domestic workers in this study preferred to speak English rather than Afrikaans (the 'other white language' of apartheid dominance). Among the coloured sample, however Afrikaans was the first language. Although most members of urban coloured populations also speak English as a second language, in some cases, it was clear that a participant's ability to speak her own first language would have facilitated greater ease in communication, heightened conversational understanding and further depth in the interview process. Therefore, if I had developed fluency in Afrikaans and isiXhosa, the nature of the interviews with all worker participants and some employers would have certainly been enhanced. Yet the reality that most South Africans are either bilingual or multilingual minimized the complexities of the use of English in this research. At times when participants wanted to use their first language to express a particular thought, experience, or emotion, I encouraged them to do so and later had the transcript translated. In other cases, language differences were eased by my elementary conversational skills in both Afrikaans and isiXhosa, which fostered both relationship-building and further ease in communication.

Of the 40 interviews, 25 were transcribed by a hired South African research assistant from the University of Cape Town. All transcripts were reviewed for accuracy with the original taped interviews while in the field. The support of a local transcriber became highly valuable to the project because of the additional insight offered in terms of interpreting regional dialect and the use of specific terminology. I chose to transcribe the remaining interviews because of the sensitive nature of their content and/or the participant's need for protected identity.

In addition to the formal semi-structured interviews, I also conducted two focus groups and a series of in-depth interviews with particular experts across a wide variety of sectors. To begin my research with domestic workers, I led two focus groups of rural women outside the Cape Town central area. These focus groups allowed access to ten workers in a setting much different to the experience of domestic workers in the urban areas. Because of language differences in rural areas, however, these focus groups were conducted in Afrikaans with the on-site use of a local translator. Notes from these interviews were later transcribed after both focus groups.

To attain specific perspectives on a variety of issues related to my topic, I interviewed 30 other local experts with varying levels of exposure to the institution of domestic work in post-apartheid South Africa.[12] These interviews facilitated my desire to gain a comprehensive perspective on the multiple ways in which domestic work operates in the newly democratic nation. I identified individual participants through my knowledge of government leaders, NGO members, gender activists, legal experts and policy makers. Again, my close work with SADSAWU afforded further access, particularly through involvement with a policy reform initiative sponsored by the Commission on Gender Equality (see Chapter Six). In particular, conversations among parliamentary Cabinet members, some of whom were formerly domestic workers themselves, provided data that encapsulated the dramatic transitions of the new democracy.

One element that remained consistent throughout all of my interviews was that the quality of the interview itself was most often mediated by how I "got in." In many cases, my ability to see high-profile experts was facilitated by another relationship in a shared network. In other words, the nature of the relationship shared between the interviewee and the person who assured my legitimacy to her/him shaped the interview itself. Personal friendship referrals, for example, seemed to foster more open dialogue and personal disclosure. Professional network contacts shared with me led to more seemingly formal interactions. Therefore, the character of the relationship from which I gained access to expert interviews impacted the nature of the exchange and the information gained in critical ways.

These expert interviews were not tape recorded because of the professional affiliations of each participant. Many agreed to share information "off the record" as long as I could assure that the data would *in no way* be linked to participants' high profile position or their organizational affiliation. Confidentiality was therefore assured several times in each interview. I took copious notes during these expert interviews and logged each the same day. In reviewing the data, these interviews formed an invaluable kaleidoscope of perspectives on domestic work otherwise unavailable by talking to employers and workers alone—particularly in formal tape recorded semi-structured interview contexts.

Participatory Research

The process of collecting data grew far beyond that acquired in individual interviews. Because I was immersed in the field for nine months, living in multiple contexts to examine a highly private aspect of social life, participant observation, case study and archival research methods became integral to this project. I attained detailed data from a variety of social groups through specific methods described in the following sections.

In addition to paving a path to access domestic worker interviews, my affiliation with SADSAWU provided a daily site from which I observed a number of critical encounters at the organizational, civil society and governmental levels. The process of "getting in" with union leadership, however, had its own challenges partly because of my "outsider" status and partly reflective of a pattern of over-reliance upon key organization leaders for social research as South Africa continues to be heavily studied throughout its post-conflict transition. My active role in providing reciprocal labor resources to SADSAWU was critical to 'proving' my integrity and research intent—particularly as an outside white North American researcher. Engaging the core reciprocal tenets central to action research, I wrote grant requests, created databases, consulted to organizational meetings and worked with union members on various projects throughout the fieldwork. These interactions fostered daily contact with unionized domestic workers over the course of six months as well as exposure to multiple environments in which the union functioned. For example, I attended parliamentary sessions and meetings of the national Labour Portfolio Committee through my alignment with SADSAWU. My work with this organization also spanned beyond the Cape Town region through involvement in education/planning meetings with National Office Bearers in Johannesburg, where I interviewed each member of the national leadership at length, along with affiliated colleagues in other workers' unions and civil society organizations. Through these ongoing contacts within SADSAWU, I was able to follow up with workers and participate in several aspects of their life outside of the formal interviews.

My affiliation with SADSAWU also afforded opportunities to work with the Gender Monitoring and Advocacy Coalition of the national Commission on Gender Equality, a Parliamentary Commission central to the national Gender Machinery established in 1996. In this capacity, I observed a central network of policy makers and NGO advocates lobby for the inclusion of domestic workers in unemployment insurance and maternity benefit coverage as well as the initial planning phases of a minimum wage campaign. My role in this capacity also allowed for observation of the Congress of South African Trade Unions (COSATU); a controversial employment agency for domestic workers; the Black Sash (a feminist, human rights, formerly anti-apartheid organization with a particular investment in domestic work issues); and the Domestic Workers' Association (DWA), the most historical organization devoted to domestic workers' rights. Each of these organizational components facilitated a reciprocal research relationship that contributed to local initiatives while gathering extensive research data. Lastly, I was able to review the membership database at the national office that contained demographic information on all workers registered in the Cape Town vicinity (N=803). As these central elements of the fieldwork experience reflect, my affiliation with SADSAWU was integral to establishing a research identity among local populations, building trust, and realizing the feminist/action methodological goals of this project.

Fieldnotes

In the context of the highly sensitive, political and personal nature of domestic work in South Africa, I found my fieldnotes critical for documenting the multiple ways in which I observed the institution throughout my nine months in Cape Town. Domestic work is unquestionably considered part of 'everyday life' in South Africa. Therefore, I gathered some of the most valuable data during times when I was 'off duty'—at social parties, restaurants, weddings, shopping areas, city parks, public markets and over the course of weekly invitations to dinner in various homes. Discussions of domestic work became easy topics of casual social conversations because I was invariably asked what I was studying in the country. The commentary replies to this question produced invaluable social discourse on the widely held perceptions across various groups that were certainly withheld from formal interview settings.

Some of the most integrated perspectives I acquired about domestic work came from a series of living experiences among South African families. While these data acquired through fieldnote observations are not free from complications related to their collection in very private circumstances, their validity is essential to this project because it was in these contexts that I directly witnessed interactions between employers and domestic workers. I recorded the actual relationship, work responsibilities, pay, daily expectations, conflicts, communication styles and perceptions shared with me by both workers and employers.

My fieldnotes mapped the social landscape of weddings where I paid particular attention to how the "maid's family" engaged in the celebration. I documented the multiple incidents when children scapegoated the domestic worker when anything was missing in the household. My observations of "Anne's" acts of agency when she was asked to iron all the bedding an hour before she could catch the last "taxi" to her township home connected directly to the findings in my formal interviews. By observing and recording the actual interactions of the institution—rather than the retelling of it by employers and employees—I began to synthesize the complex layers surrounding domestic labor in South Africa.

The daily reflection process of fieldnotes also served as a critical tool to integrate my own emotions, thought processes, development and questions throughout the research. These fieldnotes captured a chronological log where my documentation of the fieldwork was paralleled with personal experiences in order to closely integrate my own research position with the data collected. I wanted to be able to look back to my own experience and understand how emotions (especially fears and insecurities) shaped the data I gathered (Kleinmann and Copp 1993; Rothchild 2002). Many times I felt more prepared for the shifting demands of immersive research after writing fieldnotes, as they became a particularly cathartic coping mechanism to the often isolated and challenging experiences in the setting.[13]

Archival Research

I collected archival data through review of several publications related to domestic labor from both apartheid and post-apartheid timeframes. The primary data gathered included a review of the past 40 years of newspaper articles on domestic work in Cape Town. Similarly, all government documents that related to domestic work or labor were reviewed to establish a history of policy changes and the broader national discourse on the institution. I also reviewed several key organizational archival libraries in order to understand how each served as advocates for domestic worker rights. These organizational resource bases included:

- SADWA/SADSAWU—the former and newly reformed domestic workers' union
- Domestic Workers' Association—an historical non-union membership group supporting the education and rights of domestic workers (1979–1999)
- The Amy Biehl Foundation—a U.S.-based NGO focused on education and nonviolent reconciliation in post-apartheid South Africa
- COSATU—Congress of South African Trade Unions
- The Black Sash—the human rights organization with the longest history of domestic worker advocacy in South Africa

In addition to thorough analysis of these organizational documents, two key journals were reviewed from 1980–2001. I analyzed coverage of domestic work issues in both the *South African Labour Bulletin* and *Agenda* (South African feminist journal) in order to situate domestic work in both the broad labor and feminist discourses over a 20-year period. Lastly, the University of Cape Town's Centre for African Studies Library provided an extensive academic archival database. I reviewed all historical records contained in this national collection that dealt with domestic work from either personal experiences, organizational advocacy, governmental or labor policy changes.

Summary of the Field Research

In total, the data that informs this research project were acquired through the following methods:

Table 3.3: Summary of Data Collection

Interviews
20 Domestic Worker Interviews
20 Employer Interviews
2 focus groups of rural domestic workers employed on farms—10 participants total
1 focus group with rural workers employed through "agencies"—5 participants total
30 Interviews with government representatives, NGO workers and labor organizers
TOTAL N=85
Participant Observation
9 months of daily fieldnotes across professional, academic, organizational, research and personal contexts
Case Study Analysis
6 months of observational work with SADSAWU, including interviews with all members of the National Office Bearers leadership (N=6)
Analysis of 600 membership records (average salary and race of members)
6 months integrated work with the Gender Monitoring and Advocacy Coalition sponsored by the Commission on Gender Equality
Domestic worker employment agency case study
SADSAWU—the former and newly reformed domestic workers' union
Archival Research
Review of all newspaper articles related to domestic work (1960-present)
Review of all documented governmental policy debates on the case of domestic workers
Analysis of the *South African Labour Bulletin* and *Agenda's* (feminist journal) coverage of domestic work issues from 1980–2001
Review of the national union's debates around the inclusion of domestic workers
Review of the historical documents of the Domestic Workers' Association, the Black Sash and the Amy Biehl foundation

Analysis

The data analysis phase began in the field with the review of each interview tape and subsequent transcript. My early analytical insights were fostered by the support of key informants and mentors in the field in both academic and applied settings.[14] After leaving the field, the data analysis process involved an initial review of 1400 pages of accumulated interview transcripts and fieldnotes to develop general overarching themes and group the large volume of data. With Emerson, Fretz and Shaw's (1998) guidance, I employed a process of "pursing members' meanings"[15] through extensive immersion in the data to find both patterns and inconsistencies. I developed 158 codes from the data and used QSR NUD*IST software to manage the analytic phase through the development of a conceptual "tree" that facilitated both the detailed process of coding as well as the broader analytical interpretation of the data.[16] In particular, I relied upon the ability to examine within-group variance through the use of QSR NUD*IST. This aided ability was particularly fitting for my data set because I wanted to examine how multiple identity factors (such as race and worker/employer status) impacted perceptions and experiences within interview responses. This analytic tool was especially appropriate to the theoretical framework of this research, which focused on *intersections* of women's experiences.

The final component of this project involved the complex practice of siphoning the data and determining those themes that appeared as most salient to my research goals. The process of shifting from participants' voices, to narrative written transcripts, to the eventual inclusion of particular passages and participant statements returns this methodological conversation to one of the underpinning complexities of conducting feminist research. To take up these issues in greater depth, this chapter now shifts from describing the methodological techniques to posing a broader understanding of the data through reflecting on particularly salient aspects of applying the *practice* of feminist research in South Africa. By disclosing these related components of the research process, my purpose is to offer a fuller understanding of the lens through which I gained and interpreted the content of this study. I include these central components of the methodology to foster a broader dialogue about the complexities of conducting feminist research through a more comprehensive analysis of the interconnected processes by which we acquire and interpret data as "outsiders" working within local communities.

THE DIALECTIC OF FEMINIST RESEARCH

The power-laden process of conducting research in cross-cultural contexts evokes extreme differentials in race, class, language, nation, citizenship,

religion and often cultural values between the researcher and her informants. Feminist methodologies add another component to this process
through their emphasis on working *with* local communities, reflective of an
underlying ideological commitment to redress gender inequality throughout the research process. Embracing these inherent complexities, feminist
methods also contain vast opportunities to impact social change positively,
particularly in women's lives. Through their shift from traditional hegemonic approaches that reinforce power differentials in the research process
itself, feminist methodological applications reconfigure the relationships
between researchers and those communities studied by valuing the *co-creation* of knowledge. This dialectic relationship between power asymmetries
and libratory practices emerges throughout the literature on feminist
methodology (see DeVault 1999).

In *Feminist Dilemmas in Fieldwork,* Diane Wolf (1996) positions
social power differentials as the core challenge to the co-creation of
research projects among scholars and local communities. According to
Wolf, these social position divides between researcher and participants seriously limit the extent to which feminist researchers can assure that their
projects are mutually beneficial to the populations from which they draw
data. Wolf further asserts that research involving women from the so-called
First World/Global North embarking on field research in the Third
World/Global South entrenches these power asymmetries through particularly challenging questions about subject-object representation. As Chandra Mohanty (1991; 1997) problematizes, the history of this practice and
its inherent "monolithic construction" of the "other" serves as a central
conflict among women positioned in distinctly disparate geographic and
social locations.

The dilemma of speaking *for* vs. working *with* women in marginalized positions remains a central discussion among feminist methodologists. To what extent can academic researchers abandon their own social
position, institutional/academic allegiances and relative privilege in the
process of making every attempt to "blend in" as cross-cultural field
researchers? While feminist researchers note several examples of downplaying the multiple aspects of privilege they bring to fieldwork among
marginalized communities, Wolf (1996) asserts that the extent to which
such differentials can be renounced remains limited, particularly in international settings. Furthermore, genuine co-ownership of the post-
research analytical production of knowledge remains particularly
unrealistic as most feminists retain control of the research process "from
conceptualization to writing" (1996:19). These realities ultimately point
to a core ethical complexity: to what extent does feminist research benefit

the population of participants as much as it does the careers of already privileged researchers?

Led by scholars such as Fonow and Cook (1991), Wolf (1996) and Gottfried (1996), analysis of these overarching complexities and the widely unspoken applied realities of feminist methods has generated a rich dialogue about the opportunities to engage feminist politics in the field and the limitations inherent to this interconnected theory/praxis foundation. According to Kathryn Ward (2002), researchers who tell the stories of their often compromising challenges in the field engender a critical development in the growth of feminist research methods that have previously been confined for fear of discrediting the quality and claims of scholarly projects by talking about the "nitty gritty" of the field.[17] I assert that the development and legitimacy of feminist methodologies can only be assured through an ongoing analytic dialogue about these applied complexities inherent to linking the ideologies of feminist politics to the realities of conducting research on the ground. To support this notion, I turn this chapter to a discussion of key examples of the complexities that emerged as I practiced feminist methodologies among a very diverse sample of women in a society that straddles a complex conflict/post-conflict transition.

Putting Methods to Practice

Nowhere is this First World/Third World divide between women's experiences more apparent than in the private homes of employers of domestic workers. Throughout my field research, I was seeking to understand the complexity of this relationship among women—both domestic workers and employers—in the post-apartheid context. This demanded a very distinct shifting of identity in order to gain access to both populations. Feminist researchers involved in cross-cultural studies often discuss the multiple ways in which they craft, or fictitiously alter, their own identity in order to be "get in" with specific research populations (Wolf 1996). In some cases, this involves downplaying researchers' heightened levels of power in order to lessen social location differentials. In other instances, hiding particular aspects of one's beliefs or values that may be different from that of the research populations' facilitates the appearance, albeit often only at a surface level, of shared experiences.

To access the diverse informant population of workers, employers, parliamentarians and activists in this study, I emphasized certain aspects of my identity in order to heighten connections among particular groups and lessen our differences in social location and lived experiences. For example, among domestic workers, I played down my social position by emphasizing that my family had *never* employed household help. Among employers, I left out this part of my history. I also utilized my choices about where I lived in the field—as well as the connected political interpretations—to heighten connections among certain groups. My local residence in a marginalized "coloured" neighborhood afforded me more trust and credibility in many sectors of the research sample. Yet I did not live in a black township. And because the politics of race became so dominant as this research developed, my geographical affiliation with "coloureds" infringed upon relationship building among other groups. To the white employers, mention of the location of my residence was generally met with surprise, and often a related comment about how "adventurous" we foreigners were.

Race and class differentials remained at the forefront of my application of feminist methods. Centrally, because of the highly racialized history and ongoing inequalities that continue to structure South African society, my whiteness shaped every social interaction. With workers, my race was initially cause for distrust, however, its intersection with my American/foreign identity assuaged the tension between white and black women contained in the social history of apartheid and the institution of domestic work. The data reveal striking examples among participants that speak to the importance of race and the impact of racial differentials between informants and researchers. In many instances, domestic workers would refer to my race in an apologetic tone, often before they would share some aspect of their experience with white South Africans. Ntutu, for example, recalled her relationship with a former (white) employer by telling me, "I'm very sorry to tell you that because you are also a white. She took me as a *dog*. I don't think she take me as a human being." Along with apologetic statements like Ntutu's, domestic workers also referenced my race by stating an acknowledged difference between me and the South African white population. In many instances, this assessment resulted from my willingness to travel to township locations, a permeation of geographical boundaries that remains highly atypical even ten years after the end of apartheid.

In contrast to the racial dynamics of interviewing workers, among employers, my race almost unquestionably afforded access to social circles with ease in most instances. Throughout my work with (particularly white) employers, I was acutely aware of my racial privilege and the intrigue that my U.S. identity brought throughout my interactions with this group. In most cases, I knew this was the only way that I got in. Jacklyn Cock (1980; 1989; 1990) discussed the fact that her shared identity with employers led to easily established rapport and higher quality data. For these reasons, she chose a black isiXhosa-speaking woman to conduct all of her interviews with domestic workers because of the heightened racial and political nature of apartheid South Africa at the time of her research.[18] In this research, however, the intersections of my own identity as an "outsider" allowed me to span both groups and conduct all of the interviews with an external fluidity that in no way connected to my internal feelings of deep conflict. I imagined my African American colleagues' inability to access that same privilege in the South African context because the euphoric transformation of the "rainbow nation" has not yet shifted the sharp racial divides that dominate social life in ways that continue to shape the formation of relationships.

The ease of my fitting in with employers often led me to question the extent to which I was colluding with white privilege in order to attain data. Even though I knew I would eventually critically position the particularly privileged employer narratives within an analysis of the severe inequality maintained through domestic work, I remained in conflict about my relationship to and strategic use of South African white privilege throughout my work with employers. To get information, I inflated my whiteness at times, especially in the homes of employers. I commented on their beautiful decor. I shared with them personal needs about getting settled in their country, which fostered their disclosure about resources and information to align our race and social class interests. In most of my interviews in the homes of employers, I was served tea by a domestic worker while I interviewed her employer about the context of the work relationship. In these circumstances, I also refrained from divulging my active role with the national union of domestic workers. These interactions with employers continually forced me to confront the fine balance between collusion in social power and the collection of data through creating the least threatening environment for participants' disclosure.

The fieldwork similarly presented situations where I experienced conflict about colluding with gender inequality in order to both "fit in" and gain data. By adapting to local gendered norms in order to be accepted (Wolf 1996), I withheld a portion of my own belief system that remained in sharp contrast to the patriarchal culture that dominates every racial group in South Africa. This dilemma played out most intimately in a series of both public and private contexts where I absorbed a dominant expectation that I "do gender" (West and Fenstermaker 1995) in order to fit in among local populations. In some cases, I withheld challenges to particularly patriarchal belief systems—held by both women and men—so as not to upset my relationships in the field. In other incidents, I experienced a heightened expectation to participate in the household reproduction in a variety of living situations. Ironically, these dilemmas encapsulate the contradictions inherent to gender inequality and the institution of domestic labor in South Africa. Furthermore, they represent another level of compromise and identity construction through the withholding of personal values for the sake of social acceptance in the field. Knowing Judith Rollins' (1985) work and her complete identity creation as a domestic worker, I retained some sense of security and justified my subtle identity alterations and willingness to "do gender" to a certain extent because it provided a direct avenue to further understanding of my research topic, particularly in private household spaces. Yet I was still asking women for complete honesty when I was only willing to share portions of myself in many situations, thus playing out the inequality of my representation within the research process itself.

Feminist Methods in Conflict Regions: The Limits of Application

The dynamics of this study's placement in a region of ongoing internal conflict and violence centrally shaped my experience in the field and particularly my ability to access data. Throughout the fieldwork, I remained continually aware of how my need to assure personal safety influenced my emotions, willingness to take risks and overall daily experience in the local context, as this fieldnote entry reveals:

> I notice bars protecting all the windows, barbed wire topped cement walls around our backyard, and heavy double locked gates outside every door. They feel obtrusive, daunting, and so blatantly telling of the ongoing economic divide in this country. I cannot get used to these visual reminders of protection even in my third visit here. I am more fearful of the conditions that will force me to employ them throughout the next year (Fieldnotes from arrival day, November 7, 2000).

For difficult reasons, this emphasis on safety shaped the extent of my full immersion in South African society.

Another critical complexity where the realities of regional violence intersected with my application of feminist methods in the field emerged in the *spaces* where I conducted interviews. The dynamics of space and location are integral to feminist methodology and the contexts of where we gain data. In the study of domestic labor, the interview site itself embodies social power differentials. To downplay these social location divides and facilitate linkages among my informants, I regularly met live-out domestic workers in their homes during the weekends when they were not working. This required a heightened management of travel to township locations where severe poverty increases the threat of crime, particularly as a white woman driving alone in such a local community. Comforted to some extent by a broad awareness of township geography in Cape Town, I was willing

Figure 3.1. Township Geography. Photograph by author.

Figure 3.2. White Wealth. Photograph by author.

to sustain the risk of driving to black and coloured "locations" alone in order to meet workers in spaces that evoked comfort and a feeling of both physical and psychological freedom from the dominance of their employment environments. Yet I evaluated risk carefully for each township interview because of this dominant psyche I developed about safety—partly absorbing the South African culture of fear, partly my own uncertainty at times, and significantly a very grounded hesitation reinforced by the daily reports of crime and the severe structures of racial division that maintain South African society.

In many ways, however, this process of meeting for interviews was logistically much easier with employers who were all more freely mobile with personal transportation. Many were professional women who made appointments with me during their work hours. I could sometimes fit three of these appointments in a day. With workers, the travel time and average three hours per interview usually meant that one full day was required per interviewee. I wanted to disown the part of me that was more comfortable meeting an employer in a coffee shop in Cape Town's central tourist shopping mall than meeting a worker in her township home, in a neighborhood where I had known three people to be killed in my nine months of study.

In South Africa, geographic location—and its embedded race and class divides—is centrally connected to personal safety. Parts of me wanted to deny this reality. As a white woman conducting research in a black township, I tried to convince myself that I would be safe, trusting the strong community ties I established in the country since 1995. Another part of me knew that my personal safety was completely dependent upon the car that carried me. I thought of Amy Biehl[19] often in these moments. During my fieldwork, one of my closest friends, a young white American woman, was hijacked in the same area where I conducted many interviews. Her reality shaped my willingness to take risk. In one case, I stopped pursuing a particular aspect of my research on domestic worker employment agencies after being warned by several NGO leaders, domestic workers and personal friends that my safety was at risk. I look back and think that what I 'uncovered' there might have been the most original aspect of my work. Yet my research was severely truncated because of my own personal limitations in the feminist pursuit of redressing power imbalances.

In another instance, while driving at dusk in the townships to take workers home from a union meeting, we got lost:

> Last night in Guguletu [Gugs], I felt really scared—it was dark, we were relying on Zora to tell us where to go and she was also lost. It was one of the most stressful moments here. I felt so responsible for the

lives of others and so alone driving down sporadically paved roads that seemed to wind in circles amongst a sea of shacks in the winter rain. The township was alive at that hour, bustling with activity as residents ran to markets and spaza shops about to close—music pounding from each. This heightened vibrance of the community's bustling hour even further exclaimed our not belonging there. Driving through the streets, I felt so exposed and vulnerable. I knew we were really standing out too much—memories of Amy Biehl crossed my mind each minute. Curious people too close to the car walked right in front of us. The roads are full of enormous potholes. I just kept driving, calling upon the intentions of my work in this country at some hopeful, naïve level. The next day we learned that Zora's brother-in-law was shot that night on the same road. As I heard this news, I found myself drawing a strict boundary about returning to Gugs at night (Fieldnotes excerpt, July 5, 2001).

While this portrayal depicts one of the most heightened experiences of personal safety risk over the course of nine months, it also illustrates the extreme vulnerability involved in simply letting the fieldwork emerge. On a daily basis, personal safety in conflict regions of the world must be negotiated and calculated within the goals of social research. In South Africa, my aspirations to 'go with the flow' of relationship-building were constantly measured by a consciousness about personal safety, trust and my ability to 'get out' of situations or geographical placements that emerged from immersing myself in social life as an outsider.

As I reflect on my own experience with this particular dilemma, I continually evaluate the extent to which bartering the boundaries of personal safety led to both the attainment of rich data and the embodiment of a naiveté embedded in my own cultural being. My assertions about entering these spaces as an outsider also reflected a sense of curious entitlement situated in my own social position and assumption about my place in South Africa after living there for a total of two years. Sindiwe Magona's (1999) *Mother to Mother* novel poignantly reveals the contradiction inherent to this paradigm I held. As the voice of Amy Biehl's murderer's mother, speaking to her mother, Linda Biehl, Magona writes:

Let me ask you something: what was she doing, vagabonding all over Guguletu, of all places; taking her foot where she had no business? Where did she think she was going? Was she blind to see that there were no white people in this place? . . . What was she doing here, your daughter? What made her come to this, of all places. Not an army of mad elephants would drag me here, if I were her (P. 48).

This "vagabonding" Magona describes is furthermore bound by a sense of social privilege evident in how particular groups transcend geographical space with fluid boundaries—a process that materializes embedded inequalities through very practical daily realities.

Leaving the Field

Further embedding the asymmetry of social location differentials, feminist researchers generally maintain the resources to leave the field whereas participants often have few options to escape the conflicts that shape the social circumstances of their daily lives. These conditions heighten the emotional experience of separation, particularly when feminist research projects establish close friendships in the field (Oakley 1981; Wolf 1996; Gottfried 1996). Such realities allude to a central paradox in feminist methods: the greater the involvement and contribution to informant communities, the larger the possibility for instilling a sense of emotional loss (for both communities and researchers) at the closure of fieldwork. Furthermore, engaged feminist research can create a sense of dependency that seriously disrupts local initiatives when fieldworkers (and their resources) leave.

Of particular concern in the process of separation is the challenge of embracing reciprocity in analytic writing phases and the eventual production of texts that re-present the stories of women's lives. As Virginia Olsen (1994) posits:

All feminist research shares with interpretive work in general the assumption of intersubjectivity between researcher and participant and the mutual creation of data. In a certain sense, participants are always "doing" research, for they, along with the researchers, construct meanings that become "data" for later interpretation by the researcher (P. 166).

The question of how this process of intersubjectivity is facilitated and who eventually takes control over the final product remains a practical debate among feminist scholars, who are often situated in traditional academic institutions that critically evaluate the production of knowledge.

My attempts to engender co-ownership of the research process involved working with local organizations to influence policy change, pursuing subtopics that were most meaningful to local populations (such as human trafficking in employment agencies), returning interview transcripts to participants for review, and regularly discussing my analytic interpretations with key informants throughout the fieldwork. Upon leaving the field and returning to New York, however, I found my attempts to engage participants in the analytic and writing phases—as well as my own ability to maintain an active contribution to local organizations—particularly challenging. In the case of South African domestic workers, some do not read English. Others do not have phones. These practical realities of long-term communication contour the reciprocal limitations of this study. In the field, I could maintain daily contact with participants and construct processes that fostered spaces to realize a genuine co-creation of knowledge. Yet the analytic interpretation of participants' voices did not cultivate mutual engagement in the process of writing. In this case, the limitations of my feminist/action research were partly a result of geographic distance, yet centrally entangled in the dilemmas Wolf (1996) puts forward about telling and owning the "story."

This project forced me to continually confront the extent to which feminist researchers can both maintain reciprocal relationships from the field and produce knowledge that informs a broader academic community. Notwithstanding the inherent complexities of this process, from my ongoing engagement with the participants in this study, I contend that a balance between feminist politics and methods is possible, even across geographic divides. Carol Stack (1995) eloquently synthesizes this possibility:

> But in the end it is the ethnographer who lays her fingers on the keyboard to play the final note in the chorus of voices. Purged of an awesome and impossible claim that we write the "subject's" truth, I still believe it is possible that the ethnographies I write reflect a progressive and feminist social agenda. As feminist ethnographers, we take on a knotty paradox of social responsibility: We are accountable for the consequences of our writing, fully cognizant that the story we construct is our own (P. 105–106).

Ann Oakley (1981) suggests that this balance is built upon the establishment of *long-term* relationships in the field. Advocating the importance of maintaining contact, Oakley contends that genuine friendship in the field fosters higher quality data as well a critical link between research and "real life." In this regard, she posits, "personal involvement is more than dangerous bias, it is how we admit others into life" (1981:58).

More recent accounts from feminist scholars underscore the importance of longitudinal studies based upon solid relationships between researchers and local communities. As Nancy Naples (1998; 2002) comprehensively depicts, such long-term relationships foster the realization of women's coalitions that connect local struggles to broader issues of global gender justice. Through the organization of women across race, class and national divides, such linkages manifest the possibility to deconstruct hegemonic practices of gender oppression across geographic divides. Throughout my experiences working in South Africa over the past 10 years of post-apartheid transitions—and returning to the population in this study twice since this research—I assert that the felt benefit of feminist methodologies that are intended to contribute to social change can only be realized through a commitment to long-term research beyond the legitimizing academic milestones (such as tenure) of scholars' careers. While this investment is more costly at both material and emotional levels, engagement with feminist research also engenders the possibility of contributing to the reshaping of social relations through the production of knowledge.

The Research Lens

By sharing these experiences of applying feminist methods to fieldwork, I offer a fuller understanding of the complexities embedded in the spaces from which these data emerged. This discussion would be incomplete, however, without acknowledging how my own identity, social position, worldview and assumptions influenced each phase of this research. As Nancy Scheper-Hughes (1992) posits, "We cannot rid ourselves of the cultural self we bring with us into the field any more than we can disown the eyes, ears and skin through which we take in our intuitive perceptions about the new and strange world we have entered (p. 28)."

I bring to this research a particular bias about the devalued nature of domestic labor, partly grounded in my own socialized experience and largely integral to my development as a feminist scholar. This research journey began in 1995 when I lived and worked with South African domestic workers whose stories were among my first direct experiences with apartheid's brutal history. Through these interactions, I realized how systemic oppression manifested as a highly gendered and racialized sector of labor that strategically divided families and communities as a means of securing minority power. Living in South Africa, I also engaged with white and coloured families who employed domestic workers with a normalcy that made me realize how deeply engrained this institution remained. Through these experiences I grew to understand how the daily benefits of paid household reproduction could outweigh the unease of entrenching privilege. Even for those with deeply instilled values of social justice, there is something to be said for the psychological freedom of returning to a tidy home and leaving the dishes at the table. While I recognize the value of this "peace of mind"[20] available to those who have the means to hire domestic laborers, my political stance is one that seeks to redress severe race and gender stratification systems through the progressive reform of the institution of domestic labor in ways that provide other viable work options for women in South Africa.

Although I cannot divorce myself from my identity or the interconnected political beliefs that motivate my work with this topic, throughout this research journey, I have remained committed to reflexivity in order to understand how domestic work exists in post-apartheid South Africa—without imposing my own assumptions that remain centered in my identity as a U.S., white, middle-class researcher who has not lived under apartheid. For these reasons, I intentionally "studied up" (Wolf 1996) by interviewing employers as well as domestic workers. As I engaged with diverse populations throughout this study, I made every attempt to contextualize the full complexity of each participant's lived experience. In particular, interviewing feminist employers as well as "newly elite" members of South African society provided a much fuller appreciation for the layered meaning of domestic labor in this rapidly changing society. At the same time, I recognize the limitations of my temporal understanding of the full complexities of domestic work in South Africa, as well as the parts of my own worldview that are inherently woven within this story.

At a broader, ideological level, I aspire to offer some contribution to the continued remarkable progress of South Africa through this research. Although this work is produced through the lens of a non-native to South Africa, I hope that my "outsider" perspective will also offer alternative insights on the empirical case of domestic work in a way that facilitates the ongoing realization of democracy and women's rights. The presentations of the narratives to follow emerge from two parts of this methodological journey—the practices I employed to document local knowledge and my own position as a variable in the research design.[21] I take full responsibility for the shortcomings inherent to both.

Chapter Four
Resisted Transitions: The Social Landscape of Domestic Work

The institution of domestic work encapsulates an inherent contradiction in South Africa. The deeply embedded, colonial social relations that normalize the reproduction of privileged households pose sharp contrasts to the human rights focus of democratization. As we examine the household as a central political space—holding the tension of social transition—striking discontinuities between workers' and employers' life experiences repeatedly illustrate how this institution sustains apartheid in everyday life. As my findings reveal, social power, privilege and severe inequality continue to define the nature of domestic work ten years after the transition to democracy. Although participants discussed some examples of change in work relationships at the micro-household level, the dominant *structure* of the institution entrenches colonial patterns and labor practices that virtually mirror apartheid South Africa. Severe inequalities in social location, privilege and status are reinforced through this normalized social institution which allows a great deal to go *unchanged* in the new democratic South Africa.

My goal throughout this chapter is to reveal the persistent and intersecting ways in which domestic labor is embedded in South African society in order to illustrate the striking contrasts between public and private transformations. By introducing the participants through a selection of particularly revealing narratives, I hope to provide a partial immersion into the private side of South African society. The data speak to a multitude of dimensions within this institution that remains central to 'everyday life.' At the same time, the inherent mutuality of the public and private spheres (Ling 2002) allows us to examine how relationships at the most interpersonal level are shaped by and simultaneously reproduce macro-structural patterns of social power and inequality. I pay particular attention to inter-sections of race, class and gender that define the nature of relationships within this private employment context in order to examine how deeply embedded inequalities illustrate a pervasive "social apartheid" that pres-ents one of the most serious obstacles to South Africa's long-term trans-formation.

This chapter is organized in the following manner. I begin with a pres-entation of the nature of domestic work in South Africa by framing the institution in an overarching analysis of social power. The relationships *among* women centrally inform this discussion of power structures and intersections of inequality contained within the household sphere. I then map this institution as a colonial icon and illustrate the persistent resistance to its transformation. Through an examination of geographical spaces and the perceptions of employers who resist power shifts in the private home, the data reveal how apartheid's colonial legacy is maintained within South Africa's private households. I close this chapter with a discussion of the way in which domestic labor entrenches sexism and does little to transform patriarchal constructions of the asymmetrical public/private duality, as we see in the global context. Throughout this chapter, my intention is also to reinforce the interconnected nature of these defining features central to domestic work and its limited post-apartheid transformation, as the partic-ipants in this study poignantly illustrated.

SOCIAL POWER STRUCTURES

In South Africa, the institution of domestic work remains structured by the severe social inequality of the apartheid era that persists in the household as black women reproduce daily life for the privileged (predominantly white) population. Although workers continually exhibited powerful individual and collective acts of agency, the extent to which structural conditions dom-inated their experience placed serious challenges on the broader transforma-tion of this apartheid icon. Limited education, severe poverty and demanded migration created a particular experience of entrapment among workers in this highly rigid institution. In addition, the firmly entrenched social rela-tionships of inequality accentuate such structural barriers as employers retain heightened power positions through the maintenance of apartheid's social hierarchies—in sharp contrast to the democratic transfiguration of South African society. My goal here is to present the narratives that most vividly depict the spaces where social power differentials manifest in the institution of domestic work. The voices of domestic workers, employers and change agents illustrate how underlying relationship dynamics in the work context embody broader social structures of ongoing inequality. As we will discuss, the data also facilitate an analysis of the extent to which social change has been actualized in the private sphere—the central question in this study.

The "Trapped" Nature of Domestic Work

The institutionalized nature of paid household labor creates an entrapment for black women who are relegated to this lowest stratum of the labor force. Workers in this study continually pointed to the contradictions between the critical labor they perform to regenerate society and its low rewards. Through my investigation of South African society "at home," my intention was to understand how the very tangible, daily, material labor tasks domestic workers perform contribute to the broader structures of severe race, class and gender inequality that illustrate how domestic labor remains the "last bastion of apartheid." Like we see in other contexts, domestic workers are hired for a range of services including childcare, cleaning, laundry, ironing, cooking, shopping and household management responsibilities such as organization tasks and various errands. Workers are also enlisted to help in the associated professional work of their employers, such as cleaning offices or in one case in this study, *managing* a bed and breakfast owned by the employer. For employers, the ability to hire full-time, live-in domestic workers to perform all of these above responsibilities reassures heightened levels of class status. For workers, employment in this institution leads to a further entrapment into the prevailing race, class and gender inequalities that continue to define South African society.

Each domestic worker in this study performed this full range of tasks, although each also noted that the additional childcare responsibilities substantially increased their workload, as well as the emotional investment in the job. In the vast majority of cases, the addition of childcare responsibilities provided no further salary compensation or shifting of other responsibilities. For example, in one employer household, over the course of three years, the family supported by one domestic worker grew from two to four members. This required the worker to change her own sleep schedule to perform evening feedings for two babies and added an additional 24 hours per week to her work demands. Yet when I asked this employer about the substantial shift in "Lucy's" responsibilities, she expressed no need to offer further compensation. Rather, she considered the additional childcare responsibilities a "normal" part of domestic work in South Africa. A perception among white employers that "we were just raised like that" justified the extensive labor demands of childcare and household reproduction—which ultimately rationalized the ongoing social inequalities in this institution of live-in domestic labor. Through these cases, repeated connections between the material and ideological reproduction of apartheid South Africa emerged in these private household spaces. Therefore, daily acts such as mopping floors and changing "nappies" are more than labor commodities—they are also the enactment and reproduction of deeply embedded class structures that have failed to transform in line with South Africa's new democracy. The study of private spaces consistently revealed pervasive contradictions of wealth and privilege in contrast to the enormous disparities between the lived experiences of workers and employers.

These inequalities structure domestic labor in ways that trap the "poorest of the poor" in this institution that particularly marginalizes black and coloured women. To demonstrate these extreme disparities that reproduce class-based inequality, let us examine the very material nature of monetary compensation. Reported salary structures from this study illustrate the severely constrained economic realities of domestic workers in the post-apartheid context. The combined reported incomes of workers and employers (N=40 in the formal interviews) show that the average salary for workers was R1130 (161USD) per month for full-time employment. This figure, however, is almost double the reported national average of R600/month (85USD),[1] most likely because of the high representation of union leaders and feminist employers in the sample (with a few outliers of exceptionally high salaries) and the placement of the study in one of the most affluent urban areas. Yet, even with R1130 as an average monthly income, women's ability to increase their standard of living is virtually impossible. For example, renting a one bedroom flat in Cape Town would typically cost at least R1000/month. Round-trip transportation to the city, even from township locations, is typically R12/day=R240/month. These local living costs represent the practical realities of domestic workers' salaries, in relation to what they can afford in the South African context. Women employed in this sector are therefore further entrapped by their dependence on the live-in context of their work because it provides many of the basic needs, including the allocation of food and accommodation. Domestic workers in this study who did live outside of the work context (N=10) reported only being able to afford residence in township/squatter camp "locations" (established in the apartheid era). Furthermore, their salaries could not compensate for basic needs in many cases—including food, utilities and school fees for their children.

Interestingly, some participants indicated a collusive behavior among employers in relation to salary. Several domestic workers in one of Cape Town's luxury apartment buildings, for example, noted that their salaries were all comparable because employers had aligned to confirm payment standards. As Tanzi noted about her employers, "When they come visiting, they ask, 'How much you give to your maid?'" Also, a privileged, wealthy white employer shared the following when asked how she determined the salary of her domestic worker:

> Well, I normally ask my friends, you know, what their salaries are. We are all on par, so, *ja*,[2] and I'm sure if she [worker] was unhappy she would *definitely* tell me.

This collusion we see among privileged class structures reveals how the maintenance of ongoing race/class inequality and the pervasive dominance of an apartheid ideology continue to define domestic labor, even in the new democracy. When employers were asked about salaries, they often shared a perception that workers were able to use all of their salary for "pocket money" because their basic needs were met with the live-in work context. The reality that domestic workers were most often supporting at least three other individuals by sending salary remittances to rural areas was not part of the general consciousness of employers, thus reinforcing the severe inequalities of the apartheid era.[3] As these data suggest, the very material compensation for domestic labor relegates women in this sector to a level of dependency that reifies the social stratification central to apartheid.

As Jacklyn Cock (1980; 1989) revealed in her early studies of domestic work in apartheid South Africa, the institution embodies an entrapment such that workers often feel they have no other options. This perception is rooted to a large extent in the reality that domestic workers, even in the new South Africa, enjoy few work options because of the severely limited educational opportunities afforded during the apartheid era that continue to impact workers ten years after the democratic transition. The curriculum throughout apartheid's "Bantu Education" system specifically trained black women for domestic labor in white households. Although the structure of education is slowly transforming to redress former imbalances, at least another decade must pass before the democratic education redress aligns with enhanced opportunities that would shift the sectoral placement of women. Even though domestic workers continually exerted bold acts of agency in both the micro-work context and at the level of structural change, the severe systems of inequality that continue to define the institution left workers in the existing context feeling extremely limited about their ability to attain jobs in other more empowering sectors because of this severe educational barrier. As Nomsa explained when asked about the extent to which she felt qualified for other jobs:

No, because I haven't got enough education, so I must do domestic
work and that's all, I haven't got enough education for the other job.

In this study, educational levels of participants ranged from Standard
1 to Standard 10 (the equivalent of U.S. Grade 3 to Grade 12). Only one of
the 20 domestic workers in the formal interviews attained a high school
diploma and the mean educational level was Standard 6 (Grade 8). For all
of the workers in this study, economic need necessitated leaving school, and
therefore, domestic work remained the primary employment sector for
black women throughout apartheid. For 19 of the 20 workers, leaving
school was required in order to support both the immediate and extended
family. Girls therefore attained jobs as domestic workers primarily because
of extensive economic need for family survival. Elize described this experience:

In my child days we was a very poor family . . . we lived on a farm and
I went to school up till Standard 3 [U.S. Grade 5] then I left school . . .
and from that moment I went to work there [in domestic labor] and
then afterwards I was crying, why can't I go to school? Sometimes
when I sit I always think why didn't I go to school? I could have done
something better with my life.

Because the structure of apartheid was built upon black women's labor in
the domestic sector, however, the system afforded few opportunities for
quality education or work options outside of the domestic labor sector.
Elize's reflection demonstrates the extent to which the harsh structures of
inequality and limited educational opportunities from the apartheid era
continue to severely impact the majority of domestic workers.

In addition to educational disadvantages, workers conveyed feelings
of entrapment in their work because of the severely limited employment
opportunities in the context of massive poverty at the nation level. Several
workers identified that the economic resources needed to enter other fields
of their choice would require initial investments far beyond their ability to
attain, given the limited income levels of their current jobs. When workers
did identify other labor options, 18 of the 20 considered sectors that were
also highly gendered such as catering, hospitality, childcare and nursing. A
few workers mentioned aspirations of more entrepreneurial fields such as
microenterprise and informal trade,[4] however the vulnerability identified
with such professions led women to limit their risk because they perceived
domestic work as a more secure profession, albeit dependent upon individual employers. As Nosipho shared:

> I can sell clothes sometimes, like a second hand clothes, like R2, R3, R4
> you know, so I think of that, that would [bring] no money because
> when I'm selling clothes, I must put the clothes outside and the weather
> is bad, then there is no money.

Thus limited resources, structural barriers, and a felt security in domestic work consistently played central roles in workers' perceptions of their ability to attain employment in more profitable and empowering sectors.

When asked about their long-term goals, for either retirement or movement to another career, only two of the domestic workers identified alternative visions for themselves.[5] Although informants were clear that they felt they had little 'choice' in entering domestic work and emphasized consistently that they would *not* encourage other women (particularly their daughters) to enter this sector, responses about personal long-term goals were almost always met with varying levels of discomfort among workers, evident through either laughter, long pauses before responding, or an admitted inability to answer the question. Workers' reluctance around this question's relevance to their own lives, however, did not impede their belief in the possibility of long-term change. A pervasive theme of more idyllic visions for either their children or other women emerged throughout the worker interviews. In each case, education remained central to these narratives:

> I've got kids and they must go to school. I don't care no matter what I
> wear. You see, my dress is broken from here [shows hem of dress]. I
> don't mind. But my children, I want my children to go to school.

> That's one of the things I want to do, go back home and help the
> women in the rural areas to help themselves. I want to teach them so
> that they can do things for themselves, they don't depend on their hus-
> bands, you know, make them stand on their own feet.

As these interviews reflect, although workers did not always articulate long-term goals specifically for themselves, it appeared that their aspirations were based in fostering the development of others, as to assure opportunities that would be different to their own lived experiences. Domestic work was therefore seen as a means to brighter futures for others through the salary it provided, particularly among the older women in the worker sample.

Workers endured this entrapment in domestic labor because in several cases their salary remained the only source of income for the families that

they supported. In the context of a severe 40 percent level of unemployment nationally, of the 20 workers, 17 supported others, namely children
and extended family members, through the primary income they attained in
domestic labor. This context points to one of the many severe disparities in
the experiences of workers and employers. For workers, associations of
being a "good mother" were linked to their gendered role in domestic service and their ability to provide for the family through salary remittances
acquired by leaving the family. For employers, however, being a "good
mother" did not require labor in either the public or private sphere of their
own homes. Rather, employers' status could be earned by hiring the labor
of another woman to physically reproduce the family.

"When I look at the little ones, then I think of my little one:[6]*"*
Migration and Domestic Labor

The ideology of apartheid manifested as distinct geographic separation (see
Figure 2.2). In order for women to attain work in domestic service,
required migration from rural "homelands" to urban areas placed particular strains on both workers' families and larger communities. Since South
Africa's transition, the required migration of workers continues to define
the structure of domestic work. These spatial location divides between
workers' region of origin and the site of their work (and required residence)
underscore another level of privilege that intersects with race and class.
Social location power is centered in urban cities because rural areas in
South Africa remain deeply impoverished, instilling an economic survival
dependency that manifests through women's migration to urban centers for
work in domestic labor—one of the few outlets for family/community survival. Limited work opportunities and heightened economic dependence
further entrap women in domestic labor.

As workers travel to urban areas, however, their rural identity
becomes a central vector of oppression—which adds another level to Hill
Collins' (1990) "matrix of domination" and Cock's (1980) "triple oppression." In addition to the triad of race, class and gender intersecting for black
women in particularly marginalizing ways, the added dimension of geographic location creates a fourth level of domination—much like Mohanty's
(1991) notion of the "First World/Third World divide." Importantly, when
women migrate across vast distances to access employment, they are rarely
able to travel with their own immediate families,[7] creating a severe challenge
and emotional demand particular to this sector. As this geographic migration pattern illustrates, physical separation from both family and community structures presents a pervasive form of dependency that intersects with
ongoing race, class and gender inequalities and contributes to the overall

entrapment characteristic of this particular labor sector. With the shared historical experience of migration particular to the South African case, physical separation from families and regions of origin emerged as a central theme in my interviews with domestic workers.

Of the 20 domestic workers interviewed in depth, *all* migrated from rural parts of South Africa to work in Cape Town. In 16 cases, women migrated alone with the specific intention of seeking out jobs in domestic service. In the remaining four cases, women relocated to Cape Town initially with their husbands and then acquired work in domestic service—which ultimately became the primary means of income for the family. Among my sample, initial patterns of migration were shaped by the nation's former racial geography such that black women migrated primarily from the Eastern Cape/ Transkei/ Ciskei regions and coloured workers traveled a shorter distance primarily from the Northern Province in order to attain work in the Cape. Regardless of region of origin, however, domestic workers in post-apartheid South Africa remain confined by the migration demanded of this sector, which shapes work structures such that living at the place of employment is still a standard requirement of the job. The combination of workers' inability to afford to live outside of their place of work because of extremely low compensation, the insular, restrictive nature of the institution, and the long distance required to travel to their respective regions of origin ties women to this sector in particularly limiting ways. Through this lens, the extent to which structural barriers challenge workers' individual agency becomes strikingly clear.

Separation from family members, especially children, presents a particular *emotional* toil in domestic work unlike any other profession in South Africa. The severe toll this placed on workers who leave their own families in order to care for other children became a dominant theme throughout my conversations with all participants, including some employers. Workers reflected the following sentiments:

> You know when the children, they are crying, you feel bad because you don't know maybe your child is crying as well, nobody can hold, your mother is sick and then the children are crying, who is going to cook for them, as you are cooking for another one?

> I'm worried when I finish to eat, I think, I wonder, my children, what is eating there by the Transkei?

In one case, a domestic worker and union activist offered a critical link between the realities of separation and pervasive social problems that particularly impact children throughout South Africa:

It is difficult to leave your child with your parents, that child grows up.
I can remember when I arrive at home my son didn't recognise me, he
said to me that I was his *aunty*. Then I start crying and my mother start
crying because the child didn't know who I was, that is what happened
in most cases. That is why today there is so many children sleeping on
the streets, doesn't know their parents, running away because the
mother was never there for them, and it is a very difficult situation.

Through this narrative, the prevalence of absent parenting—and the extent
to which its impact may be associated with South Africa's difficult development challenges such as crime and homelessness among children—demonstrates one of the many social costs incurred for the luxury of
institutionalized paid domestic labor.

These structurally imposed struggles represent a deep internal
dilemma among domestic workers. On one hand, they cope with oppressive work situations because of the knowledge that they are providing for
their family in a way that hopefully affords their children a better life. At
the same time, the daily reminders of the ways in which workers must
abandon their own children to care for more privileged children create pervasive conflicts for workers as they literally reproduce institutionalized
social inequalities through the daily caretaking they provide for privileged
sectors of society.

Paradoxically, care for the children of employers in some cases constituted a coping mechanism for workers in this study. By developing
loving relationships with the children of their employers, workers were
able to access some sense of reward, meaning and identity in their work.
As this ANC leader and former domestic worker recalled, "The child is
the only thing you can cuddle." This reflection reveals how love for children sometimes mediates the severe emotional toil of separation and the
insular privatized nature of domestic labor, unlike any other sector. In
some cases, relationships with children even influenced decisions around
employment choices. Victoria's narrative illustrates her lived experience
in this realm:

You realise how unfair our people is in our country, that they separate
you as a mother from your child and from your family and at the end
of the day they don't even appreciate it. Now you must care for their
child, you must give the love you suppose to give to your child, you
must give it to them. Like myself, I am very fond of this child, sometimes I feel like taking my things and go, but then it comes to this child,
then I decide not to go, because we are very close the two of us.

Victoria followed this statement by showing me photos of the 10-year-old boy that she had cared for since birth. And like other workers who associated strongly with the children in the workplace, she often referred to him as "my Aaron." Many workers similarly talked about the importance of celebrating important events with the children that they believed they had literally raised. As the oldest worker in the sample expressed, "Those doctors and lawyers come from the *hands* of domestic workers."

These associations of love for the children of employers represents one of the deepest complexities and most heightened emotional aspects of the institution of domestic labor. Caring for employers' children fostered a sense of meaningful human connection that transcended racial barriers among the workers in this study. At the same time, however, workers illustrated that these powerful relationships with their employers' children served as a constant reminder of the emotional pain of separation from their own children in the daily expectations of the occupation. Nothando's narrative embodies this complexity:

> Doesn't matter if you haven't been in university, you don't have those skills, but you've got the skills of the trust, that they can trust you with the family. When they go to Johannesburg, who is looking after the house? Whatever the child, during the day, they're all at work, that child has got one mother, you are the one to look after the baby. Then when the baby is 21, celebrating, the 21st birthday, they say, "no, don't come this day because you cannot celebrate with this child. You have to stay home. We are going to celebrate with the child without you," because now you are nothing in that party. There is something very sad, it hurts you.[8]

It appeared that workers' relationships with children represent one of the few spaces in South African society where racial barriers are to a larger extent overcome, albeit temporally contained to the early phases of human development. Thus, care for children, even across racial divisions, provides an important positive outlet for workers within an extremely oppressive structure. Even though workers repeatedly expressed that they would ultimately prefer that the work environment afforded opportunities for living with their own children, affection and developed feelings of love with employers' children provided some form of reward and meaning in the job. At the same time, the emotional output required to care for employers' children represents another central vulnerability particular to this sector.

Workers repeatedly asserted that the ability to live with their own families while working in their private employment context would tremendously improve their overall living conditions and reduce the emotional demands of the job. Yet the practical realities of mediating this tension represent the enormous cultural shift required to transform the institution of domestic work in ways that would redress this psychological toil that results from the pervasion geographic division sustained in the post-apartheid context. Of the employers interviewed, it was only among those who considered themselves feminists that these issues were recognized. In one case, an employer with a new baby and a demanding career refused to hire an applicant who was pregnant at the time of the interview because she believed it would create far too much conflict in both of their lives. Marlene, a gender activist, described her awareness and subsequent dilemma about providing a workspace that would both protect her domestic worker from this separation from her own family and meet the requirements of paid household labor that she expected as an employer:

> I mean just the difficulty of here is someone with my kids and her kids are in Transkei. She never sees her kids, and the other thing that she raised her child, [her] baby is like three, four months old and she wanted to bring the baby because her mother was getting a bit ill. Now I don't have a big house, I've got three rooms and three kind of small rooms in my house. We had her in our house in the third room and it became too cramped . . . and I said to her, "If you are going to bring your baby, how do you think you are going to do the work?" But she's going to put the baby down there and she's going to work. If you have a separate quarters[9] it's different. So at the one level I mean I know what it's like to have children and I understand that struggle you know between here you are looking after someone else's kids but what about your own kids? But there is also so much that I can give because I mean it is besides what you pay the person it is extra costs in terms of accommodation and food and all of that . . . and I could just foresee a situation where she would bring the child and I mean I'm not going to have another child in my house going hungry, I mean that's just—I would obviously ensure that the child would have food and that's just the struggle, I mean because I cannot cope with my own responsibilities *and* someone else responsibilities, *ja*.

Marlene's experience points to one of the many challenge of leveling the rural/urban divide by reconstructing domestic work in a more equitable fashion. Even so, her consciousness about democratizing this institution is an anomaly in modern South African social discourse. The differentials in social location and power between workers and employers (exaggerated by migration and childcare demands) emerged throughout the interviews—representing the multiple ways in which work structures encapsulate inequality and the ongoing need for social change to democratize domestic work in alignment with the national transformation.

Built on Unequal Ground: Work Relationships

Micro-level household relations between workers and employers further embody the embedded power-laden differentials inherent to the institution of domestic work. The isolated nature of the occupation itself heightens the extent to which work relationships become central to women's experience, for both employers and employees. In this study, domestic workers as well as employers identified that their relationship to one another was the most important component of the job. The meaning associated with the work relationship, however, varied substantially between workers and employers. For employers, a positive relationship meant that their workers were trustworthy and reliable. For workers, ideal relationship qualities included a demonstration of respect, interest in their lives, a willingness to offer support in times of need, and an appreciation for the labor that workers contributed. Importantly, in both groups, elements of the relationship that were shared as being critical to a positive experience were sometimes intangible attributes. For example, one employer shared that it was essential for her to experience a feeling of "peace" in her home when her worker was present. Similarly, workers described a need to feel comfortable and "free" in the workplace. Yet for workers, more tangible micro actions—such as morning greetings and the way in which employers "dished the food" for them—were associated with an overall positive relationship. In some cases, workers even expressed that a respectful work relationship and a feeling of being "happy" on the job was more important to them than salary.

Of the 20 workers interviewed, five described the relationship and overall nature of their work context as positive, indicating more hopeful models in the transition to social democracy. These participants felt that the relationship they shared with their employer was equitable and characterized by a mutual respect. In such instances, workers also identified their employers as "friends" and felt comfortable discussing their personal lives in the work context. Yet the remaining 15 formal interviews, as well as all focus group participants, identified that clearly "not much has changed" in the nature of their work relationship since the apartheid era. Conversely, of the 20 employers interviewed at length, 14 described their relationship with their workers as positive overall, indicating much higher levels of satisfaction toward the relationship among employers. The six employers interviewed who felt dissatisfied with their relationship felt so for different reasons: four identified a lack of trustworthiness and reliability in workers that impeded the relationship, while the remaining two felt uncomfortable with the relationship because of a deep sense of inequality and discomfort with their role, particularly since the democratic transition.[10]

As we examine the underlying relationships between women within this work structure, ongoing levels of social power differentials seriously contradict the national agenda of equality. For example, when workers were asked to discuss what it meant that they considered their employer a friend, invariably they associated friendship with employers giving them money or allowing them to "borrow" in times of need without any expectation of repayment. Therefore, workers who identified a felt friendship with their employer did so on the basis of perceived levels of benevolence and generosity—ultimately reinforcing structures of class privilege. In these cases, even though workers identified their employer as a "friend," none discussed personal issues on the job.

Employers, on the other hand, noted that "friendships" emerge naturally in the work relationship because of the highly personal context of the sector:

> This is the weirdest thing about domestic work is that a friendly relationship does develop, where one shares intimacies, or you know issues of concern, or a bit of gossip here or there.

> I know people always say that you have to keep work and friendship kind of separate and for a lot of people that works, whereas you know in our home I feel that when you employ somebody, that person becomes part of your life. I mean that person learns to know things that most people won't learn to know about you because they [are] in your home, you know it's your private life, they hear things, you [are] on the phone, you know, I mean so you have to get to that point where you make them feel comfortable and feel at home almost because then you form a relationship with them.

Although these narratives acknowledge a level of personal intimacy as a result of the labor site in the private household, each employer also shared a level of social *distance* inherent to the nature of the friendship they shared with their worker. For the identified feminist employer participants, this distance was based in a central conflict about either their social privilege as an employer or the cultural/language divide they experienced with their workers. For non-feminist, more traditional employers, this social distance was identified as having little in common with their workers. In many instances, the narratives illustrate a rhetoric of othering workers because "their culture" was identified as very separate to the culture of employers, which inhibited the possibility for friendships to emerge.

Interestingly, the circumstances that employers described as motivations to disclose at a personal level with their workers were most often rooted in a need to discuss issues in their marriage. As one employer shared, following an argument with her husband, she often went to her domestic worker to discuss the issue, who would invariably respond, as she recalled "oh, Madam." Another employer shared that she approached her worker to discuss personal issues when she was seeking an objective source: "I would sit and I would chat to her and Violet [worker] would agree with me and then I would feel better." These descriptions of the relationship as perceived by employers represent an obvious inequality in the extent of personal exchange. The social power differentials inherent in the relationship impede equal exchange and certainly limit the extent to which workers can discuss the nature of their most personal concerns with their employers. Of the other 15 cases where workers did not identify the overall nature of the relationship as positive, many described that they rarely had personal conversations with their employers. Workers repeatedly identified that they felt employers rarely inquired about their lives, even though the nature of the work was so intimate:

> The employers is not interested about your family or if you got children. You have to say *yourself* that you got children. They are not interested, as long as you can be a slave.

> I must tell you why I don't talk to her—because she's not interested. How can you talk your personal things when the person's not interested?

In the worst instances for workers, like Rollins's (1985) depiction of worker *invisibility*, employers did not acknowledge them during even the most casual exchanges such as morning greetings, indicating attempts to make the highly personalized nature of the work extremely professional and removed:

> When she come into the kitchen, she won't say "good morning" because I think "good morning," it's a nice word to wake up with because I didn't see you and I am glad to see [you] but *never*. She start talking about food or what's going on and things like that.

These narratives demonstrate both the context of personalization in the job and an overlapping *emotional* requirement throughout the institution.

Overwhelmingly, workers demonstrated the ways in which they strategically assessed employers' emotions in order to craft optimal work environments. In essence, like no other profession, emotional labor is required in the context of domestic work worldwide.[11] The work demands that women remain highly sensitized to the mood and overall emotional state of their employers and the dynamics within the family structures where they work. As Sonja described in relation to her (male in this case) employer:

> If he talks to me I talk to him, if he's quiet one morning and I see. You know your boss already, when he's in a good mood, when he's in a bad mood, then you know.

Sonja later described that this mood barometer indicated how she managed the work tasks, established a relative distance from her employer and evaluated when to make requests. Similarly, many workers shared that asking for work benefits, such as time off or pay increases, was always mediated through an evaluation of the emotions of employers, thus demonstrating a keen sensitivity to employers' lives as one venue to exhibit agency.

Workers also shared that the nature of domestic work demanded that they withhold certain emotions in order to fulfill the underlying, often unstated expectation of the job: to be *happy*. As Nothando described:

> I always, you act—smile . . . I never have long face[12] because I know that if I've got long face, I'm going to lose the job . . . you are the one, whatever something hurts you on your heart deeply, then when you get at work, you mustn't show that sad, you must be happy, when everyone is coming in the house, then even your employer can see that you are happy, every day, domestic worker must be happy . . . I feel proud about myself and I also feel proud because I've got love to those people, whatever, I *never* change the face as a domestic worker because I want bread, because once I change the face, they are going to retrench me.

Nothando's pride and self assurance in her ability to purposefully alter her emotions in order to maintain the job and provide for her own survival demonstrates a powerful, daily necessity of domestic work. Nosipho similarly shared her purposeful withholding of emotions in the context of the "pain" she felt around the severe economic inequality she internalized when comparing her life and that of her employer:

> When I see these things [Christmas presents], but I feel pain inside, but I don't show them. "Why you buying this and that? Why you don't buy

[for] me?" No, I don't say that. I feel pain inside, I say, "oh, it's nice," but it's pain to me because they never ever buy nothing for me, they never even helping you.

Charmaine, a more liberated coloured employer, explained how she requested that her worker not bring negative emotions to her job, because it impacted the highly personalized nature of the workplace:

> There were times when you know she would come in not very happy, or she would seem moody or whatever and I would just tell her, "Jane, have you seen anybody moody in this house? Have you seen anybody screaming in this house?" . . . and she would say, "no." So I said, "If you can, can you please try not to, because really, you know in this house we try to be happy and we try to help each other and all of this and if you can't then really, then maybe you shouldn't come in for the day." I would say, "because you have a negative effect on all of us, you know."

Charmaine's struggle as an employer echoed other employers' attitudes about the intolerable nature of negative or moody "attitudes" among the workers employed in their homes. These distinct contrasts demonstrate that in the context of domestic work attending to employers' emotional needs is central to success in the job, yet openly portraying emotions, on the part of the worker, is both intolerable and grounds for dismissal.[13]

The most striking example of the emotional requirement in the context of domestic work was demonstrated through the following worker's case. After seven years of employment with a white couple in their mid-sixties, Tanzi found her woman employer murdered in a prestigious apartment building complex garage one year prior to our interview. She disclosed that since the woman's death, her male employer specifically requested that she appease his extensive fear about personal safety by moving out of the domestic workers' quarters in the building and into the apartment with him. Tanzi shared that she often heard her employer crying in the evening and that part of her new role since the death of her "madam" was to comfort her male employer, an emotional expectation far beyond the standard description of the job.

While workers are often required to emotionally connect with children as part of the standard childcare responsibility, this level of emotional support that develops in order to support employers in various life phases represents a central condition of domestic labor not commonly identified or rewarded in the job. Furthermore, this emotional labor affords employers a particular quality of life, especially as they age and domestic workers replace health care systems of support.[14] The oldest employer in my sample described the way in which her three workers afforded her an ability to remain in her home and sustain a sense of independence by meeting both her household and physical care needs. As Norma, age 88, expressed, "Well, I'm an old duck. If I didn't have them I'd have to go into frail care."

Compounding this complexity at a related level, in many instances workers shared that their feelings of emotion toward either their employers and/or the children in their place of work were genuine. Those who recalled positive relationships in their past also shared that separation from their employers, for example when they relocated, emigrated, or no longer needed their services, was particularly painful. This emotional expenditure was not only revealed on the part of workers. Employers also shared emotions of serious loss with the separation from their domestic worker, particularly after years of service. Thus, the emotional aspect of the institution is interdependent as demonstrated by Marlene's account of her feelings, as an employer, when she was forced to terminate the work relationship:

> So, *ja*, but it's still difficult. I mean . . . I felt when I told Gloria [that she had to end the employment] you know because she was a very friendly person, a very warm kind of person. I felt extremely bad, I actually felt depressed . . . I was saying to one of my friends, I felt so horrible about it, I felt depressed until I actually called her and I spoke to her again.

These narratives that illustrate the emotional context of domestic work represent an inherent expectation not commonly identified in this particular sector. While hired to perform the daily "dirty work," domestic workers are at the same time expected to provide emotional labor as a critical aspect of their care and service roles. As we see in these cases, however, emotional work also underscores the severe power differentials between workers and employers because of the manner in which it is both performed and withheld. The juxtaposition of emotion and distinct racial stratification in the South African case presents another striking contradiction central to this apartheid icon. Furthermore, the added expectation of intimacy also complicates the personal/professional divide, as we also see in the global the literature that depicts a "regime of labor intimacy" (Chang and Ling 2002) and a growing institution of "transnational motherhood" (Hondagneu-Sotelo 2001).

Mediating Intimacy through Establishing Boundaries

In order to deal with the complexity of intimacy and emotions, I found that both workers and employers in this study enacted distinct attempts to establish and maintain *boundaries* in order to cope with the highly personalized nature of the work and its subsequent vulnerabilities. For workers, setting boundaries often involved acts of agency in refusing to perform certain highly personalized tasks requested of them by employers. Boundaries on the part of employers varied depending upon the perspective and social consciousness of the women interviewed. For feminist employers, boundaries were set in attempts to downplay the highly unequal power structures central to domestic work and maintain certain levels of *privacy*. For less socially conscious, more traditional employers, setting boundaries often related to consciously "othering" their domestic workers, firmly instilling their role as employer, and setting limits about the extent of personal interaction in the work context. In the most severe cases, employers sharply limited workers' personal lives as a boundary that further reinforced the extreme social power differentials central to this sector. The following excerpts from both interview and observational data capture these nuances.

All participants in this study recognized that, to a large extent, domestic workers know employers' most personal "business" at a very intimate level. As one (economically privileged coloured elite) employer described, her discomfort in hiring another woman to care for her home was based in the reality that domestic workers see *everything:* your arguments, your bathroom, your sheets, your medication and your underwear. This employer shared that she intentionally "straightened up" her home before her domestic worker arrived, so as not to show her actual, more sloppy, living condition. Interestingly, all of the feminist employers that I interviewed shared similar sentiments about how they felt it necessary to in some way clean or further organize the home in preparation for the domestic worker. Similarly, this subgroup of employers expressed that they found it difficult to stay in the home with a domestic worker cleaning their private spaces. Mallie (a new black elite employer) described her feelings in this regard:

> If you need to maybe you should leave because I mean I think a lot of people find it difficult to just hang around when somebody's working in your house. It's a bit uncomfortable for me too, even when I'm on holiday, when I know that she is coming, I wake up earlier and I leave because I think it probably feels like somebody is looking over your shoulder, or if I'm around I try to keep myself busy with other things so that she doesn't feel like I'm invading her space.

In contrast, I observed other more traditional white employers' lack of awareness or discomfort in allowing their domestic workers to see "everything." For example, in one of my temporary housing situations during the fieldwork, I lived in a white household with a black domestic worker. I observed that both adults in the household frequently left their undergarments and other dirty clothing throughout the bedroom when they left for work. Upon their return, this laundry had been washed, folded, ironed (including the undergarments) and neatly returned to their wardrobes. These employers exhibited little inhibition about the reality that their domestic worker engaged in the most intimate level of their household reproduction. This observation led me to question the nature of severe race and class stratification in relation to the social distancing that creates such norms where domestic workers are both "othered" and intimately involved in the most personal aspects of daily life in the most private spaces. It appeared as though those employers who had at some point experienced oppression through their own position outside of the social power group during apartheid demonstrated far greater discomfort with the most intimate tasks of domestic work and therefore drew boundaries about performing certain tasks themselves. As Elna, (a coloured scholar/activist feminist) asserted, it was just "too embarrassing" to have her worker cleaning her personal closet. Other employers noted that they washed their own underwear and made their own bed, seemingly aware of boundaries and in an attempt to lessen the intimacy and subsequent power differentials inherent to this task.

Hettie, a strong feminist activist assessed, "the price you pay in terms of loss of privacy" is completely unrecognized by employers. This awareness of the innermost lives of employers afforded workers in this study a specific level of power within the relationship and occupational context. As one (human rights advocate) informant explained, "being privy to Madam's baggage has its privileges." At times workers utilized this knowledge and enacted agency to change the structural conditions of their employment. For example, workers often recalled instances where they refused to perform certain tasks, demonstrating powerful acts of agency in the workplace. Victoria (a coloured domestic worker and union activist) shared that she firmly established a clear boundary in her workplace by refusing to soak and wash her woman employer's underwear while she was menstruating, as her employer specifically requested. Alternatively, Victoria told me that she moved the soiled undergarments (with gloves) from the floor and placed them in a plastic bag for her employer—establishing a specific boundary in the most intimate task of her work. Hettie described such actions on the part of employers as embodying a "level of slutty-ness" through the way in which privileged women expose their most personal selves to workers with seeming disregard as a means of exploiting the severe power inequalities at the most intimate level. Other workers shared their inner disgust around particularly intimate bodily tasks in their work—such as cleaning soiled toilets and sheets—which they believed crossed this personal boundary. Yet workers also perceived that refusal to perform such intimate tasks would result in dismissal, ultimately reinforcing the severe economic power inequality that leaves workers feeling trapped in this sector. Therefore, the enactment of agency—such as Victoria's establishment of firm boundaries around bodily tasks—must be measured within this particular labor sector that has yet to enjoy the protective benefits of the new democracy.

Employers also emphasized a need to create boundaries to assure that although the nature of the work was personal and intimate, it would not become "too messy" such that lines between workers and employer became blurry. In some cases, this involved employers strongly establishing themselves as authority figures in the work context. Thelma described the way in which she set boundaries in her relationship with her domestic worker as follows:

> The thing is I will tell her certain things but there is a, you always draw that line where you still show her . . . that I am the employer but I still love you and I still will talk to you as a friend but do not overstep the boundary where you become rude . . . that's where I draw the line.

This example represents a felt insecurity for employers who perceived that their power position may be threatened by the intimate relationship with the domestic worker they employed. Thelma's narrative also echoes a colonial flavor of "love" for the worker and the firm establishment of hierarchical social positions. Like Thelma, other employers interviewed also discussed the importance of establishing strict boundaries in order to mediate the tensions and vulnerabilities of these blurred personal/professional lines. Increased levels of employer insecurity, however, seemed to be directly linked to South Africa's new governance and the growing awareness of rights among workers. Thus, as workers became more conscious and asserted agency to assure fair labor practices and legal requirements mandated for this sector, employers enacted stronger boundaries to reassure their own social power. In cases where employers felt little threat, such as with extremely wealthy white sectors, the need to assert these role boundaries decreased because of the wider differential in social locations between the worker and employer. This dynamic intersects with race as new (coloured and black) employers' instilled sharper boundaries in the work context than their more traditional (white) counterparts (see Chapter Five).

In many cases, employers specifically pointed to a need to reinforce standards and boundaries around "borrowing" items in order to maintain their class privilege. In particular, *food* became a place where restrictions were enacted on a daily basis. Workers' food was often limited and different to the food consumed by employers. In contrast, workers consistently associated the rationing of food (as opposed to freely sharing food) as particularly inhumane treatment that remained fundamental to the overall employment relationship. As Nobantu described:

> Even a food . . . she says, "I'm going to buy you your bread, your jam, you not allowed to use my bread." *Not allowed!* She buy me a bread if my bread is finished, I can't take her bread. I must take my bread in my house and go back to work, was *terrible,* terrible. The other ladies [employers] I can't tell you a lie about the food, they say, "There's the fridge, if you want something there in the fridge you must eat it." And when somebody is talking like that, you can't come to be hungry so quickly. But when somebody is going to, "I'm going to buy your bread, I'm going to put your bread here," it's easy, you come to be hungry so quickly.

This boundary setting in the workplace reinforced the economic privilege of employers by limiting the extent to which workers could share in their wealth at a physical/ bodily level. For employers, food remained a place to maintain specific boundaries of privacy. Although several employers shared food freely with their workers, over half of the workers remained limited to the food that was rationed to them each day at their place of work, reinforcing power structures in particularly bodily ways for workers.

Marlene, a (coloured activist feminist) "new employer" with a very different attitude, shared her philosophy on managing both food and the intimate living space with her worker:

> For me it's about human rights . . . I mean my policy is if someone lives in my house, they wash in my bathroom, they go to the same toilet as I, they eat out of the same plates that I have . . . they watch TV, they sit on the same couches that I have, I mean there isn't that [difference] and I think whoever works in my house, if you want to eat, you eat, you know, you don't have to ask me, "Can I have this, can you have that?" *Ja,* if you are here, you are entitled to have whatever food there is in the house for you to have and I'm not going to keep a check on did you eat this or did you eat that.

Marlene's approach represents a way of managing the micro-interactions of domestic work that is much more closely in line with the democratic structure of the new South Africa. Yet in this study, it was only the progressive, activist, feminist employers who shared her view. The more traditional employers continued to ration food, set limits and reinforce race and class hierarchies in ways that much more closely represented the culture of apartheid South Africa. The predominant sentiment throughout my interactions across all sectors was a shared fear among employers that creating a work context such as Marlene's would assure that they would be taken advantage of, particularly in the context of such poverty and high levels of need among worker populations.

Another overarching theme emerged in the data that illustrated employers' need to draw boundaries was specifically linked to spaces that related to the *physical body*. In a casual conversation, for example, one employer told me that the "ideal maid won't borrow your moisturizer." Similarly, Sarah (an entrepreneur who provides domestic labor services to elite employers) shared the following about the way in which she trains domestic workers:

> [It's] really minor little things that really gets households down and when I explain the contract to the worker, I will always use examples of, "If your hands or if your skin is dry, you can't just dip your finger into her pot of cream on her dressing table, obviously that would be *her* night cream, in any case you can't even take that cream and put it on your hands because she didn't allow you or say that you could use that. That's *stealing*, that is seen as stealing and you could lose your job for that."

This approach more clearly aligns with the traditional employer, embodying extreme connotations of race and class privilege while illuminating the highly personalized intimate nature of the daily work context. This notion of boundaries and space distinctions also echoes the apartheid ideology of physical separation—as manifested in the creation of "homelands."

HIV/AIDS and Domestic Labor

One critical space where all racial groups of employers shared the need to draw essential boundaries in the institution of domestic work surfaced in relation to the HIV/AIDS epidemic. At the time of this research, estimates suggested that 14 percent of South Africans were living with HIV/AIDS (Statistics South Africa 2000). The impact of HIV/AIDS permeates the social landscape of South Africa, embedding even deeper divides according to race and class. Because the burden of HIV/AIDS falls most heavily upon economically disadvantaged communities and women (Walker, Reid and Cornell 2004), domestic workers are particularly vulnerable and unable to access healthcare protection as a result of their informal labor positions. Furthermore, the reliance on domestic workers' salaries—particularly by AIDS orphans—increases substantially because of the extensive demands on family support structures that are severely weakened as a result of the epidemic.

In this research, the intersection of a pervasive fear about contracting HIV/AIDS and the intimacy central to domestic labor exaggerated the enforcement of boundaries and the distance between workers and employers. Among employers, a pervasive fear that workers may transmit the virus became a dominant theme throughout the fieldwork. This fear can be connected to a striking paradox between the broader public discourse on HIV/AIDS and a dominant *silence* that surrounds the private nature of the epidemic. For example, in parliamentary sessions, HIV/AIDS awareness pins are worn openly by high-level government leaders. Also, the *Mail and Guardian* national newspaper provides a weekly statistical HIV/AIDS update, while billboards, television, and radio programs centralize this topic in the context of its epidemic status in South Africa. Yet in my interviews with workers, HIV/AIDS became a taboo topic. Only six of the 20 workers in the formal interviews would engage in discussion of HIV/AIDS *in any minimal fashion.*

For employers, discussion of HIV/AIDS centered around mandated testing, a technically illegal yet widely practiced measure to instill sharp boundaries in the workplace. The ongoing socioeconomic power held by employers created situations where workers were either tested without their knowledge[15] or forced to offer HIV/AIDS test results in order to appease employers' anxieties about crossing this particularly fearful bodily boundary. In one highly personal conversation, Caroline, a more traditional white employer shared that she held extreme fears that her six-month-old baby could be infected with HIV through the domestic worker employed in her home. This fear dated back to colonial periods when wet-nursing practices were normalized. Caroline maintained the fear that her worker may nurse the baby in her absence in order to replace the food provided, which she could then take for her own children who lived in a nearby township. Caroline's fear was also rooted in a perception that HIV/AIDS was a "black disease," a widely held notion throughout the country. Eventually, Caroline dismissed her worker because of this pervasive fear of crossing boundaries at a bodily level—which held the potential to infect her child with HIV/AIDS.

The fear of HIV/AIDS transmissions underscores the intimate personal labor essential to this institution and the subsequent felt need among employers to instill sharp boundaries. Nobantu, a domestic worker, described this paradoxical reliance upon intimate labor and assertion of sharp boundaries by her employer:

> I don't know why, you know Jennifer, when you are working in the kitchen you clean the dishes, you peel the potatoes, you make a food for him—but your food must be separate your cup must be separate your plate must be separate, is not nice, they make me worried, maybe they think I'm *sick* or what, but if I make a food for him I use my hands, that's a problem, that's why that lady . . . I was working for that lady and I was worried *everyday*, shew, if I wake up I'm worried I said, "Oh my god, must find a new job?"

Nobantu eventually shared that she told her employer that she was "not sick" in order to keep her job. For many workers, either proving that they were not HIV positive or refusing testing became another space to exhibit acts of agency particular to the context of the national epidemic. Yet employers like Caroline are able to mandate testing because of the socioeconomic power they maintain, regardless of the technically illegal nature of this practice. The legitimate fear of transmission amongst employers operates such that sanctions for wrongful dismissals of domestic workers based upon HIV/AIDS discrimination are obsolete. Therefore, HIV/AIDS has impacted domestic work by jeopardizing job security and further constructing substantial social distances between workers and employers. These contrasting scenarios represent the deep complexity of HIV/AIDS as a critical bodily boundary in the context of domestic labor within South Africa and yet another space where power, privilege and social inequality continue to dominate the social landscape in the new democracy.

APARTHEID AT HOME: DOMESTIC WORK AS A COLONIAL VESTIGE

As we see in the global context, severe race, class and gender inequalities underlie and encompass the structure of domestic labor. In the South African case, however, a pervasive *colonial* nature shapes the institution of domestic work in sharp contrast to the democratic tenets of the new nation. A culture of servitude ties workers to employers in ways that virtually parallel the structures of apartheid. The institution of domestic work enables privilege and entitlement for small elite portions of the population that primarily maintain their ties to a history of colonial settlement. Although South Africa has transformed at the public level, the majority of employers maintain their social positions through both economic power and the ongoing social stratification system that privileges this small minority. This lingering colonial culture takes on a physical form in the structure of everyday living situations that distance "servants" who live at the site of their employment from "madams" and "masters." My research continually exposed these contradictions between a colonial culture of servitude and the overarching human rights focus of South Africa's new democracy. This section explores how South Africa's colonial culture continues to be most accessible in the private homes of employers.

A Culture of Servitude

> But I can say at my place of where I work, there's still apartheid. [It] will never go out in that kitchen, because I still had my separate plates to eat out, my separate cup, I can't use their stuff.

This domestic worker narrative captures the pervasive reluctance to transform the colonial nature of domestic service to reflect South Africa's democracy. Rather, keeping things "separate" epitomizes the importance of boundaries between workers and employers established in the colonial era. Apartheid normalized this colonial institution where workers were tied to their employers in material as well as ideological forms. In return, employers "took care" of their workers' basic needs in ways that also controlled their daily existence. Food, shelter and accommodation were provided as a significant portion of workers' salaries—illustrating employers' paternalistic relationship to household labor. Particularly indicative of this colonial nature is the striking practice of employers managing the health and medical needs of the workers they employ.[16]

Today, the vast majority of domestic workers do not have medical care, therefore full-time employers in many cases pay for treatment costs *when* they deem it appropriate for their worker to see the "family doctor." This practice distinctly invades privacy among workers when their medical conditions are shared with employers, thus instituting a high level of colonial paternalism that continues to shape the institution today. Through these severe power differentials at play, workers' most personal lives are both exposed to and controlled by employers as part of a social contract that structures the institution. Outside of medical needs, employers shared a sense of duty related to buying personal hygiene products as part of the "package" for their domestic workers:

> In my case I supply them with shampoo and soap and sanitary towels, it's only fair . . . I also don't want to spoil the person. I said to her it will only be for a little bit of toiletries.

Workers identified employers' generosity in supplying these personal products as a strong indicator of an overall positive, more adequately compensated working environment. Fikele recalled one of her more ideal employers:

> If you work, they must buy for you, all the toilet stuff, the pads, rinse, everything, all the things in the toilet, your roll-ons, perfume, everything. Was *very very* good to me.

While these 'perks' were commonly noted by workers as important to job satisfaction, they also more specifically entrench a colonial paternalism throughout the institution. Furthermore the paradox of intimacy and distance is revealed in these highly personal components demanded of the work.

Related to this duty of "taking care of your help," associations that linked domestic workers to "children" appeared on numerous occasions in the employer interviews:

> I do not treat them any different to my children and if I want to reprimand them I would say, "it's now your mother."

> If I buy something for my children, I buy something for her as well. Even though she gets her salary at the end of the month, but you know like I said she is part of the family. She also looks for presents.

Like the imagery associated with black women in the U.S. (Hill Collins 1990; Dickerson 1995), perceptions of domestic workers as "children" illustrate the overarching derogatory construction of "African" women—a pervasive carryover from the colonial era that continues to dominate the institution in modern South Africa.

Perhaps the most daily enactments of this colonial nature can be seen in the particular *language* associated with domestic labor. Throughout my field research, I was struck by the way in which everyday language reified both colonialism and apartheid. For example, the words "maid" and "madam" remain normal references to domestic work relationships. In my interviews, colonial terms were commonly used in a possessive form such that employers discussed "my maid" and workers used the term "my master" to indicate the male head of the household. Similarly, one worker shared her experience in a brand new job where she was given a list of daily tasks by her woman employer—who asked her to "polish Master's shoes" and "iron Master's trousers" each day. Furthermore, at a highly personal level, domestic workers literally give up their own identity on the job. Ntutu is renamed "Maggie" and Ndidi becomes "Violet." These normalized practices of stripping African identities and assigning Western names encompass the intersection of colonial language and severe paternalism. Furthermore, such dominant language patterns symbolize that transformation of everyday social norms, particularly in colloquial language, has not yet mirrored South Africa's public democratization.

One feminist coloured employer shared her frustration with the paternalism embodied in the particular language related to domestic workers:

> I mean just the whole thing of why people are called maids and boy and girl . . . and my *char*,[17] like this person is a faceless person that doesn't have a name. And you know I feel quite strongly about the term domestic worker and I mean I find *char* a bit derogatory, but other people don't think like that, they don't see it like that . . . because I also believe that people use this kind of terminology to keep people in oppressed positions and to continue with the cycles of oppression and patriarchal dominance.

Interestingly, feminist employers often referred to the domestic workers they employed as "helpers" or "assistants." One predominant government gender activist shared with me that the common questions among professional women in her social circle was, "Do you outsource?" when discussing the demands of the double day. *Outsourcing* embodies a feminist acknowledgement of the professional service domestic workers provide, while distinguishing this labor sector from its colonial inception and apartheid institutionalization.

Physical Spaces Shape Social Relations

Also central to the colonial nature of domestic work, South Africa maintains a *physical* architecture that re-instills the "spatial legacy of apartheid"[18] where geographical separation was central to social stratification. These highly visual, tangible, and racialized geographies shape domestic work in particularly dominant ways. As institutionalized in the colonial era, domestic workers' spaces were distinctly separate within the place of employment, even though these "quarters" were often linked to the family home. Felicia, a white employer participant, described, "she's miles away from us"—meaning that her worker was both available to do the work at all times yet far enough away from the family that she did not invade their privacy. This practice of living within but separate from the family of employment reflects a core component of the physical structures built during apartheid. In the democratic context, most middle to upper class homes are sold with "maid's quarters" as commonly as "built in cupboards"—representing the normalcy by which domestic work is engrained and accepted as part of everyday life. In one instance, I observed a couple negotiating the final arrangements of a newly purchased house. The real estate agent offered that the "maid" could be maintained when the house sold—thus instilling individual worker's links to physical properties. Furthermore, an ideology of property ownership extends to the domestic worker—reifying extreme colonial norms that dehumanize women in this sector.

The architectural structures that remain from the apartheid era continue to frame the overall experience of workers who live at their place of employment in critical ways. Throughout my interviews with workers across all contexts, the sacrificed privacy common to "maid's quarters" as well as employers' control over the living space became some of the most challenging aspects of the work. Both the fundamental requirement of living on the employer's property, as well as the very nature of the architectural structures assigned to workers, remain strongly indicative of a colonial ideology that continues to operate through physical spaces. In Cape Town, for instance, Sea Point's prestigious high-rise apartment buildings that face the Atlantic beachfront avenue are some of the city's most valuable properties. Each of these privately owned apartments is sold with "servant's quarters" which always face the back of the property, consist of tiny individual dorm-like rooms, require shared bathroom facilities, and are removed from the residential areas of the property owners. The domestic workers for each apartment in these buildings generally reside as a collective, usually on the first floor level without visual access to the surrounding seafront.

Louise, who described her overall working conditions as the most positive in the entire sample, shared the following when asked what she found most challenging in the job:

> The most difficult thing . . . this tiny little box I'm living in. I don't know who built this block, but the rooms are terrible. It's terribly small . . . you know it's very crowded . . . and I have so much things. You know, I'm sitting now with a room and I haven't got a cup. My cups and saucers and things that I serve people tea is all in packing boxes . . . and I have a little round table with my TV on top . . . I want the carpet out of my room. I want to put new carpet in . . . actually the rooms are

so small that it does, I think it can have an effect on one's health . . .
although I would never cook there. I can't cook in a room and sleep in
it too. Some people do, I can't. It's not for me. And the bathroom situation too—you have to share it with people, that's also, I *hate* it. I bath
mostly, and I use upstairs bathrooms mostly.

Louise was able to share the guest bathroom in her employer's flat only
because the nature of her relationship was so positive. Yet the living condition afforded to most domestic workers outside of the hours of work
shapes their entire life experience and ties them to the labor through the
ongoing dominance of apartheid architecture.

Of all the workers who lived with their employer (10 out of 20), only
one found their living quarters comfortable and conducive to an independ-
ent lifestyle. In this case, the established sense of autonomy was created
through Ina's use of an entire lower level apartment within the home structure, which afforded a certainty that:

She [employer] will never come here to my place in my room if she
know there is someone here. When I'm here and I got somebody here,
then it feels like my own place, it doesn't feel to me I'm under somebody else's roof.

This living accommodation and its afforded privacy and independence
impacted the felt experience of Ina quite strongly as she emphasized
throughout our three interview conversations. Yet the nature of this living
context remained in stark contrast to all the other situations afforded to the
domestic workers that I observed. In the worst scenarios, women lived in
garages or outdoor sheds with no windows or lighting. In the most
exploitative instances, workers were denied any personal space of their
own in live-in positions. One worker's room was flooded for three weeks
before her employer would handle the situation. Another continued to use
an outdoor toilet while working in one of the wealthiest seafront suburbs in
the city. Yet a striking paradox emerged in the attitudes employers held
about their workers' living spaces. A pervasive perception among employers illustrated a belief that whatever type of living space they afforded their
workers would certainly be better than the conditions from which workers
were raised (in either townships or rural locations). This shared myth
among employers—that their worker was "better off" in her "servants'
quarter" than in "shanties"—reinforces the sharp inequalities and colonial
paternalism that elevates the social position of employers through these
perceptions of benevolence surrounding physical spaces.

As we see in these examples, South Africa's pervasive colonial ideology prevails in the institution of domestic work in ways that serve the interests of power groups and dominate social relations between workers and employers. Therefore, these physical structures created in the apartheid era support the perpetuation of a normalcy about live-in household service labor. Furthermore, the spatial geography we see in South Africa's architecture allows the paternalistic, colonial nature of the institution to thrive in everyday life. Throughout my research, in almost all live-in contexts I observed, workers were required to receive guests through the main house or apartment entrance—which afforded employers full access to workers' day-to-day social interactions. Similarly, limiting workers' privacy through the live-in nature of the job created a powerful means by which employers maintained control over workers' daily lives. Of the 20 workers, 12 believed that their employers listened to their personal conversations in either their rooms or the workspace when receiving telephone calls.[19] Controlling the living accommodations of workers also ensured that their priority remained focused on *service*. Most living quarters were governed by strict rules for workers about access, appropriate use, and limitations. For example, in some apartment complexes, the lights are literally turned out in workers rooms at 10:00 in the evening, to assure that workers don't have guests or "get into trouble" in ways that would impair employers' lives. Additionally, living structures mirrored employers' pervasive power to deny workers the ability to share housing with their own families. In most cases, "maid's quarters" remain so small that only workers can be accommodated, not their husbands, children or other family members. These physical structures therefore further isolate workers from their own support structures, romantic possibilities,[20] and their extended communities.

Improving the physical conditions of the living space became a central place where workers exhibited agency at an individual level with their employer in order to improve the overall context of their daily experience. Monica described her process of activating change:

> When I came here the bed was in such terrible condition, my bed, but I didn't want to complain and two weeks ago now I said to her, oh, but now I have to, because my body, I feel tired every morning when I got up, oh, and I can't move and I said to her, then she bought that bed, it's a new bed, *ja,* and she bought me that bed and the husband doesn't know that because she can't ask him, he is *very* stingy, oh *ja.*

Similarly, Victoria shared the following about her ongoing campaign to improve her living quarters:

When I start working here, the first night, then I walked into this room, then I said to myself, I'm a poor person, I like to be neat and clean, that's me and I don't think that I will be able to stay in this room because this room was filthy, the carpets was filthy. I remember the mattress, the spring was broken and then the night I was sleeping, the spring was sticking me in the back, that was when I was speaking to them, they must change the mattress and put that window in [points to window added to her room] because this was like a prison cell . . . but what I'm saying is that employers used to say to you when they interview you, "You are going to have a small TV and hot and cold water." Did you see that bathroom? . . . It's 10 years still the same, they don't do anything about it, the door is nearly falling off, you get tired to ask them all the time, "Can you please repair it?" . . . They will see to *their* things, but they wouldn't bother with you.

These acts illustrate the ongoing agency of workers to transform their own daily experiences within the severe structural conditions of domination central to the institution of household labor. As workers continue to challenge the ideologies of severe colonial power structures that remain in their work environments, they are also contributing to the broader transformation of South Africa by bring democracy to the household. At the same time, however, we see how ongoing structures of power from the apartheid era maintain their dominance in ways that normalize the immense disparity in the living conditions allotted to workers and employers—particularly in the most wealthy neighborhoods. For example, even though one group of workers in a luxury apartment complex collectively organized to demand changes in their living quarters, the request was denied by the building's governing association, composed entirely of employer residents who maintained an extraordinary amount of economic power. This incidence demonstrates the enormous barriers to structural change—even as women exert agency—because of the extent to which employers maintain social and economic power in the new democracy. By controlling the living space of workers and rationing out a particularly frugal means of daily existence, the pervasive colonial nature of household labor provides vivid reminders of the "old days" in ways that bolster employers' power while relegating black women to this institutionalized "culture of servitude."

Securing Inequality

An important link between these physical structures and the extremely heightened levels of security in post-apartheid South Africa arose throughout this research. Since the nation's transition to democracy, crime has elevated to such a level that concerns for daily safety and security are impossible to escape. This crime burden, however, falls disproportionately upon marginalized communities where lack of access to economic resources affords few options for daily survival. Furthermore, women pay the price for gender violence through South Africa's severe rates of rape and gender violence (Vetten 1996; Matthews et. al 2004).

Women employed in domestic labor pay a particular price for South Africa's heightened crime rates, as well as the associated fears of violence that have emerged in the post-apartheid context. The relationship between the institution of paid household labor and South Africa's increasing crime threat illustrates another paradoxical relationship where women are both othered and responsible for particularly intimate labor within the private spaces of their employment. The irony follows: domestic workers are both a perceived threat to employers' security (through their association with "skollies"[21] in their own race and class groups) and responsible for the protection of their employers' households by "keeping skollies out." Both employers and workers in this study discussed issues of security, even though it was not part of the formal interview topics. The assurance of security therefore represents a new complexity in the institution of domestic labor since the 1994 transformation.

Property security was one area where employers recognized vulnerability associated with the employment of a domestic worker. Employer participants shared a felt threat to their personal property and belongings, particularly when trust was not yet established in the work relationships. In some cases this involved "petty theft," such as workers taking food items from the cupboard, yet in other cases employers worried about more substantial threats:

> What if you come back and there's absolutely nothing in your flat . . . it happened a couple of times, they cleaned out . . . they stole most of my stuff.

This fear is linked to another aspect of the data among employers in this study. When asked what they felt was the most important attribute in hiring a domestic worker, 19 of the 20 employers responded by naming *trustworthiness* as the most important attribute. Employers' willingness to discuss their own vulnerability in employing domestic workers emerged repeatedly in relation to the very tangible threats to safety and security in the post-apartheid context.

In contrast to the potential threat of employing domestic workers in private homes, employers also felt that the presence of "staff members" protected them from threats of crime, as this employer illustrated:

Figure 4.1: Intimate Security. Photograph by author.

No, I must say out of all the houses here, I think we've been burgled the least. We've never, when I think of all the houses, here we are, and they do know that I have a staff member every day. I mean two on a Monday and two on a Friday plus Lyla, so there are three of them and I must say it makes a huge difference . . . there's always staff here and I must say, we very naughty, we don't lock.

This added security expectation repeatedly emerged in my interviews with domestic workers. Some workers described their expanded job responsibilities in relation to heightened security: locking several access gates in the evenings, double-checking computer security systems throughout the day, *polishing* employers' guns, and sitting with their employers in the evening to assuage the threat of violence. In this particularly revealing image of Figure 4.1, a domestic worker demonstrates her evening task of locking the interior gate that prevents access to her employers' bedrooms, should a criminal access the first floor of the home.

While employers' wellbeing was enhanced by domestic labor, workers' threats of experiencing violence substantially increased when they were expected to serve as "security guards" as an added requirement of their jobs. Workers also noted that these supplemental expectations came without any increased compensation. Many participants in this study were required to manage complicated household security systems in the absence of their employers. This practice has become so normalized that capitalist ventures that appeal specifically to employers now offer "training programs" for domestic workers under the marketing guise of assuring "your safety and security."

In the case of heightened security fears in South Africa, we see another cost of the inequitable physical structures at the employment site. Domestic workers' "quarters" are usually far less protected than the homes of employers. Therefore, workers felt that they would be most vulnerable should a criminal access the home. The following domestic worker's narrative depicts the paradox of security and inequality:

This burglar system that they put, that one over there by the door, and now I've got this remote thing that I must use, If I see someone in the yard at night and I'm getting frightened then I must press the thing so that the alarm can go off . . . but here [in her room] is *no* protection, that door is nothing, they can kick it open and they come in easily. That is why I am so afraid when I'm here alone . . . so you are not safe, but there's no protection, that's it.

In other interviews with workers, similar issues of safety and security—especially when workers were responsible for the home in the absence of employers—became a dominant theme. Most telling was a shared experience of three workers that had either been attacked directly or had known other domestic workers who were killed in order to access the materials goods in the homes in which they were employed.

These narratives, on the part of employers and workers, illustrate the extent to which the institution of domestic work mediates the fear of crime, considered by many participants to be the lingering price of apartheid's inequality. As domestic workers are expected to place their own bodies on the line to protect employers' physical and material well-being, we see the reification of an underpinning ideological assumption that workers are less valuable human beings. This presents a striking contrast to the intimacy and trust necessary to protect employers from South Africa's persistent crime threats. Furthermore, this case of security illustrates how the lingering physical structures of apartheid are central to the post-apartheid contradictions that surround the distinct ways in which workers and employers are exposed to threats of crime in the new democracy.

Maintaining Familiar Ties

One of the most complicated aspects of colonialism is its impact on the oppressed (Fanon 1963). Paulo Freire (1970) suggested that the oppressed, to some extent, participate in their own subjugation. In the post-apartheid context, I repeatedly confronted experiences that illustrated a certain safety, familiarity and comfort with apartheid's strict racial order among those who had been so severely marginalized. Although the political transformation was widely celebrated among these groups, social change presented a severe obstacle for those who had come to understand their place in the world through these rigid, yet *predictable* social hierarchies.

Workers in this study realized some level of comfort and familiarity with the colonial practices that tied them to their employers in servile, yet very loyal, interdependent relationships. Of the 20 workers interviewed, the average number of years of employment as a domestic worker was 27.3. The average number of jobs, however was only 4.2, indicating a low level of job change in relation to the number of years employed. The extent to which workers maintained their employment in contexts that were extremely exploitative arose in almost half of cases. Of the 20 workers, nine expressed deep feelings of conflict, disappointment, and complete disrespect for their employers but remained in these positions because they believed that the next employer could be worse. Maggie revealed this complex position:

So I'm proud of my domestic job and I love it. It doesn't matter how they hurt me, I have to be quiet, I have to swallow. And one thing of our coloured people, we don't want to change from month to month, another job. It gives you a bad reputation. Doesn't matter what the madam do in the house, you stand there. You don't want to change from job to job.

In South Africa's first local democratic elections of 1995, the coloured population voted the National Party (NP) into office, even though it represented the reformed apartheid era of extreme white dominance. The popular rationale for this alignment of a non-power group with an oppressive regime was that "It's better with the devil you know rather than the one you don't know."[22] Domestic workers justified their persistence in jobs with oppressive employers by adopting similar rationales. Lena revealed her reasoning for staying in a particularly difficult work context:

I can't go now. Where I'm going to find a job now? Maybe I leave this bad people, I go to the other bad one. Let me stay by the bad ones I know. So I stayed there.

As this illustrates, workers often felt insecure about leaving even oppressive situations because of a degree of security and familiarity within it, albeit also embodying the racial power dynamics of the apartheid regime as they recognized.

Cecil, whose work context was one of the most exploitative, shared the following emotions in relation to her employer:

You know it's not nice to say, but sometimes I just hate, I just hate the way she treats me. I can't say I hate her, but the way she, it won't be a nice word to say you hate people, but it makes you really feel that you are just there, just to keep things for her nicely and you are a nothing. You are there to make things, just do things right for them, but when it comes to you, it's, you feel upset, you feel hurt. It's not nice, because I know when I grow up poor, I never ugly to, never, never in my life did I treat people like that. I mean, I'm a human being and so the next person is also a human being so you must treat him the way you'd like people to treat you, you see? But, I cope. I can say I cope and I just put it behind me. And that, I think this makes me strong. I say, "tomorrow it's going to be better," you know. And I'm just looking forward for the next day. And that's going to make me going because I have children and I have to be there and just don't look back, just trying to go on.

Regardless of the fact that her salary was far below average, she was forced to work seven days per week, and her food rations were absolutely minimal, Cecil did not consider leaving her employer because she felt that the next context could be much more exploitative and she wanted to insure that her children would be protected.

Closely connected to this interdependent relationship is a deeply engrained sense of *loyalty* between workers and employers, which prevailed among my sample in even the most exploitative work contexts. Employers shared that they often provided for workers' needs with the expectation that loyalty would be assured. For example, Sarah paid for her workers' children's schooling, even though as she recalled, it was "nominal in comparison to the school fees that we had to pay for our daughter." However, with this benevolence, an underlying expectation that Lyla would remain in the job until her children finished school became clear in Sarah's expectations of Lyla. Employers expressed deep feelings of betrayal when workers either left the job or jeopardized established trust in some regard, demonstrating another strong link to dominant colonial mentalities and the interlocking culture of servitude. Furthermore, loyalty is so deeply engrained in South African domestic service that it is not uncommon for generations of workers to be linked to the same family of employers.

This resistance to transforming the colonial nature of domestic labor is centrally connected to employers' unwillingness to lose the daily comforts that accompanied the apartheid era through the institutionalized nature of domestic service. This colonial system therefore embedded a normalcy around live-in domestic labor in the private household that was constructed as essential to the particular entitlement of the white minority. In exchange, however, employers were expected to uphold a certain level of caretaking for their domestic workers as part of the social contract embedded in this colonial institution. In this study, the association made by employers about domestic workers being "one in the family" exhibited a distinctly contradictory ideology in comparison to numerous patronizing practices that reinforced severe differentials in social location. For example, 'soft rewards'—such as "gifts" of used clothing, toiletries, food at the holidays, and new uniforms—remain common practice in the modern institution of domestic work. Similarly, employers' benevolence for long-term care in retirement is implied because of the nature of the colonial relationship, yet never *formalized*. In many cases, this resulted in workers receiving no compensation after years of service.

In the new democratic legislation, providing retirement benefits is not required of employers—which leaves workers reliant upon their own family structures for long-term survival. When workers in this study reported that they were assured of some form of retirement compensation based upon years of service, they also shared that their employers withheld the details of such plans. Workers assessed that discussing the material conditions of their long-term retirement was off limits in the eyes of their employers. In one of my interviews, Lena, who had worked for her employer for over 20 years, reflected upon the following scenario in relation to her preparation for retirement that same year:

> I don't know how much, so, she said to me she's going to give, she's going to put a little bit more money in for me. So I don't know how much she's going to give me.

Tanzi shared her similar experience:

> He said he is going to give me a lump of money, but he doesn't want to tell me how much, because he say I want to give you something, we look after you when you get old, then I said how much? He doesn't say.

Union leaders also consistently reported that interventions in salary, benefit and retirement conditions were the most common aspect of their caseloads in each regional office. In these instances, it was implied that employers would care for their workers following retirement, yet withholding the details of this benefit indicated another strong link to colonial practices of indentured service that reified the substantial power differentials in this private labor context.

These dominant features described above reveal the overarching colonial culture of servitude embodied in domestic labor, even within the new democratic governance. One of the central complexities we see in the enduring power of apartheid ideology is the participation of marginalized groups in structures of inequality that are both oppressive and familiar. Further examination of the underlying processes that maintain this colonial institution must involve an analysis of prevailing power structures sustained in micro-household relations. In this regard, let us move to a fuller analysis of employers' particular roles in upholding the virtually unchanged nature of domestic service within the new democracy.

Contested Power Transitions

A central explanation for the reality that the transformational ideology of democracy has not yet impacted the institution of domestic labor in substantial ways is based in the governmental transition terms that assured the maintenance of economic and social power for the white population, even though the racial structures of governmental representation shifted dramatically. These macro structural patterns play out as both female and male employers reinforce patterns of racism and gender stratification constructed in the colonial period through their daily social interactions with domestic workers in the private household. Through very tangible labor tasks, the relations between workers and employers remain embedded in a culture of servitude:

> She does all the cleaning, all the washing, all the ironing and all the cooking . . . I will decide basically what's for supper. I'll go in and decide at 4 o'clock and say look, we will have x, y and z for supper and she will [gestures, prepare it]. No, she does everything for me, and I mean her cooking is excellent, so I don't have to worry. She was able to cook when she came here and she runs her own routine. I never have to say to her, like at the moment I know today she's doing brass, so she's going probably on a Tuesday and Wednesday for about an hour or so, she's cleaning these little brass things today.[23] Then, she works through all my silverware, and then it will be the windows and then, you see I never actually tell her what to do, you know.

The extent to which domestic workers' labor affords privileged sectors of the population both material luxury and emotional freedom from the daily tasks of household reproduction is powerfully depicted in this narrative. Like Isobel above, the majority of the white population's daily existence is supported by the way in which domestic workers' labor is owned by the upper and middle class. In South Africa, these sharp distinctions between who purchases domestic services and who performs the labor continue to embody what I assert to be the sharpest racial classification system remaining in the post-apartheid nation.

While these formerly completely racially-based inequalities have shifted with the integration of economic privilege in black and coloured populations, the services that workers provide continue to embody a colonial culture of excessive luxury that remains difficult to alter for the small minority that continues to experience it on a daily basis. Thus, the democratization of the private sphere remains the most personal and challenging aspect of redressing past racial and economic imbalances. And as class structures gradually shift such that economically privilege members of formerly oppressed groups purchase domestic labor, the institution remains governed by a colonial ideology that ultimately reifies the apartheid stratification system at an economic level. Mallie, a young new elite black professional, shared her experience after hiring a domestic worker of her same race for the first time:

> She came the first day and it was like another house when I came back
> from work. I thought, oh my god . . . it can't be where I live. It was
> *amazing!* I mean she, and she takes such initiative, she just . . . I don't
> know, she was magic. There is no ways, once she starts working in your
> house, there's no way you can say you can't come here again.

The paid practice of domestic labor enhances both the material and
aesthetic qualities of life for those who could afford to purchase such services in ways that employers in this study, across all racial groups, found difficult to abandon, even for the sake of heightened political consciousness.
Of the 20 employers in four racial categories, only three believed that they
could manage the household responsibilities without the hired services of a
domestic laborer. And of these three, two asserted that they were "struggling like hell" during transitional times when they did not employ a
domestic worker in the home. However, the reasoning behind the way in
which employers felt unable to manage without paid domestic services varied among respondents. For some, such as Felicity, this was because:

> It's just the way we were brought up. I'm afraid I'm not very functional
> in the house, I'm spoiled I know.

Others, such as Thope, a black parliamentarian, said this necessity was
because:

> There is work, there is children, there is a house, all those things need
> me but I cannot do them perfectly, all three of them without assistance.

While Anna, a white feminist employer, described the way in which hiring
domestic help afforded her a particular psychological comfort, especially
for her childcare needs:

> If there is no extended family and you cannot afford to buy your help
> in, you must go quietly mad.

Alternatively, Sarah (another white employer) captured her rationale for
hiring household reproduction services as a recognized luxury:

> It's wonderful to have . . . and you know I am going through a phase of
> *I'm worth it!* I'm worth it not to have to worry about the planned
> domestic work and as I said at least you will be helping another family
> or two.

As I noticed the extent to which employers' lives were freed from both physical tasks and psychological concerns through the support of paid domestic workers, I also noted among employers varying levels of guilt and/or apologizing for the nature of their luxury. For example, employers often downplayed the amount of labor they assigned, sharing a perception that their workers had "quite cushy jobs" with all of the luxuries they afforded through the nature of the work that provided room, board and basic living needs. Most telling was Felicity's asking, "What more could she possibly need? She's even got a beautiful view of the sea!"

Employers seemed to heighten the perceived value of room and living expenses, thus lessening the extent of economic and social inequality in the nature of domestic labor as portrayed in these employer interview excerpts:

> She has her own bathroom, toilet, shower, and her own TV room and her bedroom with built-in cupboards and a bed and everything.

> She gets her meals, whatever is here, she can do her washing with the machine, the tumble dryer, she won't be restricted in any way, I mean I believe if someone is living with you, it's like having another daughter.

Also, employers intentionally brought up ways in which they attempted to make the lives of their domestic worker easier through either the structure of the work or a respectful management style, as Anita expressed:

> I always put myself in their shoes, and I'm not gonna go on my knees, how am I gonna feel, my back is gonna be paining, and so I try and makes things, I don't like, if the vacuum cleaner breaks, I will buy one immediately because I don't want her to use a broom to sweep out the mats. You know, I always put myself in their shoes because I can see when they are off [during] the weekend, then I have to do the work, so I know, you know, I don't want them to work hard, everything must be convenient.

At times, the extent to which employers voluntarily shared the ease they perceived in the lives of the workers they employed led to interview responses that seemed to embody varying levels of social desirability.[24] For example, Anita described the following in relation to her domestic worker's limited responsibilities in managing a household of five:

Well if I am home, then I manage everything, then she's got time to go and sit and watch all her soapies and the only time when she has to do something for me is just to wash the few dishes, but while I'm cooking, I wash up the dishes and the only time like I said, when she knows once I dish up, then she will come and sit with us and then she will tell me she is going to finish watching her other program. I said, "It doesn't matter, whatever time your programs are over." So she knows already, you know that I am quite flexible where that's concerned and then she will just do the few dishes and sweep the kitchen and then she goes to her room, so her responsibilities actually end when I get home and I always say, when her work is done, like on a Saturday or if she goes away for the weekend, on a Saturday morning, I clean the place within two or three hours, so I say if the place is clean for two or three hours in the morning, go and rest, take it easy, because tonight when it's washing up time, then you just have to do those dishes for me, you know, so take your break, relax, take it easy.

The tone of this narrative was repeated throughout my interviews when employers shared their perception about the relative ease in the workload they assigned and subsequent lifestyle their domestic workers were afforded. Closely related was a narrative regarding morality, such that "taking good care of the maid" was perceived as honorable and even associated with religious principles at times. Therefore, the belief held by employers that their domestic workers were "one in the family" was internalized as an ideal, noble trait and linked to both their living structures and the perceived light work load they assigned.

In some cases, employers told me that they were "spoiling the maid." Yet throughout participant observations and particularly in the living contexts I shared, a much different reality emerged. In a (coloured) home where I lived for a short period of time, a repeated familial discourse that Melanie, the (live-out) domestic worker, was "spoiled" came up in individual and group conversations. The woman employer, for example, claimed that Melanie always ate at the table with the family. Yet, I repeatedly observed Melanie's rations put to the side, while the family ate independently. At one point, Melanie was cleaning the kitchen floor on her knees while the rest of the family shared a meal in close proximity. Melanie would also remain in the house for hours after the completion of her tasks to wait for her pay and ask for a ride to the local "taxi" stand. Yet, within the family, the perception that Melanie was "spoiled" because she was "much better off" than other workers appeared very genuine. This disconnect between employers' self perceptions and my own participant observation data attained within family structures afforded a particularly insightful lens into the daily enactments of power within South Africa's private spaces—posing a severe affront to notions of democracy "at home."

This disjuncture between perceptions among employers and the lived realities of workers represents a central component that partially explains why little has changed in the context of domestic work. As a result of the reality that no structural mechanisms are in place to democratize the household, employers maintain both social and economic privilege such that they continually recreate the colonial nature of the institution of domestic work. Furthermore, this severe economic inequality fostered a shared rationalization among employers that they were contributing to the alleviation of poverty through the employment of a domestic worker, as Sarah reveals:

> They say that ten people benefit from one person's employment. So it's, you know, at least then you are doing your bit to help spread an income.

This narrative arose continually, even among the most socially conscious feminist employers who could not see any "problem" in hiring a domestic worker. The notion that the maintenance of this institution, at least in its colonial form, reinforces structural dominance and the severe oppression of black women in particular was only acknowledged by two extremely progressive employers. All others in some way justified their employment of domestic workers through this discourse of helping another family as a moral undertaking in the context of national poverty.

Another rationale that emerged as a representation of how employers deal with the hiring of less privileged women was a depersonalization of the intimate labor provided within the institution. Rather than acknowledging the extent of their reliance upon domestic workers in the most private aspects of daily life, employers adopted a business-like rationale for their employment (and unacknowledged reliance upon) domestic workers. Wardah, a gender activist, shared her perspectives about "outsourcing" by contending, "I want this service. I need this service." Gertrude, a traditional white elite employer, when asked about the extent to which she feels any sense of internal conflict about hiring other less privileged women similarly stated:

> They need jobs and I need them. I can't see anything wrong. I've never had a conscious about employing people.

From a much different life experience, Thope, a black parliamentarian, shared her primarily economic approach to the employment of another woman in her home:

> It's not a matter of her helping me only. I am helping her as well because I am paying her. She is not doing it for free—I am paying her. She is doing her own things that she wants to do with her money. Like I am working, so she is helping me in order to be able to work.

Those employers who did associate the employment of domestic workers with the reinforcement of social inequalities of the apartheid era provided valuable insights that linked the daily practice of household labor to institutional structures, as Elna depicted:

> I mean it does come down to who then reproduces the domestic worker's household? So in a very material, economic, grounded, bodily way, it is a double burden for someone like Valerie [her domestic worker]. She leaves my home, she's got to go home and assist in the reproduction of her own household, unless her daughter is probably doing that, so it becomes a bit of a [pause]—the luxury has to stop somewhere and the cost is in *that* household.

Other socially conscious employers similarly deliberated on the severe class-based inequalities between women in South Africa when they confronted the daily experiences of their domestic worker. For some this led to internalized guilt, as Sharifa (a coloured employer) shared:

> There are times I feel guilty, I sometimes feel, I often wish I didn't have to employ another woman you know, I would like to see her get on with life, get a good education.

Similarly, Charmaine (a coloured employer) expressed:

> I think also it's just . . . I tend to feel sorry for people because I always feel that they could've done so much more in their lives you know and now you know she has to clean, like, our home.

Felicity, a more traditional employer, expressed her feelings of conflict as such:

> You do feel, guilty—terribly guilty. I mean I drive this fancy car and I
> live in this beautiful house and I think, "What does she have?"

Although the costs of the colonial nature that continues to dominate
domestic work are certainly most severe for workers, employers also incur
costs. Two interviews with highly politicized feminist employers revealed
an awareness of the loss in privacy that is often overlooked by employers.
Yet the costs incurred in employers' dependence upon the labor of another
woman to reproduce the household—as well as its subsequent connection
to reinforcing patriarchy—were not addressed in 18 of the 20 formal interviews. Rather, employers talked about their challenges in ways that related
directly to their management roles regarding domestic workers. Training,
enforcing standards and authority, reliability among workers, fear of theft,
and issues of household maintenance quality comprised employers' perceptions of what was most difficult about employing domestic workers.
Employers did not, however, associate these challenges with costs to themselves at a personal or societal level. The unknown loss of parental investment in raising children, another cost of domestic labor, was not mentioned
in any of the interviews. And most important in the context of reshaping
patriarchal norms in the newly democratic nation, the multiple ways in
which domestic work further instills unequal, socially constructed gender
relations was only acknowledged in two employer interviews. Not coincidentally, both of these participants were purposely sampled for their
heightened level of feminist social consciousness through their work in gender activism. This institutionalized process therefore creates a nationwide
social structure such that "a huge gender battle is not being fought"[25]
because of the way in which labor associated with women's work can be
purchased rather than addressed directly in the household, where many
theorists suggest real change must occur (Britton 1999).

Domestic Labor and the "Gender Battle"

> A lot of women that are from middle class positions don't realize that it
> reinforces their own gendered exploitation. It just removes the tension,
> you know, and the contradictions, it holds it off for a time but as far as
> I am concerned it further entrenches it in a way, because you don't have
> to deal with it, you don't have to challenge it.

Elna further described an example from her own life:

> In the past, and the reason I guess I employ a domestic worker is because Clinton, my husband and I quarrel sometimes, dishes being done or (laughs) "but I did it last night," "yeah but I cooked" you know, *ja*, it alleviates some of that tension, and of course I mean as I said, my goodness it's a luxury of time that it buys you, time to go to Kirstenbosch Gardens because you don't have to hurry home and do laundry, so *ja*, so it does buy me precious time, it certainly does in that way.

Anna, the second feminist employer who recognized the way in which paid domestic labor further instills patriarchal gender norms, described a culture among "semi-socially conscious" middle class women who share "a rather grim acceptance of shifting women's second role onto a second woman." These participants recognized that the practice was much less optimal than actually shifting roles to men in the household.

The institutionalized process of domestic labor in post-apartheid South Africa frees both men and women from the reproduction of their own households at a task level. Its consequential reinforcement of sexism and gender oppression, however, harms women rather than men. Both women and men enjoy an elevated class status through their ability to purchase paid domestic labor. Yet this practice reinforces the gendered nature of household labor, which continually frees men from participating in or sharing responsibility for what remains constructed as "women's work." And while labor tasks themselves might be lifted from women's daily lives, the extent to which women maintain complete responsibility for the management of the household remains unchallenged.

In this study, 19 of the 20 female employer participants believed that they were completely responsible for household management, even though they paid another woman to actually perform such labor.[26] The following interview response illuminates this dominant perspective among employers. When asked if she still felt responsible in seeing that "everything gets done, even though you don't do the work," Isobel replied:

> Oh, absolutely yes, my husband says x-y-z and it's not done, it's up to me to see that it is [done]. Yes, it's definitely my responsibility (laughs). I also like to see that my house is run correctly, so it's *definitely* my responsibility.

Similarly, a gender activist shared the following in relation to men's roles:

> What goes unchallenged is the man's responsibility in terms of household chores, etc. So you know it increases the feminization of household labor, rather than challenges it or takes away from it . . . because what they see is improved class status or class position so they function because their social status in society is enhanced by having them [domestic workers].

This ongoing patriarchal structural dominance can be partially explained through the central positions of economic power maintained by men in South Africa. In relation to domestic labor, although as Hettie (a white employer) described, "the maid is always the madam's department," management for domestic labor tasks within the household is far less valued than public labor that can be exchanged for economic power—which continues to be ascribed to men in this sector. Therefore, in the context of paid household labor, women supervise domestic workers, but men pay their salaries. This dominant splitting of the management of paid household labor creates an unequal context amongst employers that values men's economic contribution to the sector over women's participation in applied management roles. This dynamic reinforces the devalued nature of women's labor in the household, both for those who actually perform it and those who manage it at a task level.

In this research, when asked who they viewed as their employer, ten workers said that they perceived the man as their employer, even though they did not interact with him about any household management tasks directly. When asked if she viewed her employer as more the man or the woman, Nana contended, "the man, because he give me money, it's never the madam that give you money." This splitting of roles functioned in ways that triangulated relationships between workers, male employers and female employers among my sample. In eight worker interviews, a narrative emerged that created an 'evil woman/generous man' discourse and illuminated the ways in which workers felt more affinity toward the men in their household employment contexts as opposed to the women who managed their daily work tasks.[27] I believe that this splitting of 'good master' and 'evil madam' was influenced by the way in which men held the power to sustain workers' livelihoods through their control over material/economic resources. This association is based in further interpretations of depictions such as Elize's, who shared her experiences of both employers:

> If I go to him for help, when I need money I go to him because that is the only thing that I always need is money in my life, for my struggles you see, when I go far away, maybe when there is a funeral for my family,

they die, and I have to go there, maybe I haven't got taxi fare or bus fare to go, then I go to him and ask him [for] R200 for the taxi or for the bus and when I come back at the end of the month, then I have to pay him back. And when I go to her and I said that I borrowed and then she always send me to him, the boss, he's the boss, you see. And like Saturdays I go off, I work till 10 o'clock in the morning and I maybe ask her [for] R10 or R20 for me for the weekend, then she said wait for him, go to him. So he is there for me, much more than she, but I'm there for her *all the time* when she needs me, but when I need her for this small things, she always push and she push me to her husband.

Elize's narrative portrays a paradox about gender relations and the nature of paid domestic labor in South Africa. Men maintain power through the way in which they control economic resources while women participate in their own gendered subordination by reinforcing these economic divides that establish men as "head of the household" and thus perpetuate patriarchal constructions that devalue unpaid labor. Furthermore, although women must manage the day-to-day responsibilities of domestic workers, they are often not afforded full authority because men maintain economic power, which not only lessens female employers' roles in their own households and marriages, but also in their relationship with the domestic workers employed in their homes.

Closely related is the reality that the ability to purchase domestic services that allowed men's wives to be "happy" affords men even further positions of power in family structures because of the way their economic power is linked to their purchasing power. Neil, an employer's husband who joined an interview briefly, expressed a sentiment that, "As long as Loretta [the domestic worker] stays, I'm happy." In this case, Neil referred to the fact that his ability to buy Loretta's services afforded him a comfort in his own marriage because his wife was also "happy," which ultimately further establishes his own authority and power in the household.

This power differential similarly poses a serious threat to transformation in the domestic work sector. At the time of this research, initiatives in place to formalize this sector included implementation of a minimum wage standard, work contract requirements, and domestic workers' inclusion in promulgated labor benefits such as unemployment insurance. Yet the split roles of employers, with men holding enhanced economic power, complicates this shift to formalizing domestic labor. Contracts, for example require discussions of both salary and tasks, which becomes even more complex with such divisions in place regarding roles assumed by employers. Monica, a domestic worker, clearly illustrated this complexity in her attempts to institute new labor legislation in her own place of employment:

> I talk to her about the contract that time, because I said to her, "I went to that meeting" and I said to her that they gave me this contract and I want them to go through it and they must sign it and then she said to me alright, they will go through it . . . then she said, "I must give it to Master." You see, so what can I do?

Monica's experience captures both her own agency to transform the context of her everyday work life and the way in which men's roles complicate and impede processes of transformation. Therefore, as accountability for change must occur in white power groups in order to breakdown apartheid ideology, men must participate in the democratization of the household in order to deconstruct the ongoing patriarchal norms that dominate South Africa and the institution of domestic work. As Marlene shared:

> You know as a feminist, my husband doesn't do and I don't know of in fact men who do the 50 percent thing. You know, it just doesn't happen. It's a whole process of re-socialisation, re-orientation, and as much as my husband is extremely supportive of my work . . . your first priority should be your kids, your first priority should be your home, your first priority should be your husband, not your work.

This re-socialization process Marlene described appears daunting, particularly as colonial patriarchal culture dominates the social landscape of South Africa. Yet her recent experience of not hiring the paid labor of another less privileged woman to perform household management duties, forced this re-orientation process at a micro-level in the household:

> I realise also, it forced, it has forced me and my husband to take more responsibility in terms of our house, which is a good thing, especially for him I think. Like I've just been to Jo-Burg and when I came back . . . he actually did clean up quite nicely and did do the washing, so, and there is also a sense that we know there is no one else is going to do it and *ja*, so we have to do it.

While complete abandonment of paid domestic work in South Africa is unrealistic, isolated experiences such as these at the micro-level illustrate important processes to engender a broader democratization of the institution. In any case, domestic work must be examined beyond the way in which women interact in the institution. Economic and patriarchal power structures continue to shape domestic labor, and remain a critical components of the ongoing neo-colonial culture we see in this institution. As the data suggest, shifting men's participation and responsibility for household labor remains one of the greatest obstacles to realizing congruence between South Africa's public transformation and the structures of race, class and gender-based power that continue to shape everyday social relations in ways that are particularly salient in the institution of domestic labor.

CONCLUSIONS

As we see in the narratives throughout this chapter, domestic labor plays a central role in the maintenance of "social apartheid" in South Africa. Even though the democratic transition realized enormous political change, everyday social relations in this colonial institution of paid household labor remain virtually unchanged. My data suggest that both employers—and to a certain extent domestic workers—were not prepared to transform the private sphere, where the reproduction of daily life continues to reinforce the familiarity and predictability of apartheid's rigid social order. The severe power asymmetries contained in this colonial institution led to a pervasive discourse about the way in which "not much has changed" in South Africa's institutionalized sector of domestic labor, regardless of the broader national transformation. In this sense, many of the narratives in my study echoed the central conditions of domestic labor we see in Cock's (1980) *Maids and Madams*. Domestic work therefore contains an incredible amount of power in maintaining apartheid structures of inequality. I suggest that this 'holding on' to apartheid in the private sphere renders much of the public transformation inconsequential to those portions of the minority population that continue to enjoy the privileges established in the colonial foundation of domestic service in South Africa.

The particular history of apartheid and the recency of the nation's transition to democracy distinguish the institutionalized nature of domestic labor in particular ways. First, race inequality embedded within this institution is distinctly defined by the apartheid era's policies of sharp segregation. The education system, for instance, channeled black women directly into domestic labor and reinforced control over this particular sector through highly gendered and racialized policies of social governance. Second, a prevailing colonial ideology in the South African case—seen through the overarching patterns of privilege, language and physical architecture—reinforces employers' extremely paternalistic relationships to domestic workers. Furthermore, a prevailing *culture of servitude* continues to tie workers to employers in ways that sustain the institution much like the colonial apartheid era. In particular, the required migration of this sector establishes a structure of dependency that reinforces the privilege of employers whose daily life is reproduced by women who provide live-in service labor. The combination of these social historical conditions underscores the reality that domestic work remains in most cases the only viable work option for black women. Like Britton's (1999) assertion that gender oppression operates in specific ways through the legacy of the apartheid era, the institution of domestic work illustrates the prevalence of a particularly racialized sexism that reinforces former structures of power in the most personal spaces central to everyday life. Changing this normalized "social apartheid" that persists most strikingly in the institution of domestic work therefore presents one of the greatest challenges to South Africa's full transformation.

Paid domestic labor entrenches the severe imbalance in gender power relations that persists in the private household realm through the ongoing dominance of patriarchy—presenting a distinct contradiction to the gender rights central to South Africa's public democratic achievement. My interviews illustrate how paid domestic work reinforces sexism at the micro-level by relieving the "tension" of negotiating household labor, as this employer depicted:

> My husband and I, when she [domestic worker] is not there, we *argue!* Because it's like he's doing more, I'm doing more than him or he's doing less than me, you know that type of thing.

The dominance of institutionalized domestic work at a structural level affords men even greater social power and privilege. Not only are they relieved from household labor, but their own social status is also reinforced by their ability to hire "other" women to perform the necessary reproduction of the private sphere. As Lorber (1994) illustrated, this allows more privileged women to participate in social processes such as charity work and "volunteer" labor to reinforce the status of the entire family—thereby embedding the social stratification functions of domestic labor in its institutionalized form. One of the most salient themes from these data was captured in one participant's assertion that, "a huge gender battle is not being fought" because of the power the institution of domestic work contains in maintaining race, class and gender inequality through the shifting of household labor to women who remain most severely marginalized in South African society.

I want to emphasize that this "gender battle" transcends the paid institution of domestic work and creates a double burden for women employed in this sector. The normalcy we see surrounding black women's relegation to the least valued positions in society shapes the status of domestic workers within their own families. Even though they provide significant economic resources, domestic workers are positioned within an overarching social stratification system that persistently reinforces the devalued nature of feminized household labor. It is important to note that patriarchal structures constructed in the dominant power group have a powerful impact on the social inequalities that are maintained *within* marginalized groups. Therefore, because of their marginalized gender positions in their work and private lives, domestic workers experience an interconnected oppression stemming from the expectations surrounding black women's roles in the reproduction of households—in both paid and unpaid forms.[28] As we see throughout this chapter, domestic labor is structured by severe power asymmetries that maintain a "triple oppression" (Cock 1980) for women throughout this sector. Although the narratives of "newly elite" and feminist employers demonstrated particular acts of democratizing the household, the extent to which the wider population of employers problematized the institution of domestic work as an affront to South Africa's democratic human rights values remained marginal. Rather a rhetoric of "taking care of the domestic" suggests that the overall improvement of working conditions for this sector remains contained by the paternalistic culture of domestic labor. Furthermore, my data reveal the importance of establishing rigid boundaries in order to maintain the sharp divisions between workers and employers—as we see in the dominance of physical structures that reify distinct social stratification patterns. This dialectic of intimacy and social distancing is particularly striking in the context of what has arisen as South Africa's most pervasive social concerns in the post-apartheid context—HIV/AIDS and human security. These emergent issues illustrate the overlapping complexities between the firmly embedded colonial nature of domestic labor in the face of new social problems.

Based upon these findings, I suggest that in the existing context of social change in South Africa, until domestic work is reformed, the full realization of democracy remains seriously jeopardized. Without a radical leveling of class-based inequality and a shift in the dominant colonial ideology, the largest employment sector for women will continue to embody gender oppression, apartheid dominance, and incongruence between the private and public actualization of transformation. Therefore, as the data reveal, transfiguration of the institution of domestic work encapsulates

South Africa's greatest challenge because of the interlocking levels of the "former regime" contained within it.

To facilitate South Africa's transformation in the private sphere, we must take a closer look at power structures within this apartheid institution. In this case, employers are central to the development of a fuller analysis of the role of paid domestic labor in the new democracy. Importantly, however, employers are no longer a monolithic group. In the South African case, particularly within the Cape Town region, another complexity emerges as "newly elite" employers move into power positions through the shifting of class-based structures of inequality. As social stratification gradually transitions in this direction, domestic work becomes an important means by which social status is accentuated, particularly among formerly disadvantaged groups. The next chapter moves to an analysis of these shifting race and class relations within the institution of domestic labor. Drawing upon data from "new employers" and within-group employment contexts, I illustrate both the embedded nature of the colonial legacy discussed in this chapter as well as new patterns of employment that provide revealing insights about the shifting texture of social stratification in the democratic context.

Chapter Five

Intersections at Play: Complexities of Gender Location

The point that I would like to make is that some of the women that employ domestic workers should realise that they are also women and they are not children or they are not slaves. They are just women like they are. Some of them are still thinking they are children or like robots that can just run around.

—Cecil

What amazed me as a worker is that she is a woman just like me, but when she want to shout at me, she will shout at me. Then it seems to me that I am a child. And one day I stood up and I said to her that she must remember and she must also respect me as a worker and as a woman, because I am a woman just like she is.

—Victoria

Regardless of the extent to which women share a gendered experience, paid domestic labor remains distinctly characterized by social constructions of *difference* centered in social location divides, as illustrated by these domestic worker narratives. Like Cock (1980) suggested, the sharpest challenge to sisterhood is the bifurcation created through the institution of domestic work. In the context of South Africa's democratic transition, as the identity of employers gradually shifts to include formerly disadvantaged groups, race, class, rural/urban location, and religious distinctions emerge to divide women through even more pronounced enactments of difference. In this study, social location differentials *among* women became central to the nature of domestic labor—particularly in the spaces where the institution had changed since the end of apartheid.

As I talked with South Africa's "newly elite" employers, as well as domestic workers who shared the same racial location as their employers, I began to conceptualize a new social hierarchy that captured the complexities of the nation's transition through the nature of social relations in the private sphere. The work relationships among urban coloured employers and rural coloured domestic workers, for example, illustrated how the intersection of class and geographic location structured the nature of household employment in these "formerly marginalized" groups. Drawing upon Ling's (2002) notion of the mutuality of public and private spheres, the complex web of relations we now see in private employment contexts—defined by the distinct social location differentials in South Africa—explain broader stratification patterns as the nation continues to transform from apartheid's rigid order to a human rights-based democracy. As Cock (1980) suggested, domestic labor is a "microcosm" of broader social relations that operates at both material and ideological levels. I wish to also suggest that paid household labor brings these complexities into sharper focus through the daily processes that encapsulate structural patterns of inequality within this central social institution.

This chapter describes the multiple contexts in which women's *difference* continues to dominate the institution of domestic work and further entrench patterns of racial categorization inherent to the apartheid era. By exploring the regional nuances that position the coloured community in Cape Town in very distinct relation to the broader national transformation, my findings illustrate very particular intersections of race, class, gender, religion, and geographic location. In addition, I analyze data from "newly elite" black parliamentary employers who shared an intimate history with the institution of domestic labor during the apartheid era. As one employer assessed, "The whole relationship of women across colour lines in this country is very, very complex." The voices of South Africa women in this study—situated in a variety of social locations—disrupt former construction of the "white madam/black maid" relationship. By providing a lens into the spaces where domestic work has changed, participants in this study repeatedly illuminated the very particular meaning of this institution in relation to South Africa's ongoing democratization.

CONSTRUCTIONS OF DIFFERENCE

While the majority of participants in this study indicated that the "old regime persists" in the household through the institution of domestic work, the emergence of economically privileged sectors of "formerly disadvantaged" groups creates both a "new employer" and some level of change within the institution through the shift in the identities of employers. Black women in parliament, for example, rely upon the labor of domestic workers in order to participate in broader processes of social and political change. Similarly, the coloured population is defined by divisions *within,* as rural/urban location and class divides afford certain sectors of this racial group the ability to hire domestic workers, while other coloured women are employed in this sector. These interplays restructure the colonial racial power relations that positioned white women as employers and black women as workers—thereby encapsulating Mohanty's (1991) "First World/Third World" divide.[1] Examining the intersections of race, class, religion and rural/urban location therefore offers an important vantage point from which to understand the complexities of social change within this institution and the possibilities for democratizing the private sphere.

In the ongoing process of social change, some participants suggested that South Africa might be moving to a class-based stratification system as racial divisions gradually loosen. Yet the pervasive discourse across all sectors of this study was that race remained deeply engrained as the primary social stratification structure, regardless of the extent to which class shifts are slowly reconfiguring relations. Class-based inequality, however, remains central to divisions *within* groups, particularly as economically privileged subgroups emerge from racially disadvantaged sectors of South African society. In this study, the "new black elite" and "bourgeois" coloured employers were frequent topics of discussion across all participant groups—who emphasized that these new roles challenged the ongoing racial divisions established in the apartheid era. What arose as particularly striking and discomforting, however, was the extent to which these formerly disadvantaged groups were perceived as the *most* exploitative employers of domestic workers, once afforded social privilege in the context of democratic change. To understand these prevailing belief systems, let us first turn to an overview of the distinct divisions between African and coloured populations in South Africa.

The Coloured/African Divide

The apartheid era strategically constructed the social position of the coloured population through a closer alignment with the white minority. Through the ideology of strict racial categorization, government issued subsequent privileges to this mixed racial group that were not available to the indigenous black majority, including expanded work options and the rights to live closer than blacks to city centers. This enhanced social status afforded to coloureds (as compared to Africans) facilitated the success of apartheid ideology that was founded upon strict divisions between the four

racial groups. Furthermore, this higher value assigned to the coloured population created a particular sense of loyalty to the white governance and a
shared group identity that valued being "partly from the whites." The construction of this "in between" race was also strategic to the success of
apartheid because it *divided* two extremely marginalized groups through
distinct conflict—which fostered greater government control over both
populations.

The struggle to end apartheid unified the interests of coloured and
black populations "to a certain degree"[2] in the search for liberation. In the
new democracy, however, expert interviewees in this study indicated that
moderate alignment no longer characterized the relationship between
coloured and black sectors of the population. Rather, severe conflict and
intergroup prejudices reify the ideological divisions between both groups
devised in the apartheid era. Therefore, constructions of separateness from
the black population remain essential to the collective racial identity of the
coloured population, as Sonja expressed:

> How can I put it . . . I mean in those [apartheid] years they used to say
> that the coloureds and the whites was more together, but the black peo-
> ple never ever exist actually, put it that way, and for us still now, look I
> mean I've got nothing against black people you know, I've got *nothing*
> against them, but some of them got no respect, and those years we
> never used to mix with black people. It's very hard, and still now you
> know lots of coloured people doesn't like black people, they doesn't
> like black people. I can tell you now because even if I go out with a
> black guy and we go somewhere, you can still see the people look at
> you, you can feel it that they are still staring at you, really that happens,
> you feel uncomfortable.

Another coloured employer shared that this separateness is further identified by a closer alignment to the white population:

> In the Western Cape, and the coloured people generally have a great
> prejudice against black people . . . that's how it is, which means that
> they actually don't really have much of a place, so they have to choose
> which way to go, so they will choose to go more toward the white side,
> that's why the language is also Afrikaans, you know it's better to go
> this way than that way . . . the black people will always be with their
> "one foot in the bush"[3]—that's how they put it. So to have a black per-
> son work for a coloured person, it's almost like you know you have this

kind of power over this person as well, you know, it still gives you that power that you are actually a bit better than that person.

And in a narrative of racial purity, which defined the apartheid era and further aligned the coloured population to structures of white status, Louise described her heritage as a coloured woman:

> We were also raised in a certain way because . . . we were not supposed to mix with them [Africans] because we, I am directly from the white people, you know.

This sense of power over less privileged groups has fueled a history of severe conflict between black and coloured populations, particularly in the Western Cape where the coloured population maintains a distinct 56 percent majority over the 22 percent black representation.[4] According to one trade unionist, these regional dynamics shape the division between black and coloured groups within Cape Town in comparison to the rest of South Africa where coloureds with minority representation immerse themselves within the black population to the extent that even language is sometimes shared. In Cape Town, however, the coloured population is strongly associated with the Afrikaans language (of the apartheid engineers). Nkensani, a black worker and political activist, openly shared her similar experience of the concrete nature of these divisions and suggested that the prejudices within these two formerly oppressed groups are even more severe than the racism held by the white population:

> The coloureds and the Africans are playing apartheid more than the white people because the people who have got this apartheid is not the English speaking. Those people are talking Afrikaans . . . the apartheid is in the coloureds and the English people are better now. The apartheid is here to us now. We don't like each other. We are full of nonsense, we are full of stories, we are full of jealousy.

This conflict and jealousy described by Nkensani is based in perceptions about heightened privileges held by both groups at different times. In general terms, for the black population, the predominant alignment of the coloured population with white dominance—as opposed to black liberation during the struggle to end apartheid—remains a severe source of tension. This created a perception about the unearned privilege of coloureds, which motivated the group's perpetuation of apartheid's oppression of the black population. Furthermore, black participants in this study were sharply critical of the coloured population's ongoing support for the Democratic Alliance (DA) in the Western Cape—the only national province where this reformed apartheid party continued to govern through the support of the coloured vote.

Sources of conflict expressed by members of the coloured population were based in a felt reality that since democracy, "the black people come first now and we come last" because of the central position of the ANC governance and the national movement to "Africanization." This shift in relative privilege through government change reconfigured social power such that the coloured population's status decreased since the end of apartheid, whereas the black population became more central, particularly in structures of governance. As this coloured activist described, "We were once not white enough, now we're not black enough." As a result, an "identity complex" was repeatedly named within the coloured community. Lena, a coloured domestic worker described her lost sense of social position and national identity since the democratic transformation: "Since we come in the new South Africa, I don't think it's nice. You don't feel you belong here."

This ongoing division creates a context such that even though black and coloured populations might have shared positions of lesser power in the apartheid era, their relative experiences and identities remain quite distinct. An ascribed apartheid separateness between coloured and black populations continues to be deeply embedded in the social fabric of everyday life in South Africa. For members of both groups, asserting differences in identity continued to frame the collective group experience as separate from the "other," as described by this coloured employer: "Don't mistake a coloured person for a black, because that's the biggest insult, you know." Therefore conflict, rather than alignment, predominantly defines the relationship between these two marginalized groups.

In the context of domestic work, these distinctions constructed clear preferences among all groups of employers about the racial identity of the worker they employed. These hiring patterns demonstrated both an ongoing allegiance to the racial categorization system of apartheid and further constructions of difference between black and coloured women, as illustrated by the following (white) employer:

> I am definitely more toward the African population . . . I grew up in
> Queenstown which is purely African in that sort of sense and I've
> understood them a lot more than the Cape Coloured and certainly I

would always rather have an African . . . I feel more at home with them
. . . I think in my home, to me, they are completely different in my eyes.

Other images emerged about preferences toward coloured workers because
of the closer affiliation to the white culture, as revealed by these two
(highly privileged white) employers:

I think they [white employers] can relate more to the coloured lady, *ja*,
whereas the black culture to them is a strange culture.

I really get on much better with the coloured people. I've found very
respectful Africans, and they are very proud people, very very easily
offended, you've got to be very careful, your manners has to be good
and very firm, you can't be mate-y with them, you know, sort of on
their level. You can be mate-y with coloured people, they will still serve
you very well, but if you are mate-y with the average Xhosa-speaking
person, they will think you are weak and won't respect you. That's a
generalization but that's what I've found in my long life of employing
people and I had all Africans until we came to this house, so I've had
30 years of employing Africans and I've had 24 years of employing
coloureds. They [Africans] have a very strong culture which is very different to ours, whereas the coloured people have a culture which is very
similar to ours and they get on much better with whites than they do
with Africans. They are terrified of Africans.

Sarah repeated this theme through broad overgeneralizations about the
nature of domestic workers in the employment context based upon race:

The black culture, those ladies are more inclined to sulk than your
coloured lady. The coloured lady, she will swear at you [laughs],
whereas the black lady would *sulk* [laughs].

In congruence with these racial assumptions articulated through South
African employers, other research on domestic work identified distinct preferences based on the racial constructions of workers. In the U.S., black women
were perceived as having a "natural" disposition to domestic work—reflecting a particular imagery that reinforces assumptions about the appropriate
labor of black women in mothering roles (Thornton Dill 1994; Hill Collins
1990). Both white and coloured employers in this study similarly articulated
examples of imagery associated with black womanhood and domestic work,
as revealed in the following (white) employer narrative:

> I just think the Africans, not necessarily the *new* African now, the ones
> that are up and coming, [they] are more home-ly you know, bringing
> up children, they've had normally lots and lots of kids on their own
> and that's where I sort of got it from because they are always wonder-
> ful second mothers to my children.

Similarly, negative cultural associations about the perceived "attitudes" of
the black population since democracy governed some employers' decisions
around racial hiring practices. As one coloured employer depicted, "They
think they deserve something in the new country."

These narratives reflect a clear and ongoing apartheid construction of
difference between black and coloured populations. We see the applied
impact of these divisions among women through the domestic labor hiring
practices of employers across all racial groups. In a parallel fashion, workers also repeatedly demonstrated deeply held preferences about the 'ideal
employer,' which they based upon race and class constructions that continue to dominate South Africa's social landscape. The following emergent
themes indicate the extent to which the race of employers was perceived as
having much more power than the race of workers in defining the nature of
household employment contexts. Of particular interest, I draw upon the
data that illustrate how these pervasive constructions were linked to a particular discourse about employers' abuse of power in the new democracy.

Constructing Difference Within: Coloured Workers and Employers

Repeatedly throughout this research, the narrative of racism being most
severely enacted within the coloured population emerged across *all* groups
of participants. In the context of domestic work, this belief system revealed
a construction of coloured women as particularly exploitative employers,
even though they had themselves experienced oppression as a result of the
social order of apartheid governance. These narratives applied to coloured
women hiring black women, yet the predominant reference was to hiring
practices *within* the coloured population, where privileged employers hired
other coloured women with less access to social power. Strong divisions
within the coloured community remain firmly embedded through class,
region, geographic location and religion differentials. Domestic labor
embeds these divisions even further based upon coloured women's location
as either worker or employer. The ability to purchase domestic labor, therefore, becomes another means by which power and privilege define variant
social locations within marginalized groups. As this coloured employer
assessed, these divisions manifest through the dominance of class-based
inequality.

> I know a lot of [coloured] people that do have domestics but they don't work, they also at home, they have a life of pleasure. They drive around and they shop while the domestic cleans up. They are actually not working but it is, it's not so much an aspiration of being white but it's, people associate it more with being *bourgeois*.

Similarly, another coloured informant shared the perception that the "newness of the acquisition of affluence" remained central to the belief that coloured employers were the "worst oppressors of other blacks" because of their unfamiliarity with heightened class status and the subsequent role as employer.

Importantly, 75 percent of the workers formally interviewed (N=20) stated that they would *not* consider working for a coloured (or black) employer, even in the context of the new democracy. This general sentiment manifested from feelings of uncertainty about the newness of such a work relationship, beliefs about exploitative employment practices, and perceptions that workloads would be increased with this sector of employers. Specifically, this resistance to working for non-traditional employers was linked to strong beliefs that the nature of the work environment would be much more challenging because of the perceived lower class status of employers. Therefore, workers believed that they would need to support more people in the household, decrease their salary severely, and enjoy far fewer "luxuries" because coloured employers did not generally own appliances to ease household labor as a result of their own marginalized class status. The following coloured workers illustrated these shared sentiments when asked how they felt about working for another coloured employer:

> I think the white employer got money and if she don't want to give to me what I think she can give me, a better wages, how will that coloured lady? Where would she get the money to pay me better than that white lady? . . . If that one, the white lady, is stingy to pay, how can the [coloured] one? Because we all struggle, you see.

> You know our people, what can I say, sometimes they want more of you and you are there for them, but they want more of you, and like for the white people, in their ways, they got rules, the coloured or whatever haven't got rules [regarding fair work standards] . . . sometimes they overdo it, you know, about taking advantage or let you do things that you not suppose to do, you know, yes really . . . honestly that's why you won't see me working for them, and it's not that I don't think anything of them, I think a lot of them, because we are all I mean

one blood, but really it would be better for me to work for white people, honestly.

As these narratives suggest, when coloured workers were asked about
their feelings in relation to working for more privileged coloured employers, the predominant sentiment was "I'd rather work for a white person."[5]
Underlying associations related to this rejection of employers within their
same racial group indicate strong links to class structures that continue to
operate such that white employers are perceived as more desirable because
of their access to economic resources. Workers therefore directly associated
the class status of employers with the benefits they could expect in the
household employment context. The following coloured employer further
articulated these perceptions based upon her observations of other employers in her same racial group:

> I personally agree that most people still want to work for a white fam-
> ily because I can be very honest with you when I tell you that if you
> have to choose between the two, that most will still choose the white
> person because your own people, if you want to put it that way, will
> treat you ten times worse and the reason why I'm saying that is there's
> always an excuse of, "I don't have money, I can't pay you, you know
> I'm struggling, you know. So therefore I can only pay you so much you
> know." And because having a domestic worker was never part of the
> deal for our people, if I had to put it this way. So suddenly to be able to
> afford one is like a big thing, so to have a domestic helper is not even
> most of the time because you really need it, but it's like a nice thing to
> have . . . it's like to have a maid, that means you are doing well, you
> know, you are the madam, you don't have to do your own thing, and
> then you just pay the maid whatever, because you can still be the
> madam.

As this narrative suggests, the employment of domestic workers provides not
only physical labor within the household, but *elevated social and class status.*
Therefore, the ability to purchase household labor distinguishes an important
aspect of social power that differentiates subgroups within formerly disadvantaged sectors. Findings from this study suggest that the heightened economic status afforded to those who can hire domestic workers is often more
important that the material value of the labor alone because of the distinct
social privilege associated with the status of an employer. In the South
African case, this enhanced status surfaced as particularly meaningful within

the coloured sector of the population that continues to experience severe marginalization in the context of broader structural change.

Social Constructions of Religion and the "Other"

In addition to these pervasive class divides emphasized through the employment of domestic workers, distinct religious divides between Muslims and Christians remain critical to defining identity within the Cape Town coloured population. In eight of the 20 interviews with employers and for ten of the 15 workers who held negative perceptions about working for non-white employers, assumptions about the exploitative nature of coloured employers were specifically linked to *Muslims*. Throughout the expert interviews and participant observation components of this research, informants continually told me to "be sure to look at the Muslims" in order to attain the "real story" on domestic work in Cape Town.

The way in which Muslim employers were identified as separate from the overall coloured community links to a particular regional dynamic specific to the Western Cape where the South African Muslim population originated through slave trade with Indonesia, India and Sri Lanka (Thompson 1990). The Muslim religious group, specifically named the "Cape Malay," became more generally classified racially as coloured in the apartheid regime. Yet the amalgamation of racial identity to this broad mixed race category least impacted the Cape Malay who maintained strong religious/ethnic heritage and an insular group cohesion. The Cape Malay population remains distinctly separate from the broader South African coloured population who possess "very few indubitably coloured cultural attributes" along with "heterogeneity and lack of an exclusively coloured culture" (Western 1996:25). Furthermore, the Cape Malay maintained a strong connection to the Western Cape as a space of geographical significance that is specifically tied to religious identity and representation.[6] The Bo-Kaap community in central Cape Town, for example, remains the oldest Muslim neighborhood in the entire country and an important ethnic heritage center.[7] Furthermore, population representation in Cape Town continues to distinguish this group from other Muslim communities in South Africa. According to national census figures, the average representation of "Islam" citizens is 1.5 percent. The Western Cape average, however was 7.6 percent, with Gauteng (Johannesburg) the second highest percentage at only 1.7 percent (Statistics South Africa 2000). Therefore, the insular nature of Muslim communities is centralized in the Cape Town vicinity because of the high levels of representation and the historical origins of this community. These distinct historical conditions continue to shape the construction of Muslims as specifically separate from coloureds, even though both shared the same racial categorization during the apartheid regime.

This cohesive group nature and specific ethnic heritage emerged throughout my sample of participants as a consistent discourse about the distinct and separate nature of Cape Town's Muslim population in relation to the broader coloured identity. In a few conversations, the group was also referred to as "the Malays," further suggesting a general awareness about within-group differences and issues of identity. Yet more commonly the label used in both interview and casual participant observations was "Muslim," thus associating specific religious identity rather than ethnic origin as "Malay" or "Cape Malay" would suggest. Furthermore, in the context of this study, what remained most pervasive and discomforting in this reference was the association of this particular group of employers to what was considered the "most abusive" working conditions. Maggie, a coloured worker described her perceptions of Muslim employers:

> I know there is a lot of coloured people who have coloured girls who are Muslims . . . they behave very bad to the people. Some of them didn't even pay the girls because they still want to give them old clothes and food, finish and *klaar*,[8] doesn't matter if they are 15, paying them the money or what. I think it's more a hard life to work for coloured people and Muslim people . . . because they haven't got, they didn't pay well, and we didn't come here for a plate of food or old clothes, we come and work for our family, to send the money there.

Nothando, a black domestic worker, further links her perceptions of working for a coloured family to issues of economic power, as the narratives earlier reveal. Yet the specific reference in this case is not to coloured employers generally, but rather to Muslim employers who were perceived as responsible for the least desirable work environments:

> That coloured woman was a Muslim, ew, find it difficult because they were still hand washing, and then that was in winter, the hand washing, whatever panties, otherwise—hand washing! Then I see the white employer, they are always constantly washing in the machine. They show you the washing machine, you put everything in the washing machine. It's only jerseys that you wash by hand. And then I say that "no"—coloured people there is extra, extra because washing by hand and here on the floors, you are still using the brush. You know the Muslim people, we have to move this cupboard, take the dust away,

move and reach, move and take all the dust. And they don't cook meat, they just cook—they are vegetarians and you end up hungry. They putting an old bread there for you. Yes the other employer, white employer, they are also putting old bread then they said "you make toast," then you do all that. That is the same.

Nothando's belief about the vegetarian nature of Muslims is a misconception.[9] Importantly, her narrative (like all the other narratives related to this issue within the sample) is based upon *perceptions* about Muslim employers rather than reality. In some instances, Muslim and Hindu employers were grouped together, indicating broader generalizations about "the other," particularly within the mixed racial group identity as similarly reflected by Victoria, a coloured union leader:

How they work, they work like slaves and then they get R200, R150 . . . the end of the month when they get that little money, then the Muslim or the Hindu or whatever, they will still deduct the money from that worker [for living expenses] and that worker is working for peanuts and old clothes, very bad conditions . . . I would *never* say to our workers to work for the coloureds or the Indians or the Muslims.

This broader anti-Muslim sentiment was repeated throughout interviews with experts and employers. Thope, a black member of parliament and employer, shared the following with me when asked how she envisioned change in the institution of domestic work:

You know I would like you to interview—I'm not trying to be racist, I'm not a racist—but to interview a domestic worker that works for a Muslim family . . . I hope you get the right people that will tell you exactly what is happening. You know those people, those people are really abusing our people. They are *abusing* our people. They've got a style now, they get people from the farm areas, they bring those people to Cape Town, and then that person works from 7:00 in the morning until 12:00 in the evening, and because on weekends, they've got nowhere to go, they stay in the house and they are treated like they are not human beings. It is very sad . . . and then at the end of the month, some are given R200 and some are not paid. They are told stories that, "My towel is missing, you are responsible for that." I mean it is something that happened to my mother. I know about it . . . my mother was a domestic . . . *ja*, and some of them, shame, you know they are told where you come from you never had a bed so you can't expect to sleep on a bed, you know? I mean terrible things. You know there is quite a lot that the government should do. We can do all this legislation, but we need to educate people. You know people behave like animals, not humans. People behave like *animals*.

Of the three Muslim employers I interviewed, two acknowledged abuses within their own communities, whereas the other placed the abuse in the Indian/Hindu community.[10] Anita, a Muslim employer shared her own experience on this issue:

> If I talk about "we," the [Muslim] community, a lot of them are still ill treating. [Referring to the situation of her worker's friend employed within her neighborhood] She was living in the, you know the garage where they park the car, so the woman parks the car on the one side and on the other side she has made like a halfway partition and she [the worker] has to sleep there . . . What year is she living in? How can you, I mean no privacy at all, and it's ice cold in that garage, how can a person, would she go and live in that garage?

Because Cape Town remains so distinctly defined by geographical space, naming neighborhoods is also a way of situating particular social groups, as place continues to be defined by race and ethnicity. Therefore "Rylands" is completely Indian, whereas "Athlone" is a widely understood way of referencing Muslim communities. Sharifa, another Muslim employer, engaged this pattern by naming a particular area of Cape Town as the center of abusive employment situations:

> I don't know if you know Rylands, you have these domestics walking around Saturday afternoons, till late Saturday evenings . . . some of them they don't have nice decent places to sleep. I knew of one lady who had this domestic living in the backyard, it's nothing! How can you have, I mean it doesn't make sense . . . and that happens here in Cape Town, because you know that these people don't have any employment, there is no work for them on the farms, they've got to be in Cape Town and they earn a mere pittance of R200, some gets R150 a month. Now if you buy your toiletries what are you left with? . . . It's still a stigma of, "oh no, that's a farm worker" . . . oh it's a real class system, really, you get it a hell-of-a-lot with Indians. As I say I don't know if you know Rylands? Gatesville? There you have a lot of maids . . . and the way they are being treated by the Indians. How fair can that be?

Sharifa later acknowledged the perceived abuse in her own community, yet maintained that the worst offenses remained with "the Indians."

Even though Muslim coloured women were most often named as particularly harsh employers of domestic workers, the pattern of placing the abuse of power in "other" communities occurred among all groups in the sample. Through this practice, informants free their own racial group from participation in the oppressive conditions that continue to define domestic work. In other words, these processes of othering allow employers to evade their own collusion in the marginalization of less privileged women by constructing the "worst employer" as outside of their own racial group. Furthermore, the way in which specifically Muslim women were identified so frequently could be associated with the close group affiliation within the Muslim population in Cape Town. Because this ethnic group is seen as separate and distinct, it may be easier for members of larger social groups to "other" Muslims by suggesting that cases of abuse are related to a religion and lifestyle that is unfamiliar to broader South African racial groups. Furthermore, the narratives emerged from the coloured Christian community, which suggests an important practice of distinguishing within-group identity.

This pervasive discourse about abusive Muslim employers remained one of my most substantial challenges throughout this study.[11] Repeatedly, as I sorted through these data, I consciously attempted to siphon perception from reality and stereotype from legitimacy. Although the qualitative nature of this study is unable to establish precise figures of representation on this anti-Muslim view, the extent to which this discourse was repeated across all sectors of participants, in both formal interviews and the most casual social conversations, leads me to believe that this completely inductive theme offers valuable meaning about race and ethnic relations in the context of post-apartheid South Africa—as well as the highly particular regional dynamics within Cape Town. Certainly the dualistic construction of white madam and black domestic worker is complicated given these representations. Furthermore, the social construction of race is centrally connected to social constructions of religion—thereby establishing distinct group identity boundaries between Christian and Muslim coloureds. These empirical data also speak to a broader phenomenon about the "oppressed" becoming the "oppressor," which was repeated in relation to black women employers. This discourse that associated the "worst employer" with the Muslim community, however, was frequently linked to a particular development within the institution of domestic labor in South Africa that has received wider attention since the democratic transition.

Trafficking Domestic Labor

Domestic work "agencies" serve as intermediary profit-based organizations that provide employers in Cape Town with domestic workers from surrounding rural areas. These local businesses have continued to grow since the 1994 transitions—in line with an overarching emphasis on entrepreneurial development promoted within South Africa's democracy. Agencies function to supply the lowest cost labor to households in the Cape Town urban area, and therefore thrive upon the excessively high levels of poverty in rural areas to recruit women into domestic labor. The clientele served by these agencies are predominantly coloured women in Cape Town's middle to lower middle class neighborhoods who employ rural coloured and black domestic workers. According to police records, NGO leaders, and union officials, these agencies are geographically based in Cape Town's predominantly Muslim (Athlone, Lotus River, Grassy Park) and Indian Areas (Rylands) areas, with smaller numbers of representation in the "Northern Suburbs" consisting of mainly coloured Christian communities. Participants suggested that because coloured employers are less likely to afford fair living wages as a result of their own class status, a higher reliance upon domestic worker agencies to supply particularly vulnerable (low-cost) workers has emerged as a specific practice associated with less privileged, namely *Muslim* employers.

Throughout this research, because the topic of domestic work agencies was continually defined as a specific, regionally-based race and class issue that had become a severe "problem" among all participants, I pursued investigation of this phenomenon in order to better understand how differences in class, religion, and geographical location among women could be further understood through this systematic organizational process of labor recruitment. Throughout my interviews with 21 experts on domestic work employment agencies,[12] severe concerns arose about the treatment of workers, the ethics of such trafficking practices, substantial economic profit at the cost of human rights, the lack of accountability regarding fair labor and business practices, inadequate state intervention on the issue, and its core practice of exploiting particularly vulnerable rural women in order to benefit more privileged urban populations. According to the employers I interviewed who used such services, however, a shared perception emerged about "helping girls find work" that would otherwise be unavailable in the rural areas. Ultimately, the most problematic issues related to the trafficking of domestic workers were strikingly similar to the broader global conversation about domestic worker trade across national boundaries at the expense of women in less developed countries (Chin 1998; Chang and Ling

2002). Yet this practice of domestic worker "recruitment" within South Africa takes on a particular meaning in relation to the construction of Muslim employers. Furthermore, it is important to examine the underlying functions of these agencies within the broader context of social change and the national emphasis on human rights.

In the democratic South Africa, national labor standards and an overarching constitutional framework assure citizens protection such that "no one may be subjected to slavery, servitude or forced labour" (Constitution of South Africa 1996). Yet women employed by such agencies (which receive business licenses from national structures) repeatedly revealed that they were approached by male "taxi drivers" in their rural locations, enticed to come to the "city" in order to work in "hotels" with "good money," and assured that "no kitchen work" would be involved in their new employment. When workers arrive (in minivan groups of 15–20) to outlying city suburbs where such agencies exist, they are housed in temporary outdoor living structures (that often violate health standards), "shown" to prospective employers who visit such agencies, and ultimately traded as these businesses collect substantial fees from both the new employer and the workers' first month's wages when each woman is placed. This enormous gap between overarching constitutional rights and women's lived realities embodies the complexities central to the existing phase of rebuilding South Africa as a democratic nation. The systematic process of domestic workers' trafficking through agencies further encapsulates this conflict within marginalized communities.

The following narrative excerpts describe the applied practices involved in trafficking domestic workers. Sharifa, a (Muslim) employer who utilized an employment agency for the first time, shared her experience of selecting a domestic worker:

> It's like a lot of cattle being herded and you've got to choose which cow you are going to use, you are going to slaughter or what, so I found it so disgraceful. There was a couple of ladies, she [referring to her domestic worker] was one of them, and this lady was selling them, sort of you know it's like, "smile at the people, give them a bright smile." You know it's so pretentious, it's so false . . . She had about ten girls there, from various parts of the country . . . it's R350 for the taxi, but I know the taxi is about R120 . . . Another thing I don't like about these people fetching these ladies, is that that R350 [fee charged to employer by agency in addition to R130 registration fee], you are supposed to give them a salary, right, then you have to deduct it from their salary. What do they sit with? But I wouldn't, I told her, "I'm not going to

deduct that money." Look, I needed somebody and if I had to go and fetch her I would've had to pay taxi fare or petrol in the car in any event, so how can I let it come from *her* money? No, it doesn't make sense.

Sharifa's depiction of her participation with an employment agency reveals the nature of profit operations. As women are placed, employers are charged both a registration fee and the workers' first month's salary. While Sharifa remained extremely uncomfortable with the use of such agencies, she also felt as though it would be difficult to find a worker from "up country" independently. Therefore, although she certainly perceived the nature of such a business practice as "disgraceful," she also maintained that the source of her workers would always be rural women in her same racial group. Sharifa later shared her associations of guilt surrounding the privilege she maintained in relation to the domestic workers she employed in her own home:

> You actually walk around with a lot of guilt nowadays after the old days because you always feel that we are a bit more privileged than the coloured people and the rural people, up country people. The way the people had to live also, even though we also had it bad, but not as bad as other people, and the blacks, you know.

Sharifa's narrative embodies how the interlocking constructions of identity are maintained by establishing oneself as *not* the other. In this case, the dominant racial hierarchy of the apartheid era and urban privilege fostered an awareness about within-group differences. Sharifa's interview also revealed several instances where her Muslim identity became central to constructing difference among the workers she employed. For example, she shared that she must train her workers to cook traditional meals, such as curries, because "they are not used to our food." In other examples, Sharifa referenced her Muslim faith as governing principles that guide her employment of less privileged women in her household.

Rita, the second employer who utilized placement agencies to employ up to four workers at a time, held much different perceptions. Rita found agencies to be highly valuable because she could "return" her worker within a three month period with no fee included if she did not work out for any reason—a practice that parallels the retail trade of material goods. This option to return workers relieved Rita of the discomfort involved in hiring a stranger to work in her home. Furthermore, because she held perceptions about the "lazy" nature of most domestic workers, Rita and her husband benefited from this agency "return policy" because, as they asserted, "We change domestic workers like laundry."

With this practice, the agency is not only freed of any responsibility of placement, but is also able to enjoy increased profits with every worker that is "returned" because each can then be placed in another home with the same fees attached. Throughout this systematic trafficking of women within marginalized communities, worker rights and equitable practices of employment are forsaken for the benefit of profit. The unwillingness of domestic work agencies to take responsibility for providing training to workers or monitoring the standards within the private employment contexts of their clients, remained a source of deep concern for NGO leaders, women's rights groups and union officials.

The following account contrasts that of the 'consumer' of such services to that of the 'provider.' Nomhle's story encapsulated the underlying human rights abuses involved in this practice. I interviewed Nomhle immediately after she "ran away" from the home in which she was placed to work through the "Spic and Span" employment agency and contacted the Gender Desk at the national union.[13]

> Yesterday I was by the taxi from Somerset [a more rural location] and they didn't tell us that they were going to sell us. So we drove with the taxi and when we arrived there, Mrs. Jacobs [owner of agency][14] called us and so she said, "You people know how the story goes" and we said, "No, we don't know how the story goes." She said, "Yes, the first month you won't get paid, your salary will go for the taxi fare." We said, "We don't know about the taxi fare" . . . They spoke to the people [prospective employers using the agency] so that we can't hear what they are saying and when they came out, Mrs. Jacobs said, "Come here, *you*" [meaning that Nomhle was chosen as the worker for the employer at hand]. Seeing that it's the first time I come to work here, I didn't know where I'm going to work. When I got to my work, the gates were locked [meaning she was locked inside the home] and I had to sleep in a small room with dirty blankets. I'm not allowed to go out and I must go to sleep at 9 o'clock and I must get up at 5:30 and I didn't get proper food. So I phoned Mrs. Jacobs and she said the madam must keep me there until Monday. I had to go back [to work] and I was told to wash the washing in the rain and so I took my bags and put it through, under the gate, and I left and when I left, the madam said, "Where are you going?" and I said, "I'm going and I'm *not* happy staying here." So she swore at me and so when I went to Mrs. Jacobs, she said I was lazy and I can't work. I said to her, "I'm not working there

because I have to do the washing in the rain and then I still have to scrub such a big house with my hands and my knees," and she said I must sit there. I sat down and I got me another job and I went to work there and it was the same. So Mrs. Jacobs took my clothes and money and said I must go on foot . . . so I left and went to phone Esther [gender representative from the national union] . . . Where would I have slept if it wasn't for Esther, you understand?

Nomhle was 18 years old, with a sixth grade equivalent education. Later in our dialogue she revealed that she was physically assaulted at the agency when she returned and that her "punishment" was sexual abuse. The acts of agency she demonstrated by confronting the abusive power structures in her place of work as well as the agency, leaving both, and contacting the national union for support were enormous. Nomhle's case, however, is exceptional. Most women do not find a support structure such as this and are often left without any resources within an urban metropolitan city geography. When I interviewed Mrs. Jacobs, she stated that she returns workers to their rural locations and posited that, "If for any reason they are not happy, I put them back on the taxi—it's part of the service." However, in the same interview, when asked why Nomhle was not returned to her rural home, a script about her being a "problem child" arose and justified the lack of services afforded to workers who "act up."

Local police indicated that in the same neighborhood, on a daily basis, 15 young women (reported age range at 15-25) ask for police services to take them back to the rural areas from which they were recruited. Union officials at times used personal resources to pay the transportation fees for agency workers, who had not received any salary and could not return to their homes. Police officials also reported that each morning at least five young women are found at the police station with cases of physical and emotional abuse.[15] In many cases, police, union and social service officials reported that women entered the sex work sector as one of the few outlets for self-survival, particularly in the context of such rural poverty. It was even suggested that particular "pimps" specifically recruit in areas where such newly urbanized rural workers are most easily accessible and capitalize on their vulnerability. Women's rights workers linked this trafficking of young women to other social problems such as homelessness, drug use and the transmission of HIV/AIDS.

Another severe source of concern across all sectors dealing with domestic worker agencies was the living conditions in the spaces where women are "housed" until placement is established. Based upon on-site visits to placement agencies, police officials equated this practice with "slave labour." In the four other interviews with workers who were recruited by these agencies, the conditions where they were held until the attainment of employment were described as "horrific" and constituted serious human rights violations:

> We slept on the floor, we [were] perhaps 24 with only three mattresses and we [were] a lot and we can't even fit in there, others must sleep on chairs . . . and then the toilet is only one and you have to wash in a small basin . . . they only give us bread, the whole day, only bread . . . no tea, nothing.

Workers also reported severe structures of discrimination within the employment agency such that coloured rural workers were placed with higher paying positions and afforded more meals and "cigarettes" while living at the agency, whereas black workers were assigned to separate quarters and much harsher living conditions. In some instances, women reported that they were not placed for months after arriving in Cape Town and were therefore forced to work in domestic service at the agency owner's home.

Another issue of concern raised by workers was their public treatment by agency owners in group contexts. Paternalistic notions of punishing one for the sake of teaching the larger group about proper work behavior were often noted and seen as particularly demeaning among the agency workers interviewed. Mrs. Jacobs told me in a personal interview that many of the workers she places to homes "steal" from employers:

> I have one woman who stole two pair of Rockport shoes, you know they are very expensive and when the employer found out, they gave her a *hiding*,[16] and I think she deserved a hiding because she stole. I would have given her a hiding for sure.

Nomhle told me that workers who were accused of stealing were physically abused in front of all the other women waiting for job placement in order to make a statement about appropriate behavior.

This practice of domestic worker placement agencies remained a top priority for SADSAWU since its inception in 2000. Both the obvious violation of women's rights and a severe lack of structures to assure fair labor standards led SADSAWU leaders to call together Department of Labour officials, union comrades, women's rights organizations and related governmental offices in order to build collaboration to close such agencies. In this coalition meeting, the structural conditions which alleviated state responsibility for these widely acknowledged trafficking organizations paralleled the many gaps between South Africa's democratic commitment and the practical implementation challenges of policy "on the ground" that remain since the apartheid era.

Governmental infrastructures technically oversee employment placement agencies through the Department of Labour and the Skills Development Act, albeit in extremely limited ways. The Department of Labour has the authority to monitor employer/employee relations through the Basic Conditions of Employment Act (extended to domestic workers in 1997), yet the Constitution protects the *privacy* of the household and therefore limits state inspection unless a court order is attained, which remains extremely difficult according to interviewed government officials assigned to all placement agencies in the Cape Town vicinity. The Skills Development Act of 1998 (established as a general advocacy measure for workers' vocational development) oversees the registration of employment agencies and their compliance with fair practices with six general guidelines to protect workers.[17] Domestic work placement agencies violated all of the six standards because they charged workers the vast majority of expenses related to their employment, whereas national policy mandates that workers may be charged only R1. According to Department of Labour inspectors, staff resources remained extremely scarce and therefore assurance of compliance in this sector is particularly difficult because personnel are not afforded time or support to actually visit agency sites.[18] SADSAWU and gender activists challenged government workers on this issue because of the obvious breach of legal standards and its predominant practice of overlooking placement agencies in this particular sector, exclusively dealing with women domestic workers.

The case of domestic worker agencies provides a direct example of policies rendered ineffective—one of the major critiques of South Africa's transition. For example, assurance of fair working conditions and reasonable living wages falls outside of legislation related to employment agencies. Therefore, once domestic workers are placed in employment homes, agencies are not held accountable in any way for the violations that may occur within the work contexts. Also central to this practice of trafficking, the recruitment of women in rural areas and the severe disjuncture between the promises made to workers and the reality of their employment placements violates both ethical and legal standards of labor recruitment. Yet government policy only mandates measures for the *registration* of placement agencies, which remains an extremely simple process with minimal fees attached. The private household labor contexts remain outside legislation that oversees agencies. Rather, employers of domestic workers are expected to follow the Basic Conditions of Employment Act, which is also not monitored, leaving workers to describe this policy as "only on paper" four years after its promulgation. These structural conditions and ineffective policies surrounding domestic worker agencies led union leaders to ask, "What is it about domestic workers that people always hesitate to get involved?" The governmental structural oversight of this "difficult" sector represents a striking example of the challenges faced in South Africa's transformation process. As we see in these cases, implementation of protective policies continually surfaced as one of the most challenging aspects of transformation "on the ground." This broader disconnect between policy and practice is compounded by the very particular institution of domestic labor. As we see in these examples, established labor policies do not extend to the private household. Therefore failure to monitor the trade of domestic workers or hold trafficking agencies accountable reinforces the pervasive structural disregard for this particular sector—illustrating a sharp contrast to South Africa's overarching commitment to gender equality at the center of national transformation.

The geographical placement of domestic worker agencies in less economically privileged coloured neighborhoods within Cape Town adds another critical dimension to understanding intersections of social location. To some degree, it appeared as though assumptions about standards in employing domestic workers were the responsibility of the Imam and community religious leaders rather than state governance structures. For example, when the Spic n' Span agency was exposed by the national media, the local Imam was called to mediate between the Muslim owners of the agency, NGO/human rights representatives, union officials, news media, and government officials. During these discussions, an ongoing association between domestic worker agencies and their specific operations within Muslim communities arose. Yet in the Cape Town surrounding vicinity, such agencies also exist in the Northern Suburbs, composed of middle class, coloured, predominantly Christian populations. According to union officials, agencies in these communities also practice similar means of recruitment, yet workers do not "flee" from these agencies to the union, as is the case with agencies operating within the predominantly Muslim coloured areas. Similarly, police reports do not indicate comparably high cases of domestic workers "running away" from their jobs, as in the predominantly Muslim areas. Therefore, local officials did not believe the same level of violations occurred in the Northern suburbs and continued to associate the wide human rights abuses specifically with Muslim recruitment agencies.

The highly contextual participant observation and interview data in this research describes a *portion* of placement agencies' operations within predominantly Muslim coloured communities. It is critical to note, however, that the scope and qualitative nature of this research did *not* include extensive research into placement agencies in *all* surrounding suburbs where they operate. Therefore, I do not wish to suggest that the abusive employment agencies exist only within Muslim coloured communities, nor do I support overly simplistic generalized claims that Muslim employers are *more exploitative* than any other racial, religious or regional group of employers in South Africa. Rather, my intent is to examine this dominant discourse about domestic worker agencies—and its particular placement in the racial politics of Cape Town—to offer a grounded analysis of how the intersections of race, class, religion and geographical location play out within marginalized groups.

To guide a further analysis of this discourse on domestic worker agencies that continually emerged through this research, I pose the following questions: Why do urban coloured—both Muslim and Christian—women employ other coloured women with less economic and social location privilege? How do agencies function in the broader framework of social relations within formerly oppressed groups? And specifically in the context of this observed practice, why are Muslim communities so severely criticized for their use of exploitative employment agencies that traffic domestic workers from rural areas? By addressing these questions through the data, I offer a broader analysis of emergent dynamics within the institution of domestic work that reflects the distinct race, class, religion, and geographic location intersections within South Africa's changing national context.

Explanations for these within-group practices were most often centered in the importance of class stratification. Coloured participants (both Christian and Muslim) repeatedly explained that the ability of formerly disadvantaged groups to hire domestic work services represented a level of earned success, as this coloured employer assessed:

> It's a way for us to separate ourselves, showing that I'm one above you because I have this help and I can afford it. I'm just one step up from you.

These class distinctions instill power and a sense of privilege within coloured communities:

> It is about asserting power, we are all, maybe they say, "Okay, we might look the same, but you know I am the boss around here," I am the *madam* kind of thing.

Yet, because access to resources remains much more limited with the ongoing structures of economic apartheid, formerly disadvantaged communities are less likely to have the economic ability to pay workers, compared to the class capital maintained in the predominantly white community, as described earlier by workers' preferences regarding the race of their employers. This economic constraint seems to force less privileged employers to utilize the services of employment agencies, who carry the reputation of perpetuating low salary structures through the workers they recruit from the most vulnerable regions of the country.

Charmaine, a coloured employer, described how the structural operations of agencies freed employers from direct responsibility for their participation in the unequal power relations inherent to domestic labor:

> I'm not even so much blaming the employer, I blame even more so the agency because they, you know these people are desperate for work, and the reason why this people [employers] treat them so badly is because they can say to this domestic worker, "Look I got you through an agency, they say it's perfectly fine to pay you R200." And now who is going to argue? I mean if you don't know your rights why would you want to argue about that? Oh, this agency says it's fine, so then it's fine. I should never leave the house because we are talking about people who have no education . . . so that is why they then exploit that because the people that is still in power is their employer because she knows, they know that they've got this power over the person, this control over the person. So therefore they would lock the person up. Then the person would work 14 days, you know they would even take the person's ID or you know or details, home details so that the person can't contact their families. So the person is totally stranded, there is nowhere to go but there and so that's then why they treat, I mean sometimes worse than animals. Because nobody is going to ask questions, nobody is going to look for them and usually they take people that nobody is really going to look for and so they have their slaves. Because for me it's slavery, they have their slaves for life if they need them to. And the sad part is that this is then how the children see the pattern, that it is actually okay, and so it's this vicious cycle that never changes that never really has much room to change because that children is going to grow up after ten, 15 years and they are going to do exactly the same thing.

This narrative extends the within-group oppression by associating domestic labor with slavery. At the same time, the tension of these severe inequalities is also alleviated through the use of employment agencies because employers are able to detach from the extreme power differentials by associating their employment of domestic labor with a more distant, formal, business structure of operation, thus disowning some of their own privilege and possible associated guilt. The institutionalized process of trafficking women's labor reinforces inequality such that it is to some extent legitimated as part of the inevitable difference in the social worlds of rural and urban populations. Thus, agencies play upon the extreme poverty and economic differentials in rural areas—as well as the mixed associations to power within marginalized employer groups—by creating an ideology that rationalizes the exploitative circumstances of the trafficking of domestic workers. Extremely low salaries, for example, are justified because agencies propagate that, "No matter what, they are much better off than where they came from." This research illustrates that domestic worker agencies operate in ways that particularly serve marginalized sectors of the South Africa's population. In the case of Muslim communities, because the utilization of agencies is practiced within a close-knit group, its "acceptability" is further reinforced.

This case of recruitment agencies represents an interesting complexity within the institution of domestic work in the context of South Africa's transformation. First, it embodies one place where class is the predominant stratification structure because women typically share the same race. Second, it certainly complicates the extent to which women's experience is universal because even within shared race groups, class, geographic location and religion play critical roles in dividing women. The practice of domestic work further instills these divisions by creating power differentials in the private household that embody social class hierarchies within communities. And third, in the highly regionalized context of Cape Town, the way in which agencies are linked to Muslim practices represents a powerful example of "othering," particularly toward a group that maintains a high degree of separateness and distinct culture with its strong representation in Cape Town.

As the Spic n' Span agency represents, women's human and labor rights were seriously violated in the context of a capitalist market of trafficking domestic workers. Although agencies such as this were identified in predominantly Muslim areas, the extent to which the entire Muslim population was then associated with such abusive practices illuminates the rigid structures of stratification and separation within racial categories engineered in the apartheid era. Therefore, the use of agencies within a certain sector of the Muslim community fueled broad generalizations about an entire world religion and an inability to perceive substantial differences *within* communities. This construction of the monolithic "Cape Malay" maintains structures that uphold the former stratification system of the apartheid era by "othering" Muslim coloured populations. Importantly, this process serves a latent function of centering whiteness. Coloured Christians are therefore more closely aligned with white mainstream power structures. Within the still disempowered coloured population, this Christian/Muslim divide creates a social hierarchy that affords certain sectors more social power through their closer alignment to the white center. The practice of utilizing employment agencies provides another means to privilege whiteness through distinct race and class constructions in relation to employers who use such services. As one white employer shared, in her community use of domestic agencies "is simply not done." Therefore, this prejudicial discourse about Muslims, emanating widely from Christian coloureds, serves an important function in both reifying the more comfortable hierarchy of the apartheid era and establishing distinct levels of difference to enhance social status within the coloured community—a racial group that continues to be marginalized in South Africa's broader social hierarchy.

In this applied case of domestic worker agencies, we see the overlapping complexities of race, religion, geographic location, and economic status that represent broader challenges of social transformation as marginalized groups uphold inequalities constructed in the apartheid era. What remained absent from this local discourse about the pervasive means by which the Muslim community was responsible for the "most exploitative" practices within the institution of domestic work is the extent to which white power structures were further freed from their own participation in the oppression of domestic workers by placing the burden of abuse on "other" communities. This critical component will be discussed in the summary of this chapter, as I propose a comprehensive analysis of new forms of social hierarchy encapsulated within the institution of domestic labor.

From this in-depth discussion of the Cape Coloured community and the discourse on its use of domestic worker agencies that emerged most repeatedly in this research, I present a highly comparable discourse that specifically criticized the "new black elite" employers for similarly instilling particularly harsh domestic work conditions in their employment of domestic workers. Let us now turn to a discussion of South Africa's most recent transition in the institution of domestic labor.

The "New Black Elite" Parliamentary Employers

Like Muslim and coloured employers, the "new black elite" or "new madam" employers were also subject to the same criticisms of constructing particularly harsh working conditions for domestic workers. Rather than the religious association to Muslim employers we see in the coloured group, references to the "new black madam" occurred less frequently and were almost always linked to members of parliament (MPs). As one Gender Commissioner described, in the Cape Town setting, this is explained through the virtual absence of black wealth[19] outside of government because of lower representation compared to the regional majority coloured population. Also important, while all groups of participants, particularly coloured and white employers, pointed to Muslim women as the "most exploitative," the discourse about MP's misuse of power was generated from other black women and union leaders. Tumi, a black ANC leader, union executive and former freedom fighter, described the following when I asked her what was most problematic about the overall institution of domestic work:

> Even MP these days, who go to parliament [say], "Must vote ANC!" I said, "I voted. I *never* vote another." But now the MPs was there in parliament, she don't ask about domestic workers, nothing, because now it's hard now, nice car, posh, everything . . . You know I see, in office [of SADSAWU] most of them working for African women, she pay R150 or R200 a month! MP! Even if you go to see about [membership] forms in office, you can see R200 in parliament, R250, no off, Monday to Monday, Monday to Monday, Monday to Monday. No off! Because she call people in Transkei, "you must work here." It's a disgrace.

Tumi's narrative captures the within-group disillusionment, particularly toward women who have achieved high levels of wealth and structural influence. As she also mentions, a central criticism of new black employers was based in the processes of acquiring workers from rural areas. While this practice also exploits rural poverty like the agencies we see in coloured communities, black women were especially criticized for hiring less privileged women within their own extended *families*—a practice which constructed grounds for extensive power abuses.

These direct criticisms of black women in governmental positions of power touch on a broader sentiment held by wider society about the abandonment of people "on the ground" by black leaders who have acquired positions of power and affluence, as Nothando shared in the following assessment of employers in her same racial group:

> I want to refer to the government, but the laws, the Constitution from the government, to the Department of Labour, the Minister of Labour, they don't recognise domestic workers . . . because even in their homes,

MP homes, they are *undermining* the domestic workers, they pay *cheap* to the domestic worker.

Although the new ANC governance was held to scrutinizing standards across all sectors, the particular practices of black women members of parliament became both a standard to measure the success of the public leadership transition and a central narrative about inner group divisions among black women. As Nkensani's interview illustrates, women members of parliament were harshly criticized because of the way in which they had "forgotten" their own former lived experience of poverty and struggle:

The problem of this people [MPs], the leaders are greedy. They forget about grassroots people . . . they forget about us because they've got houses, they've got cars. Look at my age here, I don't have nothing.

Through these narratives, it appears that exploitative practices are felt most saliently within shared racial groups—which explains why coloured women spoke about other coloured and Muslim employers and the "Afro-pessimism"[20] toward new black wealth arose predominantly from black women's discourse. Furthermore, serious concerns were raised about the extent of advocacy for domestic workers practiced among black parliamentary women. Domestic workers envisioned black women leaders as holding powerful opportunities to set agendas that prioritized women's issues, particularly the case of domestic workers. And while almost all participants recognized important gender advocacy initiatives in the governmental transition to democracy, domestic workers and union leaders seriously questioned the extent to which this sector's rights were included in the ongoing democratization. This concern was also reflected by workers and union leaders as a perception that women governmental leaders were unwilling to uphold democratic values in the *household*. The disillusionment we see in this case is also directly connected to a broader pessimism about the extent of South Africa's actual level of social change, particularly in the domestic sphere. In other words, the question embedded throughout this critical discourse on black women government leaders was, "If they can't practice democracy, who will?"

In my interviews with three black women members of parliament, two of whom employed black women as domestic workers, this perception was acknowledged and countered by placing it among certain women and not all black parliamentary employers. Importantly, one of my interviews with a Parliamentary WHIP reveals that a strong movement was initiated within ANC women's structures of governance to set standards for the

employment of domestic workers among MPs because of this broadly recognized "exploitation" and negative party criticism related to black women
employers. Yet, as this leader described, even women within the new government rejected this notion to set standards of employment. The predominant resistance was based in a belief that such a practice impedes the
private lives of employers. Therefore, the case of domestic workers was
seen as "just too personal" to take up at a structural level among women
MPs. Perhaps these leaders were colluding with male power structures or
an internalized belief that women's household labor remains a lower priority than other public decisions. Alternatively, the legislative work of government directly related to domestic work may have been identified as a
more appropriate venue for implementing fair labor standards. Yet at some
level, this proposal to standardize parliamentary women employers' household labor practices reveals an internal recognition of this broader criticism
of black women MPs. As is the case with the exploitative employment
agencies and the sweeping generalizations about Muslim employers however, it appears that the practices of a few women in power may also be
dominating the social narrative about an entire group of women. Furthermore, I suggest that this prevailing critique about black women's acquired
power and privilege is likely based in maintaining whiteness as the status
quo for employment. Strongly connected is the repeated displacement of
accountability for "fair working conditions" on the "new wealth," which
holds black parliamentary women accountable for their private employment in the household in ways that are still not expected of the traditional
"madam."

Black parliamentary women employers shared their own experiences
of, and subsequent complications with, hiring women from their same
racial group to reproduce the households that they were required to leave
in order to maintain positions in central government urban locations.[21] A
predominant theme emerged among parliamentary participants about the
challenge of balancing the enormous demands of parliament with the maintenance of the household responsibilities. In all of these interviews, women
felt they had no other option than to hire the services of domestic workers,
as this interview with a second term MP revealed:

> Maybe the question of having a domestic worker in someone's place is
> not something which we might end. Because you know development,
> you know it differs, and this was developed to that level, these ones are
> still here. So those who are at that level maybe are supposed to be in
> parliament for this session, and so in this home place there is no one. So
> somebody has to be there. So even if maybe my family wants to move

down to Cape Town, you know when I leave the offices I am *tired,* I am fucked up. When I arrive at home maybe I watch the news maybe for the next set of news follows, I'm already asleep. You see I'm *tired.* So I think having a domestic worker is a good thing, but we need to take care of them. They need not be slaves. They must be happy, you know?

With the excessive demands of parliamentary life, employers also recognized a sense of loss in their ability to be present in the domestic sphere as well as their public role, as Nomonde shared:

I think it's a tough thing, you know in parliament. You know you forfeit your roles as a mother . . . Even if we can send maybe somebody there at home, doing whatever you are supposed to be doing, you know the biological role cannot be replaced . . . Hey, it's not something, I cannot say I'm happy. I can't say I'm 60 percent happy but let me say I'm 45 to 50 percent. Because as I said earlier, on that, you know my role as a mother, she [domestic worker] cannot replace it. I'm a bit more strict on my kids and she is lenient. The last one is 15 years old. She is a teenager and she is now in the streets you see and she doesn't have those powers to say, "no." So at least if I'm around she tries and sits next to me, you know, as though she is an innocent girl. When I'm gone she goes out, you see? *Ja* it's good for the government to be having women working, women as parliamentarians, but there is a gap that has opened and this gap has created some damages which we might not be able to repair. For instance, right now I'm unable to go along to take her and follow this teenager age, these stages, you know to tell her this and this. Though I do it but the fact that I talk to her and go away for two weeks, go back, talk to her, go away for two weeks. You see? So there are those things there are damages that cannot be repaired. But if maybe we had also opted for another option of saying I would like to sit home and do, you know all the best as a mother, we would not be having woman in parliament. Men would be taking decisions on our behalf and they would be prioritizing that which is more important to them. For instance, they would go for roads when I would opt for a clinic, you see [laughs].

While all employers certainly uphold social constructions of gender in the household through their employment of domestic workers, black women parliamentarians expressed a particular relationship between maintaining "our culture" through the gendered division of labor and the subsequent need to hire another woman to do so in their absence. This cultural expectation presented enormous internal conflicts for black MP employers because of the customary, deeply engrained "role of the wife" and the rigid norms about the inappropriateness of men performing domestic work. As one participant explained, black women have realized enormous public victories, yet the reality that they must return to communities and patriarchal family structures that are "steeped in culture and traditions" underscores the ongoing need for transformation in the private realm.[22] Therefore, maintaining "culture" for black women parliamentarians was outwardly recognized as one of the key functions of hiring domestic support services, as Thope described in the following caption:

> Well, the husband will help if he wants to. If he doesn't want to he doesn't. I mean from our culture, our culture says a house is a woman's problem. Your husband can buy a house for you, but cleaning the house is a wife's responsibility. So if, well my husband is old, so I don't expect him to go to the kitchen and make breakfast for himself. I must make sure that he gets a good breakfast. And then lunch, he can look after his lunch, ah, but I make sure that he gets a good supper. There are two meals in my house that I am cooking, the breakfast and the supper.

Thope went on to describe that even though she hires domestic workers to clean her home, she maintains her mother and wife roles through preparing meals that are available for the family in her absence. This compromise between parliament and domestic expectations was possible for Thope because she resided in the Cape Town vicinity with her husband and children. For Nomonde, her immediate family lived in the Northern Province, a 2-hour flight away from her parliamentary work in Cape Town. Therefore, she hired the services of another woman to literally take on the role of the "woman of the house." This created an intimacy between Nomonde and the domestic worker she employed as well as subsequent boundary issues in relation to her husband. The following narrative captures Nomonde's response when asked what was most important for her domestic worker to maintain in the home while she worked in parliament:

> Number one, the first one, I would not like my house to be seen to be an old house, abandoned, dilapidated, you know with that utmost fear that there is no one here. I want my house to be a bright place, you know? Or when you look at it in the morning you can see that there are people in here, the windows are opened you know, curtains are opened and they are clean, shows that there is life here. Even the gardening around, it's clean there is *life* in this house that is what I want. And

then the other thing which I want, I'm having my husband, my husband is a sugar diabetic somebody and I'm also a sugar diabetic somebody. He is supposed to have his meals. At no stage should he not have his meals because the wife is in Cape Town. You know such things, we still cook for our husbands, they are still enjoying sitting back [laughs]. So I would like a situation where he has all his meals and then I would also like a situation where he goes to school [work] clean and should be having his shirt clean on a daily basis with his tie on. The dry cleaning, he takes care for himself. I also would like to have my kids clean, the house clean, them having their meals. Sundays, them getting to church. Then there are other activities in the community, them participating. And at the end of it my home, or my house to be a place where people say, "Well the mother here is not around, but when at times we do see her, but everything seems to be okay." You know? That's the situation I want when I come in. I look at my house, "oh" and then it shows me there are people here that's what I want.

Nomonde further described that a close relationship with the woman who takes on her role of wife and mother of the household was essential:

I'm saying you know the relationship now has grown to a level where I can say she is my sister. And when I left home I said, "My dear I'm leaving the family with you," something which is not usual in our culture. And everybody around will be saying, "She left the husband with this woman" . . . So I said to her, "Do me one favour you can do whatever evil or whatever bad thing as a human being but please do not fall in love with my husband, do whatever." So she has a boyfriend. The boyfriend does come and then there is an outside room. I felt that she is a human being and I can't be saying to her, "Don't bring this one, do that," because I also have a husband. So the boyfriend does come and fortunately since she came there is [only] this one boyfriend . . . So, well she is a consistent person you know and she really cares.

These narratives of black parliamentary women capture a central component of the essence of social change and gender transformation in South Africa's continual democratization. Although women have taken on prominent positions of power at the public level, the ongoing expectations that they maintain full responsibility for household labor—by either performing it themselves (thus adding to the "double burden") or hiring it out through the labor of less privileged women—indicates little change at the private level. As Nomonde shared, her community's perception of her relative success would remain measured by her ability to maintain the appearance of her house, regardless of her public role as a parliamentarian. This reality demonstrates that even when women transition from the household to work in such prominent positions, men remain freed from responsibility for domestic labor. Therefore, as Britton (1999) found in her research among parliamentary women, the real challenge to integrating democracy in the private sphere involves the ongoing transformation of household relations, and in particular, sharing the domestic responsibility with men.[23]

A final important distinction which contrasts domestic labor in coloured and black communities was the way in which, although both groups employed less economically privileged women, only black employers were associated with hiring members of their own families. One of the parliamentary employers I interviewed had employed a distant family member at one point, which she found very complicated. However, the more predominant script among black women employers was that they attempted to institute some level of mutual relatedness in the work context because of shared life experiences, rather than a required familial relationship. Because these MP employers either had direct experience themselves as domestic workers, or were raised by a mother who was a domestic worker, each stated that they wanted to lessen in some way the power differentials in the work context—a dynamic which contradicted general perceptions of the exploitative work conditions instituted by parliamentary employers. Thope described her own experience in this regard, as well as its subsequent challenges:

> I like to stay in harmony with people around me. You know when I come home, I don't expect her to make tea for me. I make my own tea. In fact I'm not even a tea drinker. I drink coffee in the morning and that's all, but like when it's cold, I feel like having tea. I make my own tea. She doesn't make tea for me. I'm not used to that. Then sometimes if she is doing ironing, then I tell, "Now I am going to cook." Then I do the cooking. I also like, I like to be responsible for my family, so I like that my children, when they come home from school, they have got warm cooked food to eat. So I don't expect her to do that, because I also think about her children. Her children are at school, they come back from school, she is not there. She is here with me. Sometimes when I come home early I tell her, "You can leave. Go have a rest," because I also think about her kids. It's nice, it's really nice, it's a good thing when you come home from school and you find your mother or your father at home.

This narrative reveals an internal conflict about the inherent inequality of the domestic work relationship. At the same time, Thope also acknowledged that embracing this more democratic, empathetic approach presented particular challenges regarding the extent to which she was taken "seriously" by the workers in her same racial group:

> It's such a problem for us to have helpers. Also I think that there is that, "Ah—black people working for black people." I think our people are used to being bossed around. They are used to being bossed around! Because I don't see myself as her boss. I see myself as a friend, a friend to her. But because our people are used to that "boss" type, then they tend not to care. They don't care whether they come or don't come, or whatever she is doing, she doesn't care, you know. So that's another problem. But when it comes to payment, then they don't take "no" for that.

Thope's narrative illustrates that although diverse employers now exist in South Africa, workers remained conditioned by a colonial system such that former structures of power are taken more "seriously." This fear of becoming vulnerable as an employer who either shares too much of the burden of domestic work or appears "too nice" was repeated across all sectors of employers and became one of the dominant challenges in managing the role. Yet because this sample consisted of predominantly newly emergent employer groups, perhaps this struggle to establish some combination of a shared connection as women, democracy "at home," *and* being taken seriously as an employer further explains the narrative and partial reality about both black and coloured employers. Because the status of these groups remains marginalized within an ongoing social stratification system distinguished by the apartheid era, the need to assert power appears to be greater in many instances because of the lower social status of both coloured and black women. Furthermore, the social distinctions instilled in the apartheid era continue to dominate the landscape of modern South Africa such that women with less privileged social positions must assert their partial power more visibly through enacting it in the household. As my data suggest, this dynamic is accentuated when women employ domestic workers in their same racial group where ascribed power is not as firmly embedded—unlike the status of white employers who maintain power through the ongoing dominance of apartheid hierarchies. Thope's experience of both embodying "sisterhood" and its shared vulnerability when employing women in her same racial group—regardless of her elevated social power as a parliamentarian—exemplifies the complexity of the relationship between formerly disadvantaged groups and perceptions about their particularly "harsh" treatment of domestic workers.

Building upon these within-group complexities we see in the case of coloured employers, Muslim employment agencies and the "new black madams," I turn to findings from in-depth research among a third group of "nontraditional employers." Women who identified as feminists revealed another particular complexity encapsulated within this highly personalized institution of paid domestic labor. By exploring these central themes that emerged among women positioned outside the "traditional employer" identity we see both the opportunities and challenges to democratizing the private sphere.

The Feminists: Portraits of Change

The employers who identified as feminists offered valuable insights that further explained this persistent theme about the "most exploitative" work contexts practiced in either coloured, Muslim, or "new black elite" communities. By deconstructing the racialized nature of this discourse and the monolithic associations of the "other," feminist employers—including coloured, black and white informants—shared a perception that the *difference* in domestic work contexts was not primarily based on the race of the employer, but rather on her personal characteristics. Mallie, a young black feminist, described this perspective as follows:

> In my experience, I really think people are people. I think that there are some really terrible white employers and there are some really terrible black employers. But I think black domestic workers get much more hurt when they get that kind of behaviour from black employers. I think that's what the difference is because they don't expect it, they expect them to understand and to treat them in a human way. I think that's where the problem, you know where the perception comes through. But I really don't think so much of it has to do with the fact that black employers are more nasty or anything like that . . . I mean I've thought about it in terms of other things that happen in life and that's how things are, *ja*. You are most likely to be angry if it's another black person ill-treating you than you are with a white person doing it because you expect it, that type of thing.

Based upon Mallie's interpretation, perhaps this discourse about the "abusive" black employer is not as much based in the extent of its practice as much as it is the associated within-group conflict when such treatment occurs. The heightened intensity of this impact therefore facilitates the pervasive nature of this narrative among disadvantaged groups. Also, the intimate nature of the household as an employment sector creates particularly personal enactments of power differentials, such that the "ill-treating" Mallie mentions manifests through daily social interactions in particularly salient ways.

Julia, a white feminist human rights professional, offers a complementary explanation by acknowledging the race and class differentials among workers and employers, yet rejecting the racist assumptions directed at new employers. Rather, Julia asserts that structures of past inequality account for these abuses in employment practices, as opposed to the predominant racial constructions:

> You know the differences are differences, there are cultural differences in that I have not been brought up in a traditional Xhosa home. So there are very real differences about what her [black worker's] experience of life has been and my experience of life. I don't think that we are different employers . . . because there are just different human beings and I don't think that racial connotations—it's more about whose had the power to employ before and how do they handle it as a human being? And again, how aware are they of the realities of the people that they are employing? Because very often it is straight ignorance. It's an ignorance that arises out of local norms of employing people and sucking their wages, you know, and we are really only just slowly making our way out of it and still leaving a huge amount of people unemployed. So I don't think that the difference as employers is a racial thing. I think that's a very racist statement. I think to say that the abuses are the new coloured bourgeoisie is *bullshit*. It's about one's attitude toward other people and their right to employment and their right to decent wages.

The way in which these self-identified feminist employers moved the conversation about the exploitative "other" black/coloured employer to structural levels of inequality was extremely valuable in deciphering this complex and often discomforting discourse among participants. In particular, these narratives also afford opportunities to examine white employers' behaviors in a way that holds this group, with its continued social power, to the same standards.

Elna, a coloured employer, reiterated the problematic racialization of employers and offered the following critical analysis which situated this pessimism toward black employers in the context of a broader disenchantment about the new government and the extent of actual change realized since democracy:

> I think you are probably going to find exploitation cutting across the board. You are going to find people who are black who are concerned about paying living wages, and you are going to find people who are black who aren't. And it's the same for people who are white, but I

think what that theme [of the exploitative black employer] probably is saying is we *thought* that when we have a black government that things would change because blackness was equated with a struggle for freedom. But actually it hasn't happened, so I think what is being expressed is a sense of bitterness at being betrayed . . . It's a betrayal that is being racialised in a sense that people who are working class and black are saying, "Oh we've got a new government that is black that *does* now have access to resources to become middle and upper class and nothing has changed for us, in fact things have worsened." I mean things have worsened for structural reasons, the GEAR policy, the you know defeat in the sense of the unions, globalization, there are structural reasons. And of course, I don't deny, I am sure there are black employers who are as exploitative as their counterparts who are white, you know. But I think what you are hearing is a racialisation of a sense of betrayal, a deep sense of betrayal, because I mean the struggle wasn't just about race, I think it was about class too. So it's a class issue that is becoming racialised and that is the way it is getting expressed.

Elna's narrative explains the way in which the slow nature of social transformation is particularly difficult for disadvantaged groups whose lives would be most significantly impacted with such democratic ideals realized. Therefore, emphasis on these "abusive" employers who shared less access to social power also becomes a way to voice overall disenchantment with democracy's slow implementation process, particularly for disempowered groups. As these narratives suggest, isolating extremely negative employment practices to formerly disadvantaged groups masks more structural explanations for continued severe inequality and the ongoing stratification systems that have not shifted in ways that hold white employers accountable to the same standards.

From these data a central question transpires—are black and coloured employers actually more abusive or do whites exercise the same practices without such scrutiny because of their maintained social power position at the center? In response, I draw upon participants' assertions to offer a structural analysis for this complex, yet predominant, discourse about "new employers." The notion of class struggle at the center of this institution emerged repeatedly among feminist employers who criticized national development through neo-liberal policies that specifically disadvantage working women, particularly in the informal sector. The burden of this focus on economic development falls most heavily on domestic workers, who remain the least protected sector of labor in South Africa's new democracy.

Marlene, a coloured employer, similarly integrated a macro-level class analysis as we discussed this pervasive negative discourse about "other" employers. When asked about her perspectives on why black and coloured workers would continue to prefer to work for white employers, Marlene suggested:

> To what extent do people understand our position in society as women and also how the economy is structured? Why do you have white people paying more? Because they *get paid* more, they earn more in the first instance . . . at the same time one needs to recognise the internalised oppression and part of that whole thing of, "I'll continue to work for white people," is also part of internalised oppression. And the other thing is also, that there isn't this homogenous black group of women that okay because we are black, we are going to treat all domestic workers better. Because it's also got to do with class, you know, it's not just got to do with race, and essentially a lot of black women who can afford domestics are middle class women . . . I think it's a combination of, between internalised oppression and on the other side it is a reflection of the truth of the reality that a lot of white people do pay their employees much better. But on the other hand, the whole thing about how I am being treated is nice also because of a lot of white guilt that you know . . . maybe I wasn't part of the apartheid state, I didn't impose all of these kinds of things or I didn't do anything to hurt any black person or I wasn't a racist in any particular way now I need to show or at least ease my own conscious in terms of the way I treat my domestic worker.

Marlene's integration of continued structures of white dominance through her presentation of notions of internalized oppression demonstrates another level in which the former apartheid power structures continue to racialize social relations in even the most private contexts. At the same time, both Marlene and Elna illustrate how broader structures of class and severe economic inequality further explain this negative discourse about "new" employers, particularly among disadvantaged groups. Marlene's narrative offers an intersectional analysis by illustrating that the treatment of domestic workers among the white community can also become a way to relieve employers' sense of guilt in relation to their position throughout the years of apartheid oppression. While my findings suggest that domestic work is primarily an institution that allows white employers to retain their social power ascribed during apartheid, as Marlene's narrative illustrates, in some cases embracing a 'new democracy' in the household assuages employers' internal conflict about the prevalence of white power in the new democracy.

Therefore, as employers "ease their conscience" about racial inequality through their more democratic treatment of domestic workers, they also reproduce the class inequalities that lead workers to prefer to work for white employers. This notion is supported through my data among workers who continually identified the "perks" of employment with "white madams" almost exclusively in relation to their heightened economic resources that would substantially improve working conditions: household appliances, better salary, more "gifts," paying for school fees, and less work.

This structural interpretation also suggests that the institution of domestic work may be one of the few spaces in South Africa's post-1994 society where stratification processes are shifting, such that class is becoming more central than race. Of the five workers who stated that they *would* work for black or coloured employers, each said that they would do so *only* if they were assured of a fair living wage. As Nomsa asserted, "It's only the money I need, to do my things, solve my problems, I don't mind what colour, as long as I've got a job."

These class differentials between workers and employers demonstrate the intersectional nature of women's relationships in the context of domestic work. As the profiles of employers shift such that women in the same racial group are positioned as both worker and employer, we see that class moves to a more central position in defining the power relations within the institution of domestic work. Therefore, this dominant theme that emerged as pessimism toward the "new employers" can be explained through the shifting forms of social stratification within the new democracy. As one feminist employer explained, when examining social inequalities, gender remains "much easier to talk about" because there is an "awfulness in class snobbery" that impedes its further study. The final section of this chapter takes this class discussion a step further by proposing an intersectional stratification framework that describes the complexities of social location contained most vividly within the institution of domestic labor.

NEW PATTERNS OF STRATIFICIATION

These narratives about the perceived abuses of power among new employers illustrate the rigid categorization of the apartheid era that continues to dominate the social landscape of South Africa's democracy. As the data illustrate, formerly disadvantaged groups are held to the highest standards in terms of their behaviors and employment practices in ways that the white population is not. As these "new employers" are rejected, particularly by less privileged members of their own racial groups, a pervasive allegiance to colonial structures continues to privilege the "white madam" in ways that reflect minimal transformation within this embedded institution of paid household labor. As formerly disadvantaged group members acquire power to hire domestic workers through their heightened class positions, however, complexities and class-based stratification is woven into the texture of domestic work in this newly democratic context.

Based on the data surrounding the "new employers" in this study, I propose a model of stratification within the institution of domestic work that constructs particular hierarchies for both employers and domestic workers. My research illustrates that the social positions of both workers and employers are defined by the way in which they engage with the institution of domestic labor. In this regard, the positions of workers and employers are mutually connected and dependent upon one another to uphold central forms of social power. For example, the more services employers can hire, the more their own social positions are elevated. Therefore, full-time, live-in domestic work is associated with the highest levels of social status, whereas the hiring of part-time, live-out domestic workers is associated with decreased social status. Furthermore, hiring from domestic work agencies is ascribed to race and class groups with even less access to social power. Domestic workers participate in this ranking system through their construction of ideal white employers—modeled from former apartheid structures of power. As my research illustrates, workers maintained that employment with a white family remained the most prestigious and desirable circumstance within their sector of labor. In this respect, the social status of domestic workers is constructed by the race and class positions of their "madams"—which accounts for the criticism and rejection of black and coloured employers from domestic workers within their own group. For employers, hiring 'below' their class status—such as whites hiring part-time *chars* as opposed to full-time live-in domestic workers—threatened social positions established during apartheid. These interconnected dependencies illustrate that the institution of domestic work is bound by and actively reproduces broader social power structures. In the context of South Africa's rapid transition, the power dynamics within this sector inform a broader interpretation of shifting patterns of social stratification, particularly as we see in the within-group divisions based upon the intersections of race and class positions.

The following typology summarizes the findings from this research by demonstrating the existing race and class-based hierarchies within the institution of domestic work. I draw upon the racial categorization system of the apartheid era to reflect the social divisions that remain dominant in South African society ten years after the national transition to provide a fuller analysis of the intersections of race and class within this colonial institution.

Table 5.1: Social Stratification and Domestic Work

Worker Category	Social Power	Employer Category
Live-in Nanny	↑	"Old Elite" Employer (traditionally white)
Live-in		Elite Black Employer (typically members of parliament)
Live-out		Coloured Employer (Christian)
"Char" (Part-time day labour)		Coloured Employer (Muslim)

This stratification system, based on the cumulative data across all sectors, indicates that colonial employers remained most desirable for workers, whereas the least desirable employer characteristics were associated with coloured Muslim women. Black women were perceived as slightly more desirable because those who could employ domestic workers were specifically associated with parliament. Based on these constructions of the ideal employer, workers' status is determined by the race/ethnicity of their employer. In a parallel fashion, employers' status is reinforced through the type of worker they are able to hire, with most privileged groups typically hiring live-in services. Furthermore, those groups with the least race/class privilege may heighten their own social power and status by hiring "up" within the social hierarchies of domestic workers. Domestic worker agencies therefore provide a means for less class-privileged groups to acquire a service associated with higher social class positions—the live-in domestic worker. These hierarchies demonstrate that the institution of domestic work assumes a central role in the attainment of social status, for both workers and employers. In the context of South Africa's rapid transition, my findings also show that the relative ability to access particular forms of domestic labor elevates the social status of employers, particularly among formerly marginalized groups who remained confined by the ongoing racial inequalities constructed in the apartheid era.

CONCLUSIONS

As we see through the discourse that emerged around the institution of domestic labor since the end of apartheid, changes have occurred within this institution that position women in distinct relation to one another based upon their relative race, class, religious, and geographic location divides. At the same time, the prevalence of colonial structures of employment continues to define the institution of domestic work, even among those groups that were formerly marginalized, through the severe racial order of South Africa's history. Particularly salient are the findings that illustrate the power of *within-group* marginalization processes that seriously complicate the traditional black maid/white madam dichotomy. The narratives on South Africa's "new employers" suggest that within this institution, as the country gradually shifts to democracy, class differentials become more central than race to some patterns of social relations. We see this in the "new black elite" parliamentary employers who hire other black women as domestic workers in order to maintain both their public role and the ongoing expectation of household management responsibilities. These data underscore the importance of an intersectional framework of analysis to interpret power differentials among women who are situated very differently in relation to the institution of domestic work.

The importance of class, religion and geographic location differentials emerged throughout the data on the within-group domestic work practices of the "middle layer" coloured community. With the dominance of this group's representation in Cape Town, participants repeatedly pointed to labor practices among coloured employers as most exploitative and problematic. The perceptions held by both domestic workers and employers were widely critical of coloured employers for instilling the most severely oppressive domestic work contexts. This case also revealed that religion was central to the construction of the "most abusive" employers, as we see through the repeated references to Cape Town's Muslim coloured community.

The highly regionalized practice of domestic worker recruitment agencies motivated much of the critical discourse directed specifically at coloured, mainly Muslim, employers. Although this practice appeared to be centered within this group, the wide sweeping claims about "all Muslims" indicate a level of stereotyping and overgeneralization about this particular group. Perhaps certain groups become a point of convergence for the tensions within society, particularly at times of transition. With this concept as a basis, the data in this study reveal that a great deal of the conflict on the part of both employers and workers was specifically transferred to the Muslim community. By placing abuse in this highly distinct insular religious community, all other groups are then absolved of their own participation in similar exploitation through the institutionalized inequality that continues to exist most strikingly in domestic work.

Analysis of these dominant regional intersections of women's experiences based upon social location differentials affords original insight about within-group marginalization not yet addressed in the literature on domestic work. Why do communities who have experienced severe oppression re-enact it when ascribed greater social power through the acquisition of heightened class positions, or in the South African case, the shifting of national structures of governance? In this study, the private household became a pivotal space where social power was exercised to elevate class status through the employment of domestic workers. As my interviews reveal, attaining the ability to hire domestic workers to perform the "dirty work" of the household indicates both the achievement of a particular level of success and an associated heightened class status. In the shifting South African context, such increased class positions become even more central for marginalized groups as a way to distinguish within-group difference and hierarchies.

Throughout this discourse about "new madams," and its subsequent association with the "worst employers," it is clear that, while the experience of domestic work does not seem to vary based on the race of the worker in the employment context, the race, class and location identity of the *employer* is perceived as critical to the working conditions, salary, and level of exploitation on the job. While within-group practices are not addressed in the literature on domestic work, two key theorists in other contexts point to domestic workers' parallel systems of preference that castigate employers outside of the dominant white group. Pierette Hondagneu-Sotelo (2001) describes worker perceptions about "other" employers based upon her research with Latina immigrants in the U.S.:

> Latina immigrants also operate under racist assumptions, many of which they learn in the United States. They quickly pick up the country's racial hierarchies and racist stereotypes. "Jews are cheap," "Mexican Americans and blacks are lazy," or "*Los chinos* are too bossy," they say. The regional racial hierarchy also fixes Jews, Armenians, and Iranians in low positions. "*Los Americanos,*" the term they typically use to refer to employers marked only "white," are almost never singled out by ethnicity and are rarely criticized or negatively labeled as a group. Conversely, Latina domestic workers single out the race of particular employers who happen to be both "bad employers" and "racialized" as non-white (P.58).

As the data portray, in the South African case, the processes of singling out, racially identifying and rejecting nontraditional employers similarly dominated the discourse among workers. Judith Rollins (1985) found a comparable circumstance in her study of African American domestic workers:

> Like employers, domestics have definite preferences. There was the expected anti-*nouveau riche* remarks . . . and there was the expected preference for younger women, seen as less prejudiced and less "picky" (P.147–148).

In South Africa's new democracy, these preferences continue to be shaped by the colonial dominance of the apartheid era. With minimal shifting of social and economic power structures, whites remain the majority of employers as well as the model from which other employers are compared. Those sectors of the coloured and black populations with economic resources to hire domestic workers were subject to broad assumptions about the expected stereotypical conditions of employment imposed by such "newly elite." Just as Rollins described in her sample's preference toward "old money," South African domestic workers maintained strong affiliations to "traditional" (white) madams.

With this allegiance to former hierarchical models, marginalized communities in urban Cape Town are able to access the privileges of domestic labor through the severe poverty of surrounding rural areas. Therefore, coloured communities enhance their own relative social power by hiring rural women within their own racial group who are further disenfranchised by class and geographic location divides. Certainly domestic worker agencies capitalize on this exploitation through their systematic abuse of poor rural poor women. Given the severe economic limitations within the national structure of unemployment and poverty that particularly impact rural areas, unless other viable means of work outside of household labor are afforded women, South Africa's democracy remains seriously challenged. With the existing structural inequalities between urban and rural economic circumstances, it may be unlikely that this geographical exploitation—upon which agencies thrive—will be abolished in the near future.

Closely related to the repositioning of social status through the institution of domestic labor, the data suggested that those groups with lower social status more strictly reinforce their positions as "the boss" or "madam." The relative close proximity of within-group coloured workers and employers in the spectrum of social power creates conditions where employers' statuses are more vulnerable, thus in need of strict measures of reinforcement. This dynamic is related to the last important analytical point. In both cases of "othering" new black and coloured employers, the interviews illustrate that the harshest evaluations emanated from workers within the same racial groups. Therefore, the "Afro-pessimism" perceptions about new employers came from mainly black workers, whereas more marginalized coloured workers distinctly linked the highest levels of exploitation to other privileged coloured women.

This leads to a conclusion that shared group identity is strongly related to perceptions of abuse by "newly elite" employers. This is not to suggest that employment contexts where employers and workers share the same race *generally* enact oppressive working environments. However, in the South African context, where class is gradually emerging as a primary social stratification structure, within-group exploitation may be linked to a heightened need to exercise social power in the employment context. For example, as one participant in this study explained, when employers and workers share the same racial identity, social position differentials are severely lessened. Therefore, those in privileged positions must strongly assert their social power because it is far more threatened when only class defines privilege. Like this participant described, those with less power must do more to continually demonstrate "who is the boss around here." Unlike the traditional "maid and madam" (Cock 1980; 1989) relationship—where power was concretely established through both the racial order embedded in apartheid and the disparate economic positions of women in the employment context—when workers and employers come from the same racial group, social power can be established only through other structures of privilege such as class and rural/urban location. In the South African case, as the data in this study illustrate, the complexities of within-group power relations draw more heavily on differentials of economic position—which importantly are far more vulnerable to slippage down the hierarchical social ladder than the more deeply engrained racial order. Furthermore, the national transformation threatens formerly embedded structures of power. Therefore, the household becomes a critical space to hold on to social power through the micro relations between domestic workers and employers.

As South Africa gradually shifts away from the dominance of apartheid's residue of prevailing racial stratification, it appears from these data that secondary constructions of social status, such as class and rural/urban location, continue to surface as important components in the reconfiguring of difference and social hierarchy in the emerging democracy. This chapter demonstrates that domestic work remains a powerful institution that situates social hierarchy, constructs severe power differentials among women based on intersections of identity, and illustrates the barriers to actualizing democracy in the private sphere. Furthermore, we see that these power relations that play out at the household level reflect broader patterns of stratification that encapsulate the ongoing obstacles to engaging democracy at all levels.

These structures, however, are not static. As the texture of social power relations is continually reconfigured in South Africa's new democracy, women are actively engaging in processes that challenge the nation's reliance upon the colonial institution of paid household labor and its reification of the "former regime" in everyday life. The next chapter explores the context of collective mobilization to democratize the institution of paid domestic labor in the spirit of South Africa's broader transformation and public attention to gender rights.

Chapter Six
"Women Will Not Be Free Until Domestic Workers Are Free!"[1]

For domestic workers, "the struggle continues" to access the public gender rights that are central to South Africa's democracy. Even though women have made tremendous progress in terms of government leadership and the implementation of policy, domestic labor illustrates that the campaign for gender rights has not yet reached the household. The largest sector of working women in South Africa continues to experience severe marginalization because their labor is situated in the private household where apartheid inequalities prevail. These conditions led domestic workers in this study to repeatedly express that to them, democracy was "only on paper."

Participants did however, discuss "moments" of change: when workers described employers who embraced particularly democratic acts in the household, through dispute resolution venues that address unjust retrenchments,[2] and as "laws for domestics" are gradually taken more seriously. Although the institution remains bound by apartheid structures, it is also slowly transitioning in South Africa's new democracy. Both worker and employer participants acknowledged a *gradual* loosening of the colonial culture of domestic labor in ways the impacted their daily lives in the private sphere. As one participant suggested, in the post-euphoria of the 1994 transformation, the "real work" of democracy begins *at home*. The spaces where change has occurred provide valuable lenses into the relationship between public and private transformation. In South Africa, women's collective organization continues to facilitate these transitions—offering a model of mobilization across divides that can be applied to the global context.

This chapter presents my findings on social change *within* the institution of domestic work. Three central questions concern us in this investigation: In what ways has the institution of paid domestic labor become more democratic? What challenges remain the strongest barriers to *accessing* gender rights for domestic workers? How are women organizing to transform the institution of paid household labor? To address these topics, I draw upon data gathered in participant observation and action research with the South African Domestic Service and Allied Workers Union (SADSAWU) and a Commission on Gender Equality (CGE) government/NGO alliance established to specifically address domestic workers' access to protective labor policy. My findings demonstrate how civil society organizations aligned with domestic workers "on the ground" to formalize legislative protection for this "casual labor" sector. The success of this policy reform offers a model of collaboration to merge South Africa's public gender rights victories with social change in the private sphere. Throughout this chapter, I also consider implementation barriers in private households—a challenge widely named as the greatest obstacle to democracy in South Africa. I begin this discussion by examining collective organization within the institution of domestic work.

OVERVIEW OF CHANGE IN THE INSTITUTION OF DOMESTIC LABOR

Formal labor policy extended protection to domestic workers initially in 1993, one year before the national transition. When asked about the extent of actual change in their employment since democracy, however, domestic workers in this study indicated that transformation at the national level had only minimally changed the conditions of their daily labor. Employers' attitudes were named as one site of change. However, as Nothando shared, this in no way improved the material conditions of her work:

> What I say is till 1994, the employer, they smile, they give us smile, which during the struggle, they didn't get that smile. And also we can use their cups. We can cut the same bread, but when it comes to the minimum wage, or it comes to the Basic Conditions of Employment Act, they are still staying . . . nothing has changed, and the way that we are working, very hard. The pile of ironing, the windows, it's the *whole* house.

This disparity between social policy reform and change in private household employment contexts remained the widest concern for all workers in this study. Of the 20 formal interviews, 15 domestic workers indicated that they felt *no change* in their work contexts since the democratic transition, even though two central labor policies were extended to domestic workers in 1994 and 1996. The remaining five indicated that domestic work had either changed "100 percent" (based on particularly sensitive employers in two cases) or moderately (in three cases). Nomsa's response, when asked about the extent to which she felt domestic labor had changed since 1994, captured the predominant sentiment among workers:

> Little bit, little bit, little bit, because employers now they just don't throw you out, say, "Go now, take your things and go now." Even if it's a live-in domestic worker, if the employer don't want you, "Now! you pack your things and go!" But now they know they have to give you a notice and they must have a good reason, before it was not like [that]. If the domestic worker wants to change a face, she's tired of your face, tired of you, just, "No, I don't need you anymore" please, take another one. But it's not like that now, there's a little change, there is a change.

Across all sectors of participants, two specific impediments to change in the institution of domestic work were identified: 1) employers' unwillingness to change in accordance with labor standard reform, and 2) policies rendered ineffective because of a lack of compliance (on the part of employers) and implementation (on the part of government). As this employer articulated, the power imbalance that continued to dominate the institution of domestic work created a normative culture of policy non-compliance:

> What we have in theory is one thing. What we have in practice is a whole other story and the challenges are really around implementation and what are we doing around the issues of implementation? Because I know there was a whole out-roar, especially from the conservative white community, around domestic workers and their rights is simply, "Ok they are going to impose these things on us, conditions, requirements, then we simply won't employ them." . . . I think that comes with an arrogance, that of the relationship of dependence is very skewed and I think we do depend a lot on domestic workers and we do have very different power relationship, but because they aren't organised as other union workers, we don't feel it, we don't feel or we don't, or we aren't so much aware of our dependency.

This narrative captures the critical connection between policy implementation and employers' recognition of their own dependency on domestic labor. Because workers are primarily seen as dependent upon employers for economic survival, power relations within the household render labor policies ineffective. Employers' inability to recognize their own dependency on domestic workers therefore creates a labor context where severe social inequalities govern working conditions, rather than formal labor legislation.

This gap between policy and implementation points to the need for alternative systems of accountability to protect workers' interests and monitor policy compliance within the private household. Although governmental institutions and national unions are most directly positioned to assure implementation, the enormous demands on both parties have facilitated a different process of advocacy and ongoing social change. Women's rights organizations assume the most central role in both shaping and implementing policies for the domestic work sector.

Leading this movement, the South African Domestic Service and Allied Workers' Union (SADSAWU) reorganized in 2000 to collectively challenge government on the extent to which the "poorest of the poor" were included in the national commitment to gender and labor rights central to democratization. While SADSAWU continues to push for recognition of domestic workers' contribution to social and economic development, unionization of this sector remains extremely challenging because of the isolated nature of the work environment and the private, individualized context of employment conditions.[3] Because of these severe structural barriers, unionization is even more critical among domestic workers who remain the most severely marginalized sector of working women in South Africa. The strengthening of domestic workers' unions is therefore pivotal to the ongoing challenge of actualizing gender rights in the private household.

Brief History of Resistance through Domestic Work Unionization[4]

The apartheid era institutionalized severe obstacles for women's unionization by outlawing the organization of domestic workers until 1996 when the Labour Relations Act was extended to this sector, two years after the national democratic transition. This exclusion, however, did not impede women's organizing around domestic work, which began in 1970 through the establishment of the Domestic Workers and Employers Project (DWEP). By including employers in this project and shaping its goals as non-threatening to the apartheid government, women's mobilization in this sector evaded state scrutiny. Ironically, this organization also fostered one of the few spaces for working relationships between black women and liberal white employers. Several regional collectives of domestic workers formed soon after DWEP's inception including the Domestic Workers' Association (DWA) in Cape Town, which similarly diverted its libratory goals by identifying as a "Christian" organization.[5] In 1982, DWA, along with six other regionally based organizations of domestic workers, merged to form SADWA, the South African Domestic Workers' Association. These collective organizations developed women's activism in this sector at a national level, affording more visibility for the institution of domestic work as a central component of the nation's labor resources.

In 1986, these regionally-based organizations emerged and identified as a union, in alignment with the national labor union movement of that era. Although working class, predominantly black unions were banned during apartheid, subverted operations and ongoing alliances in the labor movement served as a key site of resistance and women's collective activism throughout the regime's governance. The South African Domestic Workers' Union (SADWU) formation marked a critical shift from domestic workers' organization around themes of workers' education and improved worker/employer relations to a focus on collective activism as part of a broader labor movement. This ideological shift materialized through SADWU's formal affiliation with the national Congress of South African Trade Unions (COSATU).[6] The goals of this first union of domestic workers were based upon assurance of labor rights within this sector, such as pay and fair working conditions. Furthermore, SADWU operated within a broader framework of national liberation struggle to end apartheid. Notably, the organizational goals of SADWU, from its 1986 inception remain part of the agenda for the existing post-apartheid union—a reflection of the extent to which little structural change has resulted in the realm of domestic work and labor policy reform.

SADWU upheld its position as the national union for ten years during the height of apartheid. Yet, just at the time of national transformation, it began to experience critical issues of dissent and organizational debilitation, which eventually led to its closure in 1996, two years after the realization of democracy.[7] Paradoxically, domestic workers lost their organizational platform through SADWU's disbanding during the same year that the Labour Relations Act legalized domestic worker unionization. This closure symbolized not only a critical juncture in domestic workers' unionization, but also a key historical event that continues to shape the emergent context of women's mobilization in the post-apartheid context.[8]

SADSAWU: The Current Context of Unionization

> It is our interest now in the union to build this union because we are
> quite aware that the struggle is still continuing, whatever is the new
> South Africa, nothing has changed.

As this SADSAWU National Office Bearer depicted, the goals central
to domestic workers' unionization in the post-apartheid context reflect the
ongoing struggle to realize democracy in the broader context of South
Africa. Since the 1994 transition, women's collective organizing for domestic workers emerged in April of 2000 with the launch of SADSAWU in Durban. Hester Stephens, SADSAWU's first President, described the vision of
the new organization in her acceptance speech:

> As a woman, as a domestic worker, I made a vow to myself. I said, "One
> day we are going to return even stronger than ever before, and we are
> going to show the world, that domestic workers have got South Africa in
> their hands." And today, in front of you, I want to repeat that vow. We
> are going to empower ourselves. We are going to free ourselves, and we
> are going to look for justice for domestic workers. Justice free from preju-
> dice and the oppression past, justice free from everything.[9]

As suggested by this public speech and reinforced throughout my interactions with SADSAWU, a new identity and established separateness from
SADWU remained central to the organization's foundation.

Although the union had outwardly transformed in the new democracy,
it faced strikingly similar structural challenges because of the very particular
nature of this labor sector. My research with SADSAWU illustrated four main
organizational constraints that limited the collective voice of domestic workers in South Africa: membership recruitment, economic sustainability, overex-
tended leadership and compromised relationships with the national Congress
of South African Trade Unions (COSATU). The following discussion touches
on the most salient aspects of these organizational challenges to establish a
context for domestic workers' union participation in the broader labor and
gender rights movement central to South African's transfiguration.

Breaking down Barriers to Membership

> I was in the union. We were always in the struggle, you know, and peo-
> ple always didn't, you know you were always scared of your white peo-
> ple because when they find out you're in the struggle—even that lady

[employer of 20+ years] didn't know I belongs to the union. Because I never spoke to her about the union, because you know when you always used to tell our employers you belongs to the union, they can chuck you out *straightaway!* They didn't like, so this, for many domestic workers, they are very scared.

Lena's narrative depicts the extreme power imbalance between workers and employers present throughout the liberation struggle that placed severe limitations on union membership. In the post-apartheid context however, Nobantu's case illustrates ongoing structures of power that continue to admonish sectoral mobilization and its perceived threat to the employment context:

That lady [the employer], she is coming from Johannesburg. The other day I was wear a t-shirt from union. She started to be cross for me, she take like that to me [gestures disgust from employer who then grabs her t-shirt], she says, *"never, never, never* wear this t-shirt in my house again!"

Nobantu's employer's attitude illustrates the ongoing struggle for many women employed in the private homes of individuals, where union membership is neither appreciated nor even tolerated. In many instances, women described a very real threat to their ongoing employment if union membership was discovered by the employer.[10] These social location differentials illustrate Nobantu's enormous acts of agency to overcome historical power imbalances by confronting her employer and later contacting the national Department of Labour and SADSAWU for advice on this case. After receiving an endorsement from SADSAWU about her legal right to wear a union t-shirt at work, Nobantu was empowered to leave her job specifically because of the inability to tolerate union membership on the part of her employer:

[Employer stated] "I don't want to hear about union otherwise I'm going to chase him [union representative] away." I said, "I'm ready. You must chase him away." I go to, in the kitchen to wash the dishes. I didn't care about that after that, they talking a nonsense to me about union, that's why I leave that lady like that.[11]

Throughout our interview, Nobantu directly connected a broader commitment to women's empowerment with her own decision to join the union and exercise her own power in the workplace. She shared that the strength and support she acquired as a member of SADSAWU allowed her to confront her employer and eventually leave the oppressive work context.

Nobantu's case illustrates a critical benefit of unionization for domestic workers—the power of collective voice in the face of ongoing structures of domination. Domestic workers clearly developed a sense of collective purpose and support through their union membership, much like unionized labor's more standard function in public workplaces. Through their enrollment in SADSAWU, workers identified a strong knowledge and power base about their rights in the household as centrally connected to broader gender and labor priorities in the new democracy. Like Nobantu, these two domestic workers described the benefits they received as a result of union membership:

> I'm only involved in the union. And then I also like to go to different meetings, like the NGOs and that kind of meetings. And it's also empowering me as a worker, and not sitting here in the room and do nothing for yourself.

> Yes, it is part of the struggle, and to make other workers aware of it, that I can talk to them about the union, because I find the union like a security for myself. You know, if I got a problem, I can go there. So I also want them to be part of that union.

At the time of this research, however, of the over one million women employed as domestic workers in South Africa, estimates suggested that between 1 percent and 4 percent were enrolled in the union. Representational membership is extremely difficult to assess because the sector is not formally documented at a national level in census figures, even though every other general work category is represented. This makes a powerful statement about the extent to which domestic workers are not yet considered a legitimate sector of labor. According to government officials, the perceived *informal* nature of domestic work, as well as the frequency of part-time labor in this sector, confounded the ability to keep accurate records. The enrollment of SADSAWU, based upon paper documents of membership, totaled approximately 10,500. Therefore, using the one million sectoral total, only 1 percent of domestic workers are enrolled in the national union as of 2001. Other estimates suggest a 4 percent enrollment figure, however without national tracking of domestic worker totals, union records alone remain only partial in attaining accurate estimates.[12] Even with this 1 to 4 percent range, however, these figures remain extremely low in comparison to other sectors that maintain at least 80 percent union enrollment figures.

These low levels of union enrollment impede transformation of the household in ways that would alter power relations between workers and employers. This union leader suggested that until the union has a stronger voice, fear of employers' reactions presented a substantial barrier to membership:

> I mean if most of our workers can come out, out of the backyard and stop being scared for their employers then things will come right, but it is only certain people going there.

From an employer's perspective, Marlene illustrated the underlying threats when workers become involved with unionization:

> Who is going to give people time off to go to union meetings and to organise? Because also, people and especially employers, feel threatened by unions because okay, "You are going to become quite cheeky now because you think you know your rights. I don't like you and I don't like you asserting your rights."

Forbidding union membership therefore becomes a further means by which employers can continue to exercise power and reenact former systems of dominance in the household. Furthermore, one of the greatest challenges expressed by the majority of leaders within SADSAWU was workers' reluctance to join the union *until* they needed advocacy services in their employment contexts. As one domestic worker stated when asked if she had considered joining a union: "No because I never, you know when you haven't got a problem you don't worry about these things."

Throughout my work with SADSAWU, membership campaigning remained a top priority for the organization. The very particular nature of this sector, however, presented substantial logistical barriers to recruitment. Access to workers was extremely difficult because of the private households as employment sites. The heightened security consciousness added another layer of physical barriers to accessing domestic workers with the predominance of gated homes and sophisticated technology specifically designed to avoid solicitation. Furthermore, door-to-door campaigning placed workers in vulnerable positions within the power-laden household dynamics of their employment. Recruitment also required a great deal of organizational resources to support transportation costs.

Even though they faced severe obstacles, SADSAWU leaders remained committed to the importance of recruitment and utilized their own resources to attract membership. The most successful strategies of recruitment also illustrate the prevalence of domestic labor in South Africa. Union leaders spent their weekends at public transportation sites in Cape Town's township locations, handing out flyers on rights education and union protection. I frequently traveled with union leaders to participate in this process of recruitment and noticed that during peak hours when live-out domestic workers were returning from their jobs, almost every woman approached accepted a flyer when the leaders announced, "domestic worker rights!" Even men took flyers as leaders suggested, "give it to your mother."[13]

The ongoing commitment to membership recruitment led to the realization of substantial organizational successes, even within the severe structural barriers that dominate this institution. From 2000–2002, SADSAWU increased its membership substantially and opened three additional regional offices throughout the country. Through these acts of agency at both individual and collective levels, leaders continue to expand the organization with a vision of unionization as the only means to transform the working conditions within this sector. SADSAWU remains the only national organization dedicated solely to the rights of domestic workers in the post-apartheid context. Leaders maintained their involvement in SADSAWU and sustained the new organization because of a central belief that unionization was the only viable channel where structural reform of the institution of domestic work could take place in post-apartheid South Africa.

SADSAWU in the Broader Context of Labor

To discuss domestic worker unionization in South Africa's new democracy comprehensively, we must first establish SADSAWU's relationship to the broader labor movement. The national relationship between SADSAWU and the Congress of South African Trade Unions (COSATU) is structured by a history of severe power differentials, dependency and conflict—rooted in a struggle for recognition of domestic labor in the national union. SADSAWU leaders and gender rights activists repeatedly pointed to a male dominated national leadership in COSATU that created a patriarchal organizational culture, in sharp contrast to the goals and membership of SADSAWU. As one historical labor activist described:

> In the trade unions it's still a 50–50. Our union is the only union who's got all woman leadership, most of COSATU's unions, their affiliates it's more men. Since '93, '94 since the new South Africa has been born, they tried to fit women in COSATU's leadership and in the other unions, but

most of the unions don't have women in leadership, because they still got that culture. Women must stay inside and the man must go out.

The 1997 "September Commission Report," organized by COSATU's central executive body identified "building a movement of women workers" as one of its central goals. In line with this agenda the report stated:

We have a vision of a future where women participate equally in the labour market and the world of work without having to face gender barriers or glass ceilings. The trade union movement has a crucial role to play in fighting for justice for women in the workplace, the labour market and society as a whole. We have a vision of economic policies that include women's emancipation. We have a vision of eradicating apartheid oppression and gender oppression in all spheres of society and in the workplace in line with our new Constitution. . . . None of this can be achieved without taking into account the unequal division of labour in the household . . . We have a vision of a trade union movement that plays a central role in empowering women and challenging unequal power relations between men and women—a trade union movement which forges a movement of women workers.

This same report identified women as only 8 percent of COSATU's combined regional and national leadership structures. Therefore, although the "vision" of COSATU impresses gender sensitivity, commitment to the inclusion of domestic workers had not yet taken structural form within COSATU's national leadership. SADSAWU leaders further suggested to COSATU leaders that, "the reason you are ignoring us is because you are employers yourselves," indicating another complexity of power relations surrounding the role of paid household labor, even within progressive sectors of society.

SADSAWU's alignment with COSATU appears ideologically to be the most viable route to engender tangible change within this sector. Yet a formal affiliation between SADSAWU and COSATU remained a source of ongoing debates within upper levels of both organizations' leadership. In a personal conversation "off the record," one executive member of COSATU stated that domestic workers will never be a "viable" union because their dues will remain minimal in comparison to other sectors within the national organization (such as metal workers, mining workers, and textile workers) where dues collection is centrally located. This notion of "viability" is related to the concerns expressed by other COSATU leaders that "domestic workers are by far the most difficult to organize," and that the sector overall is "unproductive." Many COSATU leaders considered domestic worker unionization and possible affiliation more of a liability to the national union than an enhancement of organizational strength. This assumption, however, is based solely on economics. Furthermore, its sharp contrast to COSATU's public commitment to gender rights presents a parallel concern about materializing these rights, as we see in the national context.

Regional support for SADSAWU, however points to a stronger recognition of domestic workers' rights as a central concern for the broader labor movement. SADSAWU's national headquarters are operationally based at the regional Cape Town office of COSATU, which provides substantial structural support for the new organization. This geographic proximity creates valuable spaces to coordinate the interests of domestic workers with larger operations of COSATU, as well as its established "Gender Desk." Through this alignment, the Cape Town regional context provides a model of co-relationship with the possibility for replication at a national level to actualize COSATU's ideological gender commitments. Through the organizational inclusion of the largest sector of working women, the capacities of both parties are strengthened, as well as the position of labor in South Africa's ongoing democratization.

Drawing upon this foundation of the labor movement and SADSAWU's position within it, I turn to an examination of the disjuncture between the macro-level development of social policies and the micro-realities of implementation in the private household.

"OUR RIGHTS ARE ONLY ON PAPER:"[14]
REFORM CHALLENGES

The institution of domestic work embodies the space where South Africa's new democratic public policies most strikingly juxtapose the lived realities of the majority of working women. In the general public discourse, a perception of unrealistic social policies constituted one of the most pervasive criticisms of South Africa's actual transformation. In particular, failed *delivery* of impressive human rights oriented policies remained one of the widest concerns pertaining to transformation across all sectors, as captured by this NGO leader: "The legislation is good. The Constitution is excellent. The intentions are excellent, but the delivery is *quite* terrible." Along with access to rights, domestic workers face an added challenge of *inclusion* in labor policies. Although legislation was established under the ideologies of democratic human rights, because domestic workers are considered "informal labor" they were specifically omitted from key policies introduced as late as 2000. Hettie, a feminist scholar/activist, referred to the "the tragedy of the lost maid" as one of the most severe inequalities in accessing rights in the new democracy.

The following table (Table 6.1) outlines national labor legislation from 1994–2002 that applies to the institution of domestic work. I compare these policies with the number of households that implemented each in their private employment contexts.

Table 6.1: Domestic Work Legislation and Implementation Overview

ACT	YEAR PROMULGATED	REQUIREMENTS	NUMBER OF HOUSEHOLDS PRACTICING ACT (N=40)*
Basic Conditions of Employment, 1993	1994 (Revised in 1997 for further coverage, yet still restricts part-time "contract" workers)	Work Contract	3 (N=75)
		Regular Work Hours	15
		Paid Vacation	23
		Personal Leave	12
		Illness/Maternity Leave	12
		Termination Notice	N/A
Labour Relations Act, 1996	1996	Provides right to organize and unionize	3/20 workers felt open to discuss their union enrollment or interest in the workplace.
Unemployment Insurance Act, 2000	2002	Assures unemployment protection and compensation for short-term leaves, such as maternity	N/A (promulgated in April 2002)
Skills Development Act, 1998	1999	Increase skill training to address the 80% semi-skilled or unskilled sectors of the national working population	**Domestic Workers not covered**
Domestic Worker Sectoral Determination, 2001	2002	Set minimum wage and conditions of employment specific to this sector.	N/A (promulgated in September 2002)
Occupational Injury and Disease Act, 1993	1994	Protection for job injuries and long term illnesses as a result of work environments	**Domestic Workers not covered**
Employment Equity Act, 1998	1999	Elimination of discrimination in hiring practices and work standards	**Domestic Workers not covered**

=Number of households out of 40 (employers and workers) who implemented the specific above requirements.

This summary explains why such policies are perceived as "only on paper" by workers. Most striking is the 1994 requirement of work contracts through the Basic Conditions of Employment Act, which was the first to formalize domestic work as a protected sector within the democratic legislation. Yet of the 40 work contexts studied in depth, coupled with 25 additional worker participants in focus groups and observations (total N=75), only *three* utilized these contracts. Notably, these three cases were two union leaders (who had initiated the contract in their workplace) and the Director of an employers' agency that sold domestic work contracts. Even members of parliament, Gender Commissioners, and feminist scholars found the use of a contract extremely difficult and avoided its implementation in their own employment of workers, though most knew that doing so was technically in violation of the law.

Some employers attributed their resistance (and at times admitted guilt) about not using a work contract to language barriers that would make such negotiations extremely challenging. Others identified that they had obtained a contract, but had not reviewed it with their workers. Even though domestic workers performed extremely intimate labor, employers asserted that communication remained a prominent barrier to implementation. One feminist stated that she found workers resistant to signing a contract because it was atypical to both "their culture" and the long history of "casual labor" in this sector. In this case, the employer felt that presenting a formal contract would make her domestic worker feel uncomfortable and skeptical about the overall job. Interestingly, another worker who experienced an ideal, very positive work environment also resisted the formalization of her employment through a written contract, which she perceived as binding. She preferred the "silent agreement" she maintained with her employer stating, "If I have a contract, I will be the first one to break it." The work contract was one of the most widely discussed issues in relation to all of the legislative requirements that applied to domestic workers at the time of this study. Although employers recognized the legal requirements of the Basic Conditions of Employment Act, the cultural shift required to formalize this sector remained a difficult leap for most employers.

A related limitation that severely impacts this sector is that the Basic Conditions of Employment Act, while comprehensive in scope, covers only *full-time* workers. Therefore, domestic workers employed as "chars" in several different work contexts, totaling well over a 50-hour work week, do not qualify for coverage because their relationship with each employer is considered part-time. This increased casualization of domestic labor allows employers to circumvent protection when they hire workers on a part-time "contract" basis. Therefore, the legislation itself affords substantial loopholes for this particular sector of workers. As women employed as domestic workers are the lowest paid and often most exploited sector in the country, the extent to which such democratic labor policies transcend power relations in the household remains a serious obstacle. *Access* to rights, therefore embodies one of the greatest challenges in the post-apartheid context of nation building. While a formal analysis of each policy's application and subsequent complications in the domestic work context is beyond the scope of this study,[15] the structures and power relations that maintain this "gap" between democratic values and lived realities of domestic workers remains central to understanding South Africa's complex path to social change.

"Our Culture is 20 Years Behind the Constitution:"[16] *Addressing the Access Gap*

As I compared democratic policies to domestic workers' daily lives, I was particularly interested in why this sector remained so unable to access labor and gender rights, even though it comprised the largest sector of working women. First, as I addressed in prior chapters, the data repeatedly illustrated that social inequality remains so deeply embedded that employers maintain positions of power, particularly in the context of a 40 percent unemployment rate. The power asymmetries in the workplace render policy inconsequential. From a structural level, to date no measures of compliance are in place to assure that employers follow labor regulations. This allows employers to "choose" to a greater extent whether or not to implement legislation that is officially mandated in all domestic work contexts. The following domestic workers captured the dominance of social privilege over policy when asked about the extent of compliance to labor regulations in their own homes:

> Some of the employers, they do know about the laws. Some of the employers, they got their own laws. They got their own laws from the apartheid. They don't take no notice for this new laws. *Maar* [but] I think the government must force this people, employers on this laws, you know, we must force them. They don't force them—they're not strict on them.

> She [employer] take out the laws that suit her from the labour law, but when I try to do that, not try, when I *said*, "You know the law said so." Then there's a fight because I said, "I know my rights" but then there's a fight. It's always a fight.

Power and privilege facilitate a normalcy about employers' ignorance in relations to employment standards mandated in the new labor legislation. The following employer interview excerpt captures this socially acceptable lack of awareness:

> [*You've heard about the government changes around domestic workers in terms of implementing the minimum wage and the basic conditions of employment, what do you think about those generally?*]

> Well you know, I never, I don't even know what they are, I don't even know what the minimum wage is, do you know what it is?

After employing the same woman for over 18 years, Isobel remained completely unaware of all labor legislation that applied to her domestic worker. In Zandile's case, her (male) employer was fully aware of his violation because of his own profession as a lawyer, yet held on to his position of social power by determining *when* he would implement the legal requirements, even though he recognized that he technically could go to court:

> He takes the paper [on domestic worker rights] and read a little bit, after that he said, "Mildred,[17] one day I sit down with you and I must talk because I am a lawyer. I don't want to go to court because I feel you put me in court because I know I am wrong." I said, "Good if you know you are wrong."

These narratives reveal a second component of employers' unwillingness to comply with labor legislation in the domestic work sector. The nature of the work, while formalized at a policy level, remains deeply "informalized" in the ongoing culture and social norms that construct everyday social relations. The colonial mentality that structured South Africa for 350 years was built upon domestic work as a relationship of servitude. With these deeply embedded power relations, social positions were assumed. Therefore, formalizing the relationship on paper was antithetical to colonialism. This entrenchment of positionality throughout the colonial history dominates the existing collective social perception of domestic work. Thus, acknowledging and granting protection to this sector through formal processes that structure other public occupations remained an enormous barrier to the transformation of the institution.

Last, some participants suggested that the delicate nature of South Africa's new governance was partly related to the lack of accountability measures in place. In other words, the post-Mandela governance received widespread criticism, particularly about its inability to deliver the promises of the Reconstruction and Development Programme (RDP) of 1994. Ironically, even though criticisms of the new government were often associated with the creation of policy with "no teeth," it was also widely acknowledged that the enforcement of labor legislation in private homes would lead to an uproar, particularly among the privileged sector of the population.

While economic power is largely maintained in the white population, workers suggested that policy makers themselves, the "newly elite formerly disadvantaged groups," also employ domestic workers and therefore fail to prioritize compliance measures because of the potential felt impact in their own lives. Another central contradiction explains the challenges of domestic workers' access to rights. Because the overarching Constitution continues to protect the private home, under the current legislation, government is unable to monitor compliance in household employment contexts. As workers pointed out, however, during the apartheid era government *required* employers to "register" all domestic workers through pass laws. In order to assure compliance, police also regularly inspected households to enforce racial segregation policies in private spaces. As Gertrude, a white employer, recalled, "In the old days, we used to *queue up* to register our domestics." Some workers suggested that a return to this type of strict monitoring would assure fair labor practices in line with new legislation:

> I think if they [government] could put it very strict, make it very strict, like come around and see what, you know, like inspectors come and see that you got a contract like that at your workplace . . . Because the white people don't take it serious, or maybe *we* don't take it serious.

Whose responsibility is it to assure that policy is practiced? Workers demonstrated enormous agency in some contexts to pressure employers to enact at least the Basic Conditions of Employment Act. Yet social power remains so institutionalized that employers could systematically disregard policy in their own homes. These power differentials between workers and employers were reinforced at a structural level as government colluded with employer privilege and systematically ignored the pervasive lack of compliance in this particular work sector. In personal interviews, even parliamentarians identified compliance as the most delicate aspect of new labor legislation within the domestic work sector. Perhaps the new government's willingness *not* to interfere in the private home—thereby assuring the ongoing privilege of paid domestic labor for those sectors of the population that enjoy social power—is one way to assure the "peaceful" transformation. Employers feel minimal change in their everyday personal lives, even

Figure 6.1: Triangulated Relationships and Social Power

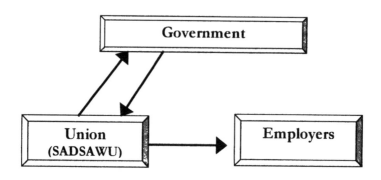

This diagram provides an overview of the relationships among parties invested in the process of domestic labor policy reform. Government and unions participate in a two-way communication process such that unions pressure government for ongoing change and accountability and government responds to union activism to some degree through policy reform. The relationship of accountability from government to domestic work employers is currently non-existent in South Africa because no measures of compliance are in place. Unions are the only organized body to pressure employers to enact policy in the work contexts. SADSAWU's low levels of enrollment as a young institution and lack of formal ties to COSATU result in less organizational influence on employers. Therefore, in order to implement labor policy within domestic work contexts, the relationship between government and employers must be enacted such that employers who maintain social power are held accountable to legislative standards in a more formal manner.

though the entire public governance structure has transformed. In this regard, domestic workers assuage the conflicts of transition by providing a security and continuity in the everyday lives of privileged sectors of the population. The disjuncture between policy and practice can be further understood through the following model (Figure 6.1) which portrays the triangulated relationships that limit employer compliance and worker access to labor rights.

Based upon the context of domestic workers' unionization, the legislative framework established for this sector, and the social relations that create conditions of noncompliance as outlined above, this chapter now shifts to models of collective organization by examining a pivotal case study of policy change to protect the institution of domestic work. This remarkable "success story" demonstrates possibilities for both legislative reform and broader social change initiated by women "on the ground" to transform the conditions of their own lives.

ORGANIZING ACROSS DIVIDES: THE UNEMPLOYMENT INSURANCE FUND

During this study's fieldwork, the union initiated reform of a major national social security policy to provide a safety net for domestic workers during periods of unemployment. In the former apartheid framework, social security remained unavailable to the majority of South Africa's (black and coloured) population. The activist work of the domestic workers' union—in collaboration with local NGOs and international supporters—transformed national labor policy from continued exclusion of this sector to full coverage in the Unemployment Insurance Fund (UIF) Act, widely viewed as the most critical benefit within the new national social security framework. This victory marked critical progress in both the formal recognition of the sector as well as the success of domestic workers' engagement with government as an active civil society organization.

The inclusion of domestic workers in UIF benefits remained under investigation within government structures from 1991–2001.[18] Domestic workers in the former SADWU leadership campaigned for full access to UIF benefits throughout this period, emphasising their heightened need for protective social insurance because of frequent retrenchments and low wages. Because of the pervasive challenges to implementation in this sector (as seen with the BCEA), government policy makers were particularly aware of the potential for severe criticisms by crafting another policy that could not assure compliance and access for workers. Since the UIF bill was formally under revision, in both 1997 and 2000, government responded to domestic workers' request on the status of their inclusion in the legislation by identifying a need for an additional 18 months to investigate the administrative implications of the recommendations of past research. In 2001, a final draft UIF bill was presented to the Labour Portfolio Committee by the Department of Labour.[19] This third draft again specifically *excluded* domestic workers and sought another 18 months to investigate the administrative challenges involved with this sector. The next step of the legislative process included public hearings where invested parties within civil society presented their comments to the Portfolio Committee in order to influence the legislation—a process which models the inclusive nature of democracy and citizenship since the 1994 transformation. Drawing upon this model of active civil society engagement with policy reform, domestic workers established a central role in ultimately crafting new labour legislation.

Building Gender Alliances

The successful reform of labor policy to include domestic workers provides a framework for analyzing models of social change, particularly within the context of ongoing nation transition. In order to impact change as a collective civil society platform, SADSAWU joined a coalition formed by the governmental Commission on Gender Equality, a human rights task force designed in 1996 as a central body in the democracy building period. This collective became known as the Gender Monitoring and Advocacy Coalition for the Unemployment Insurance Fund (GMAC-UIF). The alliance consisted of four predominant NGOs (with both gender and human rights emphases) and representation from COSATU's national Parliamentary Office. These organizational bodies merged through identification of similar platforms in response to government's exclusion of domestic workers in the announced UIF legislation. In order to strengthen participation in the newly open parliamentary process of "public submissions" on draft policy documents, the coalition centered its work on strengthening the collective submissions of each organization while co-creating a consistent platform on gender and labor rights concerns. Organizational members of the GMAC-UIF aligned with Labour and SADSAWU to present 11 submissions that clearly demonstrated the unconstitutional and discriminatory nature of the exclusion of domestic workers from social security benefits guaranteed in the new democracy. Government's contradictory social security philosophy—to protect the poorest of the poor—and its practice of excluding the most vulnerable sector of the population from unemployment insurance benefits appeared as central arguments in every GMAC-UIF submission.

The Commission on Gender Equality (CGE) led the collaboration building process from its particular position of power within the new democratic framework. As a governmental "monitoring body," the CGE assumes a powerful role as part of the broader national *Gender Machinery* in collaboration with "The Office on the Status of Women" and "The Committee on the Quality of Life and Status of Women." The rationale for establishing the CGE in the new democracy is outlined as follows:

> The mammoth challenge of transforming gender relations in South Africa requires a dedicated focus. The concept of gender equality is a relatively new one in South Africa and many African countries. Even in the older democracies of the world, issues of women's rights and gender equality have only recently taken shape. Even the notion that women's rights are human rights only found its way into the international human rights agenda and jurisprudence in 1993. Focus on gender equality thus

requires that an institution, such as ours, be specifically tasked with this mandate. Otherwise, danger exists that in an all-embracing human rights institution, issues of gender equality may fall into the cracks. The CGE exists because South Africans, when writing their Constitution, insisted that such an institution be established. But it is also there to ensure that gender issues are visible and integrated in the day to day policy and practice of state and non-state institutions. Until gender equality is a way of life in South Africa, the mandate of the Commission on Gender Equality remains.[20]

The CGE therefore works within government structures to a certain degree. Yet, its primary mandate is as a monitoring body, holding the state as well as private institutions accountable to supporting gender equality as an integral component of democratization. This model is both innovative and exemplary of the public level of gender transformation we see in South Africa. The CGE's coalition leadership on the UIF campaign actualized democracy by creating a space where civil society could actively engage with the state and collectively influence policy change.

The UIF policy reform established a new framework for the coalition model practiced by CGE. With the integral membership of SADSAWU, domestic workers were afforded a pivotal space to network with other NGOs who were taking up their cause. SADSAWU's presence as an equal party in the coalition, in turn, informed NGOs about the practical realities of policy decisions in ways otherwise unavailable had domestic workers not been present at the decision-making table to share their lived experiences. In a personal interview, Fatima Seedat, Director of the Coalition and leader within the Commission on Gender Equality, described her own perceptions of the innovative success of this model. As a result of the central inclusion of domestic workers, this particular coalition allowed Ms. Seedat to develop a heightened awareness of the impact of her work in ways she had formerly not considered, even in her role as a gender expert. The direct representation of domestic worker union leaders on the GMAC-UIF forced other gender activists to ask, "What are we actually doing this for?" and "Why are we here?" on a regular basis.

SADSAWU also benefited extensively through its involvement with GMAC-UIF. Their alignment with a collective of organizations with wider networks, grounded histories as human rights advocates, further lobbying experience, and larger resource bases positioned SADSAWU more powerfully when its parliamentary submission was backed by ten others who had outlined the same concerns and suggestions for reform. In a sense, government was forced to take domestic workers seriously once they were aligned with many of the most powerful representatives of civil society. Secondly, the

GMAC-UIF provided resources (such as buses for domestic workers to join the parliamentary process and opportunities for networking with news reporters) that SADSAWU was unable to afford independently at the time. This resulted in a much more public campaign, bringing broader awareness of domestic workers' rights as *human rights*. At an ideological level, the alignment of women's organizations with NGOs created a space where difference was very much recognized, valued and applied to inform policy reform and social change through the diverse yet powerful representation of civil society.

Transforming State Processes

We ask you to think seriously about domestic workers. You know ever since this slavery started in this country, domestic workers were there. We have been doing the work for all of you, yet when it comes to laws, there is just no way it can be extended to domestic workers ... We find it most problematic that the bill seeks to include the poor while overlooking the poorest of the poor, the domestic worker ... We feel the unemployment insurance is discriminating against us as women ... We see women that are working for 20 years. We see them walking in the streets because there is no unemployment benefits for them. There is no pension fund for them ... I am asking you this morning, listen with your heart to the domestic worker ... think of your mothers because many of you were raised by domestic workers working for you while you are here now ... I see also another person that has been with us in this struggle for so long, Comrade Olifant. He is actually hiding himself today, [broad laughter] but he has been there with us. And I am asking you this morning, yes we may laugh about it, but in here it is not nice. Looking at a domestic worker, facing them daily in my office, I am telling them I am sorry you cannot claim benefits. There is nothing for you. A poor worker leaving the employer with the R100 in her hand after twenty-four years and the employer said, "You have been such a good worker" and the worker come in with tears in her eyes and, "What can I do?" Must I send that worker to you so that you can answer, "I am sorry there is no unemployment benefit for you." I am asking you this morning, please consider the domestic workers ... If it were not for them in your houses, you would not have been here today. If it were not for domestic workers working for the people of parliament there would be no parliament today. If it were not for the domestic workers working for the factory boss, there would be no factory today, because they need us to run their houses while they are building the economy of the country. So they call us non-productive, but if we decide on a Monday morning we are not turning up for work, we will all be helpless. So please consider the domestic workers. You are going to investigate and investigate, you will find nothing new, you will find the same problems, you will find the same story. But we are asking you to extend the unemployment fund to domestic workers. Do not delay. The time is now. Thank you for listening to me this morning. I appreciate it and I hope that you will *not*

sleep comfortably tonight because you will be thinking about domestic
workers. I thank you.

—Myrtle Witbooi, SADSAWU General Secretary; Parliamentary Public
Submission in Cape Town Legislative Chambers, March 2001.

The above public submission by SADSAWU in the national legislative
parliamentary chambers shaped the future direction of the unemployment
insurance fund policy and initiated a message repeated by all GMAC-UIF
members throughout a full day of public hearings. As a result of this collective
civil society voice, less than one week after these public hearings, government
announced that the Unemployment Insurance Act would be extended to cover
all domestic workers, acknowledging that they composed the largest sector of
working women in the country. Many NGO leaders and political analysts
suggested that this bold change in government policy was a direct result of the
pressure from civil society and specifically the GMAC-UIF addresses.

Figure 6.2. Hester Stephens, SADSAWU President, reads press statement to Salie
Manie, National Labour Portfolio Committee Chair outside Parliamentary Chambers in Cape Town. Also pictured (left to right) Pumla Mncayi, Ntombizanele Felicia Msila, and Myrtle Witbooi (SADSAWU General Secretary). Photograph by
author.

Of all of the public submissions, SADSAWU's was clearly the most direct and challenging, with a distinct emotional appeal for parliamentarians to consider their "mothers" on this policy. SADSAWU also established a strong argument through the contribution of domestic workers to the economy as well as the government itself. By calling parliamentarians to task on their own employment of domestic workers, this submission pulled the private lives of government leaders into the public decision-making space. The nervous laughter in the room—particularly as a leading labor activist and prominent Member of Parliament was recognized as formerly being part of the labor struggle—personified the nature of tension around the formalization of this sector. Although domestic workers has been included in other labor legislation, the pervasive contradictions of implementation in the private households (even among government MPs themselves) were publicly challenged in an unprecedented way through SADSAWU's address. According to the perspective of SADSAWU leaders, this public submission within Parliamentary Chambers—a structure which was reserved for "whites only" throughout apartheid—fostered a belief that, "Now we are on the map," as a legitimate organization and activist lobbying group. Based upon the consequences of this Parliamentary address, women felt as if government could no longer ignore domestic workers' rights when crafting protective labor policies.

International Alliances

A shared reference to international conventions adopted by South Africa became a critical emphasis within the collective work of the GMAC-UIF. The adopted resolutions of the Conference on the Elimination of All Forms of Discrimination against Women (CEDAW) served as a central reference point and as a tool to hold the state accountable to its national commitment to gender rights. The Black Sash, for example, a human rights organization and historically progressive anti-apartheid women's rights group, stated the following in their submission on the exclusion of domestic workers in the UIF:

> It is unfortunate that neither international law nor the recommendation of the task team [referring to past research that advocated inclusion of domestic workers in the UIF] has been followed. References in international law prohibiting this type of practice are numerous. In particular, the practice contravenes the Convention of the Elimination of All Forms of Discrimination Against Women (CEDAW), of which South Africa is a signatory. Article 11 of CEDAW provides that "States Parties shall take all appropriate measures to eliminate discrimination against women in the field of employment, in particular, the right to social security, particularly in cases of . . . unemployment, sickness, invalidity, old age and

any other incapacity to work" [Article 11(1)(e)] . . . There has been a clear trend in recent years amongst international jurisdictions to bring casual workers and workers in the informal sectors within the ambit of more formal employment legislation. This trend has been brought about in recognition of the principle established under international law that to exclude them amounts to unfair discrimination. We submit that the exclusion of domestic workers from UIF benefits is in clear contradiction of international law, is at odds with accepted international practice and for all of these reasons, as well as the reasons outlined above, is unfair discrimination.

By referencing international conventions, such as CEDAW, the state's obligation to the international community was reinforced by civil society—making the contradiction between international law and practice strikingly clear. The Black Sash's reference to international documents illuminated the gendered discrimination inherent in the exclusion of domestic workers from critical social security legislation. It also provided a model of alliance among civil society to activate social change by drawing upon international documents adopted by the state.

This approach can be adapted to establish a model for further international linkages that would engender change in the global institution of domestic labor. If the global community were to align as GMAC-UIF did, such collaborative efforts would heighten impact at the local level. In the GMAC-UIF model, the inclusion of international women's rights agreements strengthened civil society submissions and activated policy change at the state level. As we see in this case, the power of drawing upon international documents holds further potential for change than civil society influence alone. Therefore, the alignment of international structures, such as unions, women's rights organizations and development agencies, could similarly act as a collective to pressure individual states to reform the context of domestic work. Because state institutions hold the greatest power to change internal standards in relation to domestic work, assuring accountability from international organizations would enhance the likelihood of change at the local level. Utilizing the success of GMAC-UIF, an international model to activate change in the global institution of domestic work is conceptualized in Figure 6.3.

Drawing upon this framework, I suggest that the alignment of domestic workers is also critical to influencing change at the global level. At the time of this study, cross-national forums for collaboration among domestic workers were minimal, particularly because of the limited resource pools and the isolated nature of the work itself. Of the 40 women workers interviewed in various contexts, only *one* mentioned an awareness

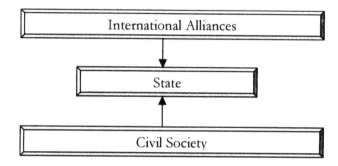

Figure 6.3: International Alliances

of domestic work as a global institution outside of the South African context—which illustrates the long path to transnational linkages within this sector. The national union, however, has expanded its international linkages and aligned with broader labor movements to "tell the story" of domestic work in South Africa and to gain the support of broader bodies that continue to hold the South African government accountable to this sector. These alignments are enhanced by globalization as organizations like SADSAWU benefit from the interconnectedness that is made available through technology and its compression of temporal and spatial relations.

The other critical level of global change involves the commitment of women's and human rights organizations to prioritize domestic work. If a transnational collective were established to serve as an umbrella body (like the GMAC-UIF), its ability to expose the injustices in this sector could influence change at a number of levels. The establishment of these networks offers enormous potential to align strategically with international domestic workers' organizations and dramatically alter the material conditions of workers' lives. While at some level this has the potential to heighten social location differentials between domestic worker unions and transnational rights organizations, as the GMAC-UIF model demonstrates, women in alignment from diverse social locations also affords much greater strength to activate change. The enactment of this model would require a collective recognition of the SADSAWU motto, "Women will not be free until domestic workers are free!" To realize this vision, international bodies will similarly have to prioritize the transnational case of domestic labor as a critical concern. This involves transcending race, economic and geographic divisions *within* the global women's movement. By transforming the institution of domestic labor, however, the broader gender movement also benefits from the recognition of the central contribution of women in this sector.

WOMEN SPEAK ON TRANSFORMATION[21]

We have explored three levels of social change that most directly impact domestic labor since South Africa's transformation: unionization, democratic policy implementation, and collective gender activism. In this final analytic section, I would like to close this chapter with the voices of South African women who spoke to me about transformation on a number of levels. I began this research journey by asking, "To what extent has the institution of domestic labor changed in South Africa's new democracy?" Underlying this question, I was seeking to understand what "change" would look like in the lives of women in South Africa. And overarching this inquiry—what could the rest of the world learn from women who have survived apartheid and continue to actively engage in ongoing transformation? Much of South Africa's success, as well as the ongoing transformation of domestic labor, has involved transnational organizational alignment, policy reform, and unionization, as we have discussed. At the same time, throughout this research I was particularly struck by participants who shared moments of change in everyday life as enactments of the possibility for broader transformation. When I work with students who are introduced to the world's inequalities and are subsequently left feeling paralyzed to influence change, I often provide reflections from these participants to illustrate the dialectic nature of change at the micro and global level. Over the course of ten years of work in South Africa, I found that these pieces do merge in particularly powerful ways. I suggest that these interconnected levels of change hold the possibility to realize democracy in South Africa.

As evident throughout this research, apartheid still exists in the everyday experiences of the majority of South Africans. The relative newness of the transition and the enormity of the task can be attributed to the pervasive lag we see between public and private democracy. At the same time, participants repeatedly expressed hope toward ongoing transformation and improved social conditions that would transcend this divide. Many participants in this study looked to future generations who would fully realize the impact of transformation. Certainly the collection of nations continuing to engage in post-conflict reconstruction illustrates similar realities about the temporal lag between policy implementation and felt change in the lives of those most severely disenfranchised. Therefore, South Africa faces the *daily* task of transformation which proves to be, in many regards, much more challenging than the public victories of 1994.

And as this research repeatedly illustrates, apartheid inequalities underlie and encompass the institution of domestic work. Therefore, as participants across all sectors confirmed, this institution presents one of the sharpest challenges to change. Yet those most marginalized within this institution repeatedly resisted its dominant structure that reproduced social inequalities embedded throughout apartheid. Each of my interviews with domestic workers depicted strong representations of women's agency in two forms: direct challenges to the work environment and joining the union to collectively influence change. In their work relationships, women described acts of agency in their approach to employers, much like those identified in former research on domestic labor such as confrontation, mockery and cajolery (Cock 1980; Rollins 1985; Romero 1992; Chang 2000). In most instances, workers felt that their ability to challenge employers resulted in some level of success in changing the conditions of their daily experiences.

In the following narrative, Thandi's account of challenging her employer's behavior through her direct acknowledgement of the power differentials at play in the underlying relationship particularly stood out as a captivating act of agency. After her employer exerted particularly harsh verbal aggression about something that was "missing" in the household, Thandi responded as follows:

> I say to her, "I don't want to talk at the back of you. I like to work in peace and I double say so, *I like to work in peace*." And I told her, "The care I give your baby is more than the care I give my one, my children. I haven't got time for my children, but I've got time for your little one." So I don't want myself to be upset. I'm so very very cross and I see she feels very sorry . . . I say, "No, I don't like that."

Thandi's confrontation resulted in movements toward more equality within her work context based upon her own agency in both challenging her employer and asserting her expectations in the workplace. Futhermore, Thandi's action influenced other domestic workers to similarly assert their own power to reshape their working environments.

Acts of agency at the group and organization levels are also central to the process of motivating ongoing change. At times, the union, for example, further supported individual acts of agency by providing education on working rights and organizational strength to support workers' individual decisions. In other instances, organizational acts of agency were motivated by workers' influence on union leaders.

Table 6.2 summarizes the critical acts of agency that emerged from this research. As it details, many of the acts of agency directed at particular areas of concern were addressed at both the individual and group level, which illustrates the growing strength of complementary initiatives to actualize change in this sector.

Table 6.2: Domestic Workers' Acts of Agency

Summary of Acts of Agency at the Individual and Collective Level		
Act of Agency	Individual Level	Collective Level
Policy change	• Joining union • Participation in protests and union lobbying	• SADSAWU alignment with women's organizations, NGOs, & human rights agencies
Policy implementation	• Initiating compliance with labor policy such as the work contract requirement and appropriate termination notice	• SADSAWU and other human rights organizations provide training to workers on rights and methods of approaching employers to access rights. • CCMA government process for dispute resolution
Minimum wage compliance	• Demanding fair living wage	• SADSAWU's lobbying government for release of the minimum wage and working condition standards
Refusal to perform certain tasks requested by employers	• Defining and maintaining boundaries regarding intimacy of labor • Denying employer requests during designated "off hours"	
Demanding equitable treatment in the workplace	• Joining union to build knowledge of rights • Contacting CCMA for unfair dismissals and dispute resolution • Identifying important needs and assuring they are met in the workplace • Demanding details of pension coverage • Assuring a livable space for workers that "live-in" • Demanding "peace" in the workplace • Asking for schedule flexibility	• SADSAWU—structural support through case management and dispute resolution work between workers and employers • Government policy revisions and promulgation providing a "back bone" for advocacy and mandating compliance

Table 6.2: Domestic Workers' Acts of Agency (Continued)		
Summary of Acts of Agency at theIndividual and Collective Level (continued)		
Act of Agency	Individual Level	Collective Level
Openly stating need for romance, particularly in live-in contexts	• Confronting married women employers on the inequity of experience and the inherent need for intimacy for both workers as well as employers	
Utilizing emotions and personal power through knowledge of intimate lives of employers	• Approaching employer for work requests at times when her emotions are best in order for a more optimal outcome • Becoming silent • Acting "cheeky" • Demonstrating an "attitude" because of awareness of rights • Wearing a union t-shirt • Abandoning the job, particularly when employers are most in need (re: childcare)	
Establishing independence	• Talking with other domestic workers, advocates, & union leaders to gain perspective and insight on personal work context	
Theft (as a means of survival)	• Overstepping boundaries to deal with massive economic inequality • Taking food	
Establishing support structures	• Talking with other domestic workers, advocates, & union leaders to gain perspective and insight on personal work context	• Support Structures in place: SADSAWU & the Black Sash Advice Offices • The GMAC-UIF Alliance

Table 6.2 illustrates the extent of change realized in the context of domestic work. Participants in each sector (including employers and experts) also noted that the work of transformation was ongoing and therefore highlighted the following critical areas for further development: 1) change at the macro and policy levels; 2) change at the social and cultural level; and 3) change at the individual level. Each of these themes is taken up in this final section to offer perspectives on social change from those who have lived through the apartheid history and democratic transition.

Participants continually pointed to the complexities of *accessing* rights that are provided in the impressive legislation of the newly democratic nation. Therefore, even though women's rights had been realized to a great extent "on paper," the majority of participants identified the need for continual change and further pressure on government to maintain its commitments to democracy. This activist shared her vision for ongoing social change:

> I think we ought to put pressure on the women's desk in parliament. I think the pressure has got to come from the unions and I think domestic workers have to overcome divisions of race within the unions . . . But I think that is where the pressure, from human rights groups, women's groups, pressure on government, like people say, we are the voters, we are not going to vote for you, or we will vote for the person who takes up our issues. We shouldn't go with political loyalty. But I think you know the ANC is still the party of the struggle and they have been the ones to put in place the legislation, albeit legislation that cannot be implemented because you don't have the political will or the person power to police it.

While change at the structural level has been implemented, its limitations are a result of the rigid nature of power inequalities and an embedded colonial culture that continues to define social relations. Therefore, although impressive policies have been put in place, changing individual mindsets in ways that value the contributions of this sector remained the most challenging aspect of transformation for many participants, as this feminist employer suggested:

> I don't see anything else happening unless you know the demand for domestic workers outstrips the supply, or the state really takes seriously its commitment to domestic workers and for the most vulnerable sectors of the labor market, farm workers, etc., migrants, refugees. I don't see the situation changing much. I think it will still come down to individuals' consciousness, which is, you know, a very shaky thing to go by.

Another employer identified that this change would have to occur within power groups in "small ways" in order to impact change in the institution of domestic work:

> The things that go into life is really the small things . . . It's essentially about can you show compassion even, I mean how do you? . . . Would you go to your domestic worker's house? Are you interested to see where that person lives? Do you ever ask how many children do you have? Do you have an actual interest in the life that this person has outside of your home or do you just assume that this person gets subsumed into your family, into whatever your world is about?

In this study, only two employers had visited the homes of their workers. Not surprisingly these women were both coloured feminist activists, much different than the more traditional madams who told me, "we just don't go there" when asked if they had visited their workers' homes. Because of the very particular nature of domestic work and its history in South Africa, effective change for this sector requires engagement at the micro-level, reinforced by a cultural shift as well as macro-level structural transformation.

While this task remains one of the most challenging and difficult to measure, five workers did point to felt change in their own experience post-apartheid:

> I see a change. It won't be overnight, but step by step . . . We grew up— you must have your own plate, you must have you own glasses. So to us, to me it really, it's a shock because even to speak in the car, at that time I must sit behind you just because you are white.

A "newly elite" black employer further identified the importance of change at the micro-household relationship level in ways that would involve a reconfiguration of household responsibility:

> It really has to start at home, people have to shift responsibility for who takes care of their kids. Who should make them free? But it starts in the family and if you can't handle your husband and your kids and your family, I mean those are the things you are sending out to oppress other people.

These changes, albeit at the micro-level of relations, did foster a sense among workers that relations were changing, "little by little." Of the five workers that had experienced change, their reflections mirrored this relationship level we see in the above narratives. At the same time, however, domestic workers frequently articulated clear visions about the ongoing work of democratizing the household at the structural level.

Domestic Workers On Change

Finally, let us turn to the domestic worker interviews. Each participant in this study was asked, "If you could talk to the government about the changes needed for domestic workers, what would you say?" From the responses to all questions, themes emerged regarding the qualities of an ideal employer, the characteristics of reformed work contexts and structural changes that would most positively impact workers' lives. In order to best convey the depth of responses to this question, the following table (Table 6.3) summarizes workers' perspectives about the most critical components of envisioned change.

Throughout my interviews with domestic workers, each participant identified clear visions of the necessary changes to democratize household labor in alignment with the national restructuring. While the work contexts themselves were more often described in terms of articulating the ideal employer or conditions of the job, workers also clearly pointed to needed structural and socio-cultural changes that represented a shared perception that real change in this deeply embedded historical tradition would need to be enacted at multiple levels. In other words, a "nice madam" or changing weekend work schedules, while beneficial, was also recognized as only one marginal level of change.

Many workers pointed to men's roles as a central source of needed transformation. Some even suggested that if men would share in the household responsibility, the need for paid domestic work at the national level would be greatly reduced. Workers referred both to men's roles in their own families (often described as being "steeped in tradition") and to the roles of the men in the families for which they worked as collectively important to change. Furthermore, some participants contended that the inability to change patriarchy remained the most significant challenge to transformation.

Workers frequently demonstrated an awareness of the historical conditions and their subsequent residue on limiting access to other labor opportunities outside of domestic work. Education, for example, often emerged as a central opportunity for future change that would allow women to move out of the institution. These data illustrate two distinct perspectives on change in the institution of domestic labor: either progressive reform of the institution or the creation of support structures (such as training and education) that would facilitate women's movement from this sector into other fields. Importantly, when asked about the extent to

Table 6.3: Domestic Workers Speak on Reform

Level of Change	Suggested Reform	Narrative Examples
Individual / Worker	Further education needed/skill building	"I need to still do other things, but my worry is I'm not educated, my standard [grade completed] is very low, but I still need to do something better."
Individual / Employer	Most desirable individual traits of employers identified by workers	• Pleasant "happy" nature • Respect for worker • Appreciation of labor contributed by domestic worker • Honest, "straightforward" (particularly re: work issues) • Financially support domestic worker and family by increasing salary and providing bonuses for special needs • Sharing of household resources, particularly food
Work Context	Increased salary/fair living wages	"I think all we need is money, money for living, you can't survive without."
	Reasonable work hours/schedule flexibility	"I start at half past 6 [A.M.] and then I go sometimes to 11 o'clock [P.M.]. It's *long* hours."
	Discussion of expectations from the beginning of the work relationship	"You must sit down and make these things [conditions of work and expectations] clear from the very beginning and treat me with respect and I'll treat you with respect."
	More flexibility with workers' childcare needs and the ability to have children stay with workers in live-in contexts	"We are giving them a better life because they got children. [We] look after the children as they stay at work . . . We also need a better life. We also need our children to come be with us."

Table 6.3: Domestic Workers Speak on Reform (continued)

Level of Change	Suggested Reform	Narrative Examples
Cultural	Changing men's socialization/shared participation in household labor	"We have to bring up the children and the man never shared the domestic work with his wife or girlfriend, he just believe that you are there to do all the dirty work, whatever and that is why we feel it is time that we as women must stand up for our rights and also be part of the liberation of the country, be part of society, be part of leadership."
Structural Government	Monitoring of fair labor standards in the work context	"They must give us a living wage and better conditions and the employers must stick to the rules of the country when it comes to domestic workers."
	Prioritize needs of the most vulnerable sector of the population in alignment with democratic vision	"Domestic workers lose their jobs, they're struggling, they're hungry, they're unemployed. The government don't look after them. The government is busy to buy new planes and people are outside, they've got no houses." "These people [government] must come to the grassroots level. We can do something there. They must [sometimes] leave that parliament."

which they would encourage other women to become domestic workers, *all* respondents indicated that they would in no way encourage others to do so. Thus the most ideal process of reform would enact macro-level economic restructuring in order to provide other viable means for women aside from domestic work.

These perspectives on change from workers depict the multilateral nature of South Africa's ongoing transformation, particularly in the institution of domestic work. Similarly, Eva Lazar's (2000) research on domestic work in post-apartheid South Africa calls for a movement beyond everyday acts of resistance to reform this "last vestige of control available to white employers" (p. 233). Lazar therefore advocates multi-layered reform from all "locations in the social fabric" as a broad scale initiative (p. 235). Workers in this study similarly indicated that while employers may implement a contract or evoke some component of more egalitarian labor practices, the underlying power differentials, enormous economic inequality, and severe marginalization of the sector remain the primary barriers to felt change in their own work contexts. In many respects, the early phase of democracy, which focused upon the political level of change, was insufficient in redressing the institution of domestic work. Therefore, workers in this study asserted that macro-level change would only be realized through long-term commitments to challenging the severe inequality and patriarchal dominance encapsulated in the institution of domestic work.

CONCLUSIONS

This chapter examined the spaces where transformation of paid household labor in South Africa has begun. Notwithstanding the challenges to unionization among domestic workers, SADSAWU's progress since 2000 illuminates the potential for women's collective mobilization within the most severe conditions of structural domination. Although SADSAWU remains a young organization, one year after its launch, critical labor policy change occurred as a direct result of women's collaboration across social location divides. The GMAC-UIF model demonstrates a critical step in aligning domestic workers with the broader public gender rights movement in South Africa. Under the guise of "women won't be free until domestic workers are free," the protection of domestic workers in unemployment insurance set a precedent for public recognition of the largest sector of working women in South Africa.

The challenges to the ongoing transformation of domestic work within South Africa lie in linking public transformations, particularly policy changes, to democratically based opportunities to *access* such rights. As Helen Moffett, a prominent national feminist writer described to me, "Our Constitution reads like a new year's resolution list." Similarly, the labor policy already in place for domestic workers on paper appears very sound and equitable, assuring that the nation has put structures in place to provide rights and redress past socio-economic imbalances. Yet this pervasive access gap led workers in this study to repeatedly suggest that their rights were "only on paper."

The massive disparities and ongoing "social apartheid" within South Africa are blatantly evident in daily social life. The challenges to redress the most severely disenfranchised sector of the working women's population remain daunting, as illustrated in this chapter. Yet it is also critical to note that South Africa's democratic change has been revolutionary in its integration of gender rights within the first ten years of democracy. By working with the national *Gender Machinery,* women in the GMAC-UIF crafted a model of democracy building that is highly appropriate to the South African case and applicable to other contexts where domestic work remains a primary institution in the oppression of women's labor. For example, like the GMAC-UIF process of civil society pressure, women in Trinidad's National Union of Domestic Workers have similarly aligned to hold state officials accountable for international standards to assure the inclusion of this sector in internal labor legislation (Karides 2002).

As many visionary activists in this study suggested, South Africa's full democratization can be realized by building upon these models of success as the new nation is continually reconstructed. The following feminist employer narrative poignantly captures these important victories, as well as the ongoing work of democratizing all levels of society:

> Well I think that if you just look at the way the ANC has first of all got women into parliament, I think it's down on the first election but it's still very high and I think a lot of those women have made a difference. I see that as all clearly positive. The second thing is South Africans tend to forget we didn't have open standing committees, that we weren't able to access government in the way that we are now and I think that those are very, very important things. I think that a lot of the legislation that we have in place is astonishingly idealistic, and very good. Our biggest problem is putting it in place. We do not have delivery mechanisms and in some ways we don't have a *culture* to deliver because some of it, and I don't really know enough about it, but my instinct tells me that some of it is terribly Western human rights based and to what extent it acknowledges culture and cultural differences I'm not terribly sure.

Through this statement on the magnitude of integrating democracy at all levels, we also see an emphasis on the importance of transformation processes built from *within*. While the international community supported South Africa's work, the "Western human rights based" approach cannot be universally applied to this nation's highly particular context. The GMAC-UIF model was designed specifically for the particular case of

South Africa, situated within the framework of a new democracy. It represents an example of successful social change from within as well as the potential South Africa holds to become a model to other nations in its ongoing process of democracy building "on the ground."

Further opportunities for realizing social change that engender women's labor rights within South Africa lie in international collaborations. A network approach to redressing the gender imbalance maintained through domestic work affords the possibility for application to global alliances not yet exercised in the South African case. If domestic workers mobilized and aligned with gender activism at the global level, states would then realize pressure from internal coalitions and international organizations. As Nancy Naples (2002) contends, the linking of local struggles with transnational activism provides the most powerful platform for restructuring patriarchal global processes Given the growing international 'trade' of domestic workers, opportunities for collective mobilization across state boundaries are crucial to democratizing the household. In the context of such severe oppression and social inequality maintained within the institution of domestic work, drawing upon international strength through coalition-building across race and class divides provides a powerful venue for structural transformation that embraces the human rights center of South Africa's democracy.

Chapter Seven
Bringing Democracy Home

South Africa's 1994 democracy motivated applause by a global audience. Redressing past social imbalances placed race and gender at the forefront of democratization. At the public level, we see these transformative victories through a revolutionary human rights based Constitution, one-third representation of women in national government, a model Truth and Reconciliation Commission process, and impressive policies adopted to engender social equality "on the ground." Yet the picture of democracy from home—where distinct gender imbalances prevail—illustrates the sharp contrast between these public victories and the lived realities of the majority of South Africans.

In the context of democratic transition, the nation faces a 40 percent unemployment rate, severe levels of internal violence, massive social inequality, and pervasive poverty concentrated among those most heavily marginalized during the apartheid regime. The task of redressing deeply embedded separateness—of racially divided neighborhoods, schools, shopping centers, languages, health care facilities and universities—daunts the ongoing work of social change. Ten years after democracy, South Africans continue to fathom the consciousness required for reconciliation and transformation in everyday life (Krog 1998; Tutu 1999). South African women at the World Court for Women hearings (2001) insisted that, "the country is walking around with decades of memory—of what happened to the brother, the mother, the son of—just under the surface." These collective memories contain the painful history of apartheid for the majority of South Africans, while at the public level the nation has completely transformed—a symbolic account of the dual realities that define the first ten years of democracy.

TRANSITIONS AT HOME

The encapsulation of this discontinuity between democratic change and severe social inequality persists most strikingly in the institution of paid domestic labor. As one domestic worker described her job, "Apartheid will *never* go out of that kitchen." Embedded in an ideology of colonial privilege and a distinct feminization of household labor, this institution remains completely normalized in the social fabric of everyday life to the extent that it is the largest sector of employment for women in South Africa. Yet, in relation to its prevalence, domestic labor is rarely problematized in the local discourse surrounding the limitations of change.[1] Findings from this study reveal how the institution of domestic work circumscribes democracy by allowing a great deal to go *unchanged* in the new South Africa. As a result, for domestic workers in particular, "the struggle continues" to transcend apartheid at the most intimate level of household relations.

Although South Africa's public prioritization of gender rights remains victorious, women employed in private households as domestic workers remain most seriously marginalized by low pay, poor working conditions, isolation, exploitation, and minimal opportunities for upward mobility. Furthermore, much like the global context, domestic work is performed completely by black and coloured women in South Africa, embodying a "matrix of domination" (Hill Collins 1990) that fixes workers in the lowest paid labor sector. Subsequently, we see that women's relative position as "maid" or "madam" (Cock 1980) to a large extent shapes their *access* to gender rights in South Africa. The relationship of domestic work to democratic transition in South Africa is therefore distinctly counterintuitive to the realization of social equality.

This research posits that domestic workers assuage the tension of national transition through their material acts that reproduce daily life in ways that remain virtually unchanged for privileged sectors of society. The *range* of tasks that domestic workers perform is completely engrained in South African society; ironed sheets, daily washed floors, unlimited childcare, household security, and served meals are readily available at a very low cost because of the severe exploitation that continues within this sector. As union leaders in this study asserted, "It's very important work. I think the country would fall apart if it weren't for domestic workers." I suggest that this dependency on domestic labor also cushions the jolt of public transfiguration by maintaining the private household in ways that fail to disrupt the embedded inequalities of the apartheid era.

Through the lens of workers' life experiences, the portrait of transformation in South Africa remains grim. Data from this research identify the severely limited options for women employed in this sector because of substantial structural barriers—such as high levels of unemployment, the pervasive marginalization of black women's labor, limited education, and workers' ongoing economic dependency on employers. The interlocking nature of these pervasive structural conditions led to a dominant theme among domestic workers that "not much has changed" in their own life circumstances since democracy. The data in this study illustrate that, like no other institution, domestic work remains rigidly bound by the residue of apartheid.

Ten years after democracy, a generation of women continues to face a labor market oversupplied by domestic workers that reproduces the dominant class-based inequality of the apartheid era. Discouragingly, many domestic workers reflected upon the career that constructed life circumstances parallel to Elize's:

> I came to Cape Town, that time I was young. I didn't think about money. But now I'm old and sickly in my leg. Now I think about it—I haven't got a cent. I said to myself I worked as a domestic worker for all these years and I am 53 years old now and I haven't even got R100 in the bank. I got nothing. I don't know what I worked for all my life.

Monica shared a similar position as she evaluated her extensive work with one family:

> I mean they had 20 years of me, of my life and what is there for me today? Nothing! There is nothing I can say, "Oh I got that for the 20 years or I got that for the 20 years," nothing! You see because we only had to work, work, work.

These lived experiences of domestic workers illustrate the exceptionally harsh *human costs* of the entrapment of women in this sector. As this coloured employer articulated, such losses are immeasurable aspects of the social inequalities contained in domestic labor:

> You know the cost of reproducing my household, because I don't think money captures the full value of that person. They are not just doing it for money. You know they pay with their *life energy*. They pay with days of their human life and that money can't buy you. Money can't buy you a day in your life. So in a very real bodily life energy way, they are being exploited, and money—it's not even an issue of money—it goes beyond money that kind of cost. So I am deeply aware and deeply uncomfortable with the situation.

This discomfort expressed in the above narrative points to the central position of the power group in the maintenance of structures of privilege and inequality. In order to deal with the "housework dilemma," (Romero 1992) like in other global contexts, privileged women in South Africa increasingly rely upon paid domestic workers to manage their household reproduction. Some employers disclosed that they were willing to purchase these services because of the increased "quality of life" it afforded them:

> For me the priority isn't around cleaning the dishes and cleaning the house. My priority is that I take my kids to Kirstenbosch [national gardens] and we spend an afternoon there or we've gone for a walk on the beach or we've gone for a walk on the mountain. That's my priority.

In the context of 40 percent national unemployment, the hiring of domestic labor in the household was overwhelmingly viewed by employers as a positive step in redressing the severe national levels of economic inequality.

Yet feminists in particular pointed to a deeply conflictual tension in their "shifting of household responsibilities" to other less privileged women for two specific reasons. First, the extent to which such practices collude with the oppression of less privileged women became a core internal dilemma—so much so that a few determined *not* to participate in paid household labor. Others pointed to a sharp disconnect between their feminist ideology and the practical realities that play out in this highly personalized context, as Julia illustrated:

> It's still quite a *fraught* sort of relationship. I mean I find it *very very* difficult because I came back [to South Africa after living abroad] with all of my egalitarian notions—which have always been there anyway—and my feminist ones *blazing*, and you actually have to come down to earth because the reality is that it's a different place. People don't have a basic income grant [social security]. People don't have the basics to live off, so you've got to try and make an arrangement that will be fair, *ja*, and that you can afford and that, it would be nice if it were more of a developmental role.

Feminist employers secondly identified a severe contradiction in their hiring of other women to maintain the household division of labor because of the extent to which men remained free from any responsibility in the private sphere. Therefore, as the data illustrate, hiring domestic workers allows a "huge gender battle" to go unaddressed within a nation that places the elimination of gender discrimination at the forefront of its governing democratic ideology. When feminists discussed men's unchanged roles, they pointed to household management responsibilities as a source of particular tension within their marriages. By "outsourcing" domestic work, employers ease this conflict over "who does more of the work at home." At a structural level, however, men's elevated social positions reinforce a patriarchal dominance that continues to challenge the actualization of gender rights in both public and private spaces.

These data offer a valuable critique of the extent to which South Africa's macro-structural change has been integrated at all levels of social relations, particularly when we examine gender rights. Building upon theories of interrelationality between the public and the private spheres (Ling 2002), one of the central findings in this study is that in order to *actualize* the public tenets of South Africa's new democracy, as Britton (1999) also posited, the real work of social change remains centered in the private household realm of social relations. I suggest that when the private realm is a pubic work space, attaining *domestic democracy* entails the most serious challenge to South Africa's public victories.

THE NEW FACE OF DOMESTIC LABOR

By capturing this moment in South Africa's transition to democracy, we see the context of change through some of the most intimate levels of social relations. My findings on domestic labor, ten years after the end of apartheid, illustrate that although the composition of workers has not changed with the democratic transition, the development of a layer of "new madams" complicates former systems of stratification contained in this institution. One of the most important contributions of this study is the emergent data on this "newly elite" group of "bourgeois" employers that suggest shifting patterns of social hierarchy as class relations begin to change. The complexity of domestic work *within* marginalized communities seriously complicates the traditional construction of the 'black maid/white madam' relationship central to apartheid South Africa. To date, the literature on domestic work has not yet fully addressed this within-group dynamic. Rather, studies emphasize the disparate social locations of workers and employers, particularly through the growing prevalence of transnational migration patterns.

In the South African context, however, a discourse about the "worst employers" repeatedly emerged within marginalized groups. In this regard, coloured participants named Muslim employers as the harshest in their employment practices, while black workers identified black members of parliament as most problematic in their treatment of domestic workers. In

many instances, participants suggested that newly emergent groups positioned as employers represent a particular betrayal in terms of the lost
ideals of South Africa's liberation struggle for race and class equality, as this
coloured employer assessed:

> I don't deny, I am sure there are black employers who are as exploita-
> tive as their counterparts who are white, you know, but I think what
> you are hearing is a racialization of a sense of betrayal, a deep sense of
> betrayal, because I mean the struggle wasn't just about race, I think it
> was about class too. So it's a class issue that is becoming racialized and
> that is the way it is getting expressed.

This castigation of "other" employers presents a striking contradiction
because a set of standards is being applied to coloured and black employers
that was not expected of whites throughout the apartheid era. As my findings
suggest, this marginalization maintains the familiarity of the former systems
of racial stratification. Because it is often too uncomfortable that "servants
have servants,"[2] the behavior of new elite employers was particularly scruti-
nized across all sectors of informants. Furthermore, the pervasive "othering"
of newly elite employers reproduces the deeply engrained social stratification
system because it frees whites from any responsibilities for maintaining the
former system of apartheid oppression within their own private households.
By placing the "most abusive" conditions elsewhere, white power groups
maintain social positions at the center, leaving hierarchical patterns firmly
intact from the apartheid regime's structuring.

Another attribute at work in this "othering" of new employers is the
intersection of hired household labor and social status. Many informants
described that the ability to hire a domestic worker was a critical measure
to establish a "bourgeois" position in society. This daily luxury in the private home therefore represented an important image of heightened class
positions embedded in the collective memory of the apartheid privileges
afforded to whites. Because paid household labor holds such meaning in
South Africa, as measures of social location are gradually shifting to class
rather than the predominant race structures from the apartheid era, domestic work becomes one powerful means by which still marginalized communities can accentuate their relative higher social positions. Furthermore, as
some informants explained, those groups with lower social status more
strictly reinforce their position as the "boss" or "madam." In the case of
both black and coloured populations that can hire household labor, the relative close proximity of within-group workers and employers in the spectrum of social power creates conditions where employers' positions are

more vulnerable, thus in need of strict measures of reinforcement. The particular dynamics of these power inequalities between workers and employers indicate that *within* marginalized groups, class at times emerges as a central differential. Therefore, this study demonstrates that domestic work is a powerful social institution that defines class positions, particularly in the South African case as processes of the transition to democracy gradually reshape structural relations.

CHANGE AT HOME

This research specifically sought to understand how domestic work informs a more complex understanding of South Africa's ongoing democratization. The general resistance to recognizing this institution as a viable sector speaks to the ongoing severe marginalization of household labor, and particularly black women's contributions to the daily reproduction of privileged sectors of society. This feminist activist described her reaction to the pervasive internal dialogue about the "unproductive" nature of paid domestic labor:

> You know the thing is when people put it in arguments about you know inefficient, poorly skilled, unproductive labor. I mean I'm like— *duh*—you know these are people who are actually spending life energy to come and reproduce other people's life energy and their offspring's life energy. You call that inefficient? Or unproductive? They are producing two households—that's not unproductive! You know what I'm saying? You know economic theory is inadequate to capture that, it can't capture that kind of expenditure.

Yet even within the gender rights emphasis of South Africa's new democracy, the productive contribution of this sector was persistently devalued. As Chapter Six discussed, the release of critical social security measures with the specific *exclusion* of domestic workers seriously challenges the nation's commitment to redressing the gender imbalance, particularly among this largest sector of working women, composed completely of black women.

One of the most pervasive themes across all sectors of participants was an assessment of South Africa's remarkable social change process as "only on paper." Or, as one participant put it, "Our Constitution reads like a new year's resolution list." For human rights activists, a "culture of delivery" was not yet in place to match the revolutionary policies already promulgated in the new democracy. For workers and the most seriously marginalized, the disjuncture between rights at the public level and *access* at the private level remained the sharpest contradiction to the actualization of democracy. While labor legislation passed in 1997 required the use of a contract for *all* domestic work employment contexts, only *three* households of 75 observed actually implemented such a practice. Central to the overall analysis of structural transformation in South Africa, the data from this research depict the enormous gap between democratic policy and the lived realities of the majority of the population.

Given these findings, from a policy standpoint, the implementation of legislation to protect domestic workers must be accompanied by processes of re-socialization in relation to the legitimacy of this labor sector. Furthermore, a deconstruction of the severe race, class and gender-based inequalities that prevail throughout the transition remains critical to the full realization of democracy. These levels of social change are certainly more challenging than political restructuring alone, and much longer-term, as this research repeatedly magnifies. Without processes of shifting patriarchal structures and redressing the severely racialized and class-based "social apartheid" that continues to dominate South Africa, policy change alone will continue to have little impact on either the reform of domestic work or the democratization of social relations.

A central component of this research also examined women's agency to transform the institution of domestic labor. Even with the enormous structural barrier challenges embedded in the residue of apartheid, this study reveals that the institution has shifted through workers' collective acts of agency and women's mobilization across social location divides. Through this ongoing resistance, union organizers are pushing for an awareness that "women won't be free until domestic workers are free!" The South African Domestic Service and Allied Workers' Union (SADSAWU), in collaboration with the Gender Machinery, won a pivotal legislative victory to assure domestic workers' access to unemployment insurance during this study. Through this policy reform, the GMAC-UIF coalition, initiated by the South African Commission on Gender Equality, established an original model of cross-sectional activism that positioned domestic workers' rights as central to the broader commitment to gender rights.

Because the inequality contained within the institution of domestic work is a gendered and racialized *global* phenomenon, the alignment of committed international organizations to realize change within this sector is therefore essential. In this regard, feminist-activist networks provide a critical opportunity to support SADSAWU's campaign on "rights for *all* women." As this feminist employer portrayed, global restructuring, although problematic in its reinforcement of inequalities, also holds the potential for engendering powerful social change:

> I think it's going to come to the organization of human rights groups
> and domestic work and women's organization across the world, I do.
> One tends to think of globalization only in a negative way but I think
> there seems to be a rising consciousness of human rights in a sense
> worldwide.

As this narrative suggests, centralizing the case of domestic labor within
this broader global movement that prioritizes "women's rights as human
rights" provides one of the most viable means to engender a substantive
transition of this institution.

LOOKING TO THE FUTURE

From this methodological approach and its subsequent knowledge claims
in this study, after ten years of inquiry about the multi-faceted nature of the
institution of domestic work in South Africa, I am left with a few com-
pelling questions that remain unresolved. First, should the institution of
domestic labor be abolished or progressively reformed? One participant in
this study suggested that at a very core philosophical level, no human being
should be made to "clean up another human being's mess." Certainly when
black women perform the "dirty work" for society, equality, "nonracial-
ism" and gender redress are severely compromised. Particularly in the
South African case, the deeply embedded apartheid ideologies manifest an
even greater challenge to realizing democracy when the majority of women
remain so severely marginalized in this highly inequitable, isolated,
"trapped" existence.

Yet, this study also revealed that for a few workers, domestic labor
was a positive means to survive economically and contribute to society.
One domestic worker in this study, Louise, received generous financial
compensation, felt extremely valued, and was well situated for retirement
through her 18-year position as a domestic worker with a particularly sensitive, egalitarian-oriented, wealthy employer. Throughout our repeated
interactions over the course of six months, and two formal interviews,
Louise told me that for her, domestic work was much more optimal to
spending her days in a factory. Louise takes walks on the beach each day
with her employer, manages a relatively small apartment, and after the
death of her male employer, has become the long-term companion and
confidant to the woman she "serves" and also considers a friend. Through
coming to know Louise's circumstance, I questioned the extent to which the
intimate nature of domestic labor could produce genuine, reciprocal, even
loving relationships between employers and workers that transcended the

deep divides structured by the particular history of this institution in South Africa. Or, does this very ideal egalitarian-based relationship still remain entangled in power and dependency such that Louise's surreal, optimistic circumstance exists only through her acceptance of and participation in her own subordination? While my personal inclination suggests the latter, Louise's life context required that I consider how domestic labor could exist as a *democratic* social institution.

South Africans overwhelming pointed to reform of domestic work rather than any illusion of its abolishment. In the context of severe 40 percent unemployment, virtual absence of other viable work options and no structural support for education and training initiatives in this sector, claiming (particularly as an outside Western academic) that domestic work must be abolished because of the inherent fixed power inequality contained within it is naïvely idealistic in many regards. Yet Hettie, a strong (white) progressive feminist scholar, and Tumi, a long-time trade unionist, freedom fighter, and current high level (black) parliamentarian, both refuse to engage in the employment of domestic workers to support their own household reproduction because of a shared sentiment that the inherent contradictions within it too painfully recreate the severe oppression of the apartheid era at the most personal level. Is the institution of domestic work in South Africa therefore always completely contradictory to the democratic tenets of the nation's transformation? At an ideological level, I believe yes. However, my experience studying this institution intensely in South African society also revealed transfigured spaces where domestic work had been, to a certain extent, democratized in ways that support the public commitment to gender rights.

In my ongoing conversations about this particular institution in the South African case, many have asked if this is the *answer*. In other words, would enough acts of human rights in private employment contexts engender the macro-level change that would restructure this institution with democratic possibility, rather than embedded apartheid inequalities? If we embrace the theory of interrelationality (Ling 2002), change at the individual level holds the potential to restructure the institution. Certainly the repeated acts of agency among workers throughout this study continue to reshape domestic labor in ways that suggest a gradual loosening of its apartheid structure. I am also reminded of a repeated theme in the data that eluded to a growing "nervousness" among employers about their responsibility to treat domestic workers differently. This discomfort was expressed across all participant groups in ways that, in my assessment, illustrated a growing awareness of change. I suggest that this "nervousness" may be the first stage of a longer-term transition in this colonial institution.

As the case of policy change illustrates, structural initiatives alone will not transform the institution of domestic work. Maggie, a domestic worker and union activist assessed, "to change other people, you know, it's from the *inside*." The data throughout this study reveal how social relations maintain more power in everyday life than macro-level political changes. Therefore, I believe there is merit to the notion that "democracy begins at home." At the same time, social institutions hold tremendous potential to actualize South Africa's democracy. Education, for instance, repeatedly emerged among domestic workers as the most important component to long-term change. By working two jobs in this sector to finance her children's education in a private school, Ntutu assured me that South Africa would be a very different place for her daughters. Furthermore, as we see in the power of women's collective organization across divides, the gradual restructuring of institutions—in collaboration with democratic policies and change within individuals—holds tremendous power to reshape South African society in ways that would also engender the progressive reform of domestic labor.

Like students who often ask about the "answer" on how to change this vestige of apartheid, I too feel a need for resolve—to conclude by synthesizing this research with a response that solves the complexities of this case in order to facilitate the ongoing work of South Africa's democratic transition. Yet, what emerged as one of my most powerful insights from this research was a realization that in many regards, the cumulative impact of domestic labor on society as a whole is immeasurable. Regardless of the approach to the study of domestic work, there is a certain quality or character of the institution that is *intangible* and escapes scientific inquiry. How does one comprehend the mutual social-psychological impacts of looking out onto the world through clear polished windows each day, of bathing in a sparkling bathroom, of having tea served upon request at any time of the day, or coming home to neatly folded, ironed undergarments placed in one's drawers, while dinner is prepared by another's hands? Certainly these micro-level encounters mutually construct and reinforce class privilege, racism, sexism and deeply engrained patterns of social stratification in ways that collectively shape the social psyche of South Africa. Yet the interwoven impact and symbiotic meanings of these acts are deeply personal and powerfully structural. For example, how does the formative connection between a child and her "black mama"[3] transform into the severe structural level of racism that continues to exist in South Africa? Furthermore, the labor tasks that domestic workers perform for privileged sectors of society are also human endeavors that connote valuable life pursuits. Raising a child, tending a garden, teaching, preparing a meal, creating a

home—these are all essential *human* undertakings that construct our existence and give meaning to individual's "life energy." Because domestic
workers perform all of these tasks for more privileged sectors of society, I
suggest that at a core level of human existence, employers barter *some* loss
of an aesthetic, thoughtful life experience for the daily privileges paid
household labor provides. Each of these questions evades the capacity of
scientific inquiry alone. At the same time, however, the very nature of these
underlying complexities provides a more nuanced appreciation for meaning
of domestic labor, particularly in the South African case where we see the
collective apartheid history so vividly contained within this institution.

Because transformation of domestic labor involves change at the
micro, organizational, structural, and socio-cultural levels, it encapsulates
South Africa's greatest challenge to democratization. The deeply embedded
nature of this "last bastion of apartheid" for many participants confirmed
that "domestic democracy" is not attainable because of the pervasive dominance of race, class and gender inequalities that remain rigidly engrained
in South African society ten years after the national transition. Yet others
repeatedly illustrated that transforming the institution of domestic work
necessitated a recommitment to the collective strength that sustained the
apartheid era, as this narrative exemplifies:

> You know I do believe in the triumph of the human spirit and of
> human rights issues over much of the exploitation and of evil, of that
> kind of evil that does exploit people, so you know one has to have cer-
> tainty and that vision all the time, of human rights at some point. And
> apartheid, the death of apartheid was something. Growing up under it,
> one *never* thought it would end and it did end and it is also true that
> this exploitation is going to end, so that's the position that I work from,
> one has to have that kind of thought.

Drawing upon this capacity to change the severe structural inequalities of
apartheid, women in South Africa are actively reshaping the institution of
domestic work on a daily basis. Their collective acts of agency continue to
engender the possibility for ongoing change at the private level to actualize the
public victories of South Africa's transition. I suggest that this resistance holds
the potential to realize "domestic democracy." As one participant in this study
astutely depicted, "When domestic workers realize democracy in their everyday lives, then we will know that South Africa has fully transformed."

Notes

NOTES TO CHAPTER ONE

1. The TRC represented a pivotal process in South Africa's post-apartheid reconstruction. Although the TRC is broadly viewed as a positive and necessary initiative emphasizing restorative justice, forgiveness and national healing, its current task of assessing reparations for the 21,000 cases of human rights abuses heard from 1996–1998 illustrates one of the most challenging aspects of societal redress. For comprehensive discussions and analysis of the TRC process, see Gobodo-Madikizela (2003); Tutu (1999); Krog (1998); and Nuttall & Coetzee (1998).
2. This deliberation emerged at Truth and Reconciliation Commission Hearings that I observed in Uitenhage; May 1996.
3. I use the term "black women" here to include both the black and "coloured" racial groups that maintain distinct identities in South Africa, as I take up later in this chapter.
4. For example, domestic workers clean most household bathrooms and floors on a daily basis.
5. Throughout this book, I refer to "domestic work" as well as "paid domestic work" as a social *institution*. What I mean to discuss here is domestic work as a *paid* sector of labor. As feminists have problematized in an extensive body of literature, domestic work is typically unpaid and highly feminized because women perform this work in the private household (see Chapter Two). Building upon this gendered division of labor, this book focuses on how paid domestic work becomes institutionalized when women are hired to reproduce the households of those that can afford these services. In South Africa, as a result of deep colonial and apartheid histories, this paid sector of labor is also a predominant social institution, as I take up throughout this book.
6. Desmond Tutu originally coined the term "rainbow nation" as an image of ideal, inclusive multiculturalism that embraced difference without the inequalities of social hierarchy. In this regard, all races/ethnicities are celebrated as a central component of the new national identity (see Tutu 1994). One participant in this research, however, suggested that the current context of

South Africa is more accurately described as a "nation of islands" because of the sharp separation of races maintained in post-apartheid social relations. For further discussions of this national ethos and comparative analysis of the U.S. melting pot ideology, see Cock and Bernstein's (2002) *Melting Pots and Rainbow Nations: Conversations about Difference in the United States and South Africa.*

7. For example, South Africa was the first country to include freedom from discrimination based upon sexual orientation as a Constitutional protection, as included in Nelson Mandela's 1994 inaugural address.

8. Because of the significance of the Constitution in South African society, I associate my usage of the term "democracy" to its meaning as defined in the "Founding Provisions" of the South African Constitution which prioritizes "human dignity, the achievement of equality and the advancement of human rights and freedoms" with "non-racialism and non-sexism" in democratic governance (Republic of South Africa 1996).

9. South Africa's Gender Machinery consists of three governmental offices with monitoring, lobbying and advocacy functions. Importantly, as a representation of South Africa's commitment to gender-based redress of social inequality, one of the branches reports to the national President. For further discussion of this democratic initiative, see Chapter Six.

10. South Africa's first national elections in 1994 result in this 26 percent representations, however in 2005 women comprise 32 percent of the national parliament (see Britton 2005).

11. According to the *Mail & Guardian* (Khan 2002) report, South Africa's rape statistics per capita remain one of the highest in the world in 2002. The figures were so shocking that the national government withheld release of the figures for a portion of 2001 because of the particularly harsh reactions from both local and international communities.

12. This group's history can be linked to sexual relationships between the colonial white settlers and indigenous black portions of the population, predominantly in the Western Cape where the Spice Trade developed. In 1950, the Immorality Act was passed, banning sexual relations across racial groups, however the coloured population was already identified as one of four racial categories under the apartheid governance of the time. While I strongly resist reifying the socially constructed divisions employed by the apartheid regime to institute severe oppression, because racial identity so sharply defines social relationships and stratification in modern South Africa, particularly within this group, I use the local term 'coloured' throughout this book in order to speak to the internal reality that continues to exist. Importantly, however, this is not to further instill the ongoing stratification or subsequent privileging through its usage. I engage this term to accurately portray the local context with admitted discomfort because its usage in other contexts is so strongly associated with racial prejudice and derogatory terminology. Therefore, I qualify its usage only to illustrate the ongoing realities of post-apartheid South Africa and the particular nuances of the Cape Town region.

13. Notably, these two groups remained in severe conflict throughout history, as evident through the Anglo-Boer war ending in 1902. The apartheid regime is predominantly associated with white Afrikaaners, while the English (who obviously participated in and benefited from such governance) maintained higher socio-economic power. See Thompson (1997) for further detail.

14. The Household Survey is the equivalent of the U.S. Census. These data most accurately describe the national context at the time this study was conducted.

15. Statistics South Africa reports the next three highest categories of women's employment as "clerks" with 699,000 (16 percent), "technicians and associate professions" with 553,000 (13 percent), and "service workers, shop and market sales workers" with an estimated 541,000 (12 percent). These three largest occupational categories following domestic work and "elementary occupations" denote a predominant service character, linked to gendered constructions of work. Also central to these estimates, the concentration of women in the *informal* sector is growing rapidly in both South Africa and the globalized world labor market. Estimates of representation in this sector, however, are not attainable because women employed as street vendors and sex workers, for example, are not counted in national statistics of labor. Therefore, as South African gender activists asserted, women's informal labor is even more prevalent than these representations suggest and a further source of ongoing marginalization because of exclusion from protective labor measures.

16. Male "gardeners" are common to the culture of domestic service and therefore included in this occupational definition, however as the statistics reveal, their representation is only 4.5 percent of the total. This study focuses only on female domestic workers.

17. This quotation is based on a personal discussion with Thandi Modise at the annual colloquium of Women Waging Peace in Cambridge, Massachusetts (November 2001).

18. This narrative caption represents my selective usage of identity descriptors to preface and more specifically situate the interview data in certain cases throughout this book. To qualify my inclusion of such identity labels, I contextualize the narratives by the specific race and/or political position (e.g., feminist, parliamentarian) of each participant in cases when revealing such information enhances the meaning of the narrative itself or the discussion at hand. This practice is in no way intended to reify the hierarchical racial categorization system of the apartheid era, but rather to foster increased understanding of the lived experiences of participants in this research and the relationship between such identities and the issues revealed within each narrative. When identity constructs are not shared, it is because doing so would not foster any further understanding of the concept illuminated through the participant's voice. In other cases identity descriptors are withheld because the narrative itself represents a more widely held view across various race, class and political locations.

19. The Western Cape is the regional province, with Cape Town's location as the urban center (see Figure 1.2). These racial dynamics span the entire Western Cape, however, beyond Cape Town.

20. I recognize the problematic nature of this term as a result of its broad categorization of women from a variety of global locations. My usage of the term here is intended to illustrate that migrant women who work in domestic labor are primarily women who experience racial oppression (e.g., Chicanas, Latinas, Filipinas, Caribbean Americans). See Chapter Two for a discussion of the relationship between race and the institution of domestic labor.

21. Throughout this book, my diversions from the actual interview conversational are noted by the (. . .) within narrative excerpts.

NOTES TO CHAPTER TWO

1. For the foundational contributions of Feminist International Relations, see Pateman (1989); Peterson and Runyan (1993); Enloe (1993); Pettman (1996); Sharoni (1995) and Ling (2002).

2. Here, I draw upon the following in-depth studies of domestic work as the foundation for these common features: Katzman (1971); Lerner (1972); Cock (1980); Gordon (1981); Jones (1985); Rollins (1985); Gaitskell et al. (1984); Nakano Glenn (1987); Ntombi (1987); Bunster and Chaney (1989); Chaney and Castro (1989); Hansen (1989); Romero (1992); Heyzer, Lycklama and Weerakoon (1994); Thornton Dill (1994); Gill (1994); Chin (1998); Andersen (2000); Chang (2000); Lazar (2000); Chang and Ling (2002); Gamburd (2000); Hondagneu-Sotelo (2001); and Perreñas (2001). This collection is transnational and comprehensive, although not exhaustive.

3. I recognize sex work as an equally gendered and devalued women's profession, however the placement of domestic work in the private household further lessens its worth and separates it from sex work, which carries other related elements of (particularly sexual) objectification through its historical and material value.

4. Rollins is also widely recognized for her methodological approach to this topic. By attaining employment as a domestic worker herself, Rollins integrated data about the treatment she received from employers into her multi-faceted analysis of the institution of domestic work.

5. *Global restructuring* is the preferred term among many feminists because it acknowledges the patriarchal tenets of globalization (Marchand and Runyan 2002). For a more thorough discussion of the underpinning processes central to globalization see (Held et al. 1999).

6. The exception here is the global nanny practice (which is more typically a short-term occupation for younger white women) or the high status level governess positions in extremely elite families.

7. Ultimately, these two practices are mitigated by strong class divisions such that women in economically privileged positions are able to purchase the labor of women in lower class positions in order to free themselves from

the burden of domestic labor. Women without such class privilege, in order to cope with the "housework dilemma," rely most often upon family support structures and shared childcare systems among kin. Romero (1992) claims that domestic work therefore embodies the site of class struggle.

8. To devise the map, patterns were drawn from the extensive body of literature that examines the international trade of domestic workers. While beyond the scope of this study to discuss the particular nuances in each region, broader patterns illustrate the relationships of dependency among nations at the global level. As I discuss, the patterns of dependency are enacted within the private households between domestic workers and employers. For in-depth discussions of this global trade of domestic labor, see Heyzer et al. (1994); Bakan and Stasiulis (1997); Chin (1998); Lan (2000); Gamburd (2000); Parreñas (2001); Chang (2000); Andersen (2000); Hondogneu-Sotelo (2001); and Chang and Ling (2002).

9. I draw these analyses from my own (2000) research with Wendy Bokhorst-Heng within the diplomatic community in Washington DC. Many of these points emerged from the 20 diplomatic spouse interviews conducted for this project (publication forthcoming).

10. For more detailed discussions of this particularly overt reliance upon exported domestic labor in the Philippines, see Chin (1998); Parreñas (2001); and Chang and Ling (2002).

11. This term was used throughout my interviews among domestic workers, referring in Afrikaans to "boss" or "master."

12. For more comprehensive national historical overviews see Thompson (1990); Sparks (1990); Walker (1991); and Mandela (1996).

13. Former residents of District Six created a "people's museum" in downtown Cape Town in 1995 that captures the vibrancy of the lost community when this area was demolished. Current initiatives in Cape Town involve rebuilding the area, which remained virtually empty throughout apartheid. Even though it was demolished under the auspices of the government's need for the land in close proximity to the city, only one technical college was ever built on the demolished area, representing a powerful example of the cruel human costs of the apartheid system of dominance. For detailed accounts of apartheid's racial ideology at play in District Six from former residents, see Linda Fortune's (1996) *The House in Tyne Street: Childhood Memories of District Six* and Richard Rive's (1986) *'Buckingham Palace' District Six*.

14. As a powerful depiction of social agency, women utilized the fluid nature of race in strong opposition to apartheid's sharply defined racial categorization practices. One Xhosa-speaking black worker in this study shared how she would often craft a coloured identity and begin speaking Afrikaans when confronted by police forces in order to avoid the mandated work pass for Africans. In addition, she straightened her hair and dressed "more coloured" which succeeded in "fooling" police and attaining domestic work without a pass for years.

15. Women's activism embodies another in-depth dialogue within South African studies. For a comprehensive overview of acts of resistance, see Walker (1991); Wells (1993); Meer (1998); and Farr (2002).

16. I believe I acquired an exhaustive collective of all academic and organizational literature on domestic labor during apartheid South Africa . I am particularly appreciative of the archive collection at the Centre for African Studies at the University of Cape Town, which provided access to a wealth of unpublished and rare sources on this case as well as research papers and conference proceedings . In addition, the historical collection of the Black Sash aided my access to the documentation of organizational advocacy and women's activism in relation to domestic work throughout apartheid.

17. "Bantu" is a colonial term for the indigenous African population. Similarly the Bantu Education system was devised in the apartheid era to strategically separate public services for black sectors of the population.

18. Gaitskell's analysis provides an important comparative lens for the U.S., where white women left the occupation and were replaced by African American women, followed by Latina immigrants.

19. See for example van Onselen's (1982) study of class relations in the industrializing (1886–1914) Witwatersrand region; Boddington's (1983) Master's thesis "Domestic Service: Changing Relations of Class Domination 1841–1948-A Focus on Cape Town" (and subsequent conference papers); and Eales's (1988) African Studies Institute Seminar paper, "Good Girls and Mine Married Quarters: Johannesburg, 1912."

20. See Chapter Six for reference to Gordon's Domestic Workers and Employers Project (DWEP).

21. It should be noted that during this time of most heightened apartheid rule, Cock's work was perceived as extremely radical and incredibly threatening to the national government. Not unrelated, she received numerous threats and destruction to her personal home and property shortly after release of this study.

22. Social/psychological outcomes of the domestic work relationship on parenting and children's socialization have been the source of Master's degree research in South Africa. See for example Nomsa Ngqakayi's (1991) "Subjectivity in the 'Maid'/'Madam' Relationship and its Effects on the Occupational Child Care-Giving Functions of the Domestic Worker." Also related is Rucksana Christian's (1998) thesis on employer involvement in parenting children of domestic workers, and Nondwe Mange's (1995) study of domestic worker children in predominantly white schools.

23. This statement is quoted from Cock's *Maids & Madams* documentary video, released in 1989.

24. Importantly, a central element in South Africa's ability to uphold a dominant role in the global market is based in the reality that its economic resource base remains centered in the white population even with the new black governance in place. The extent to which this challenges former structures of power, therefore remains somewhat marginal.

25. These analyses about the ongoing challenges to actualizing South Africa's democracy are drawn from interviews with NGO leaders and government officials.
26. This wide acceptance of Nelson Mandela's governance is also based in his charismatic leadership and personal history of 27 years imprisonment for leading the struggle to end apartheid and the almost unbelievable realization of his later national presidency. For a detailed depiction of this evolutionary life experience, see *Long Walk to Freedom* by Nelson Mandela (1994).
27. This perception of under-qualified leadership is based on the realization that many of the government's top leaders were living in exile throughout apartheid, trained as freedom fighters rather than political leaders. Thus the common perception that "fighting for freedom is much different than running a country" predominates the social discourse about the new government's shortcomings.
28. NGO leaders in this study referenced this constraint often as a particular struggle in their ongoing work toward human rights and democratization.
29. At the time of this study, 40 percent unemployment rates were confirmed by the central office of the Minister of Labour, as well as the Labour Portfolio Committee . Furthermore, the *Mail and Guardian* throughout 2001 frequently reported this rate. Importantly, this estimate is not disaggregated by race or gender . Government labor experts interviewed for this research suggested that unemployment rates in South Africa' black communities may be closer to 60 percent . Importantly, this places a particular burden on women in the informal economy.
30. While a small portion of Lazar's work overlaps with my own analysis of current policy and lived realties addressed in Chapter Six, her Gauteng/Johannesburg regional focus provides much different racial location dynamics to the Cape Town vicinity central to the content of this study. Furthermore, our theoretical frameworks diverge, as well as the methodological approaches employed. However, the possibilities of transformation through women's ongoing acts of resistance and mobilization, central to Lazar's work, most directly intersect with and inform this current research.

NOTES TO CHAPTER THREE

1. See Marjorie DeVault's (1999) *Liberating Method: Feminism and Social Research* for a comprehensive historical presentation of the development and contextual usages of feminist methods.
2. For a full description of methodological practices adopted by feminist researchers, see Reinharz (1992).
3. I am grateful to Simona Sharoni for first teaching me about this ideological link between politics and practice.
4. Action research also advocates the co-creation of the research design between scholars and community members. Importantly, while local participants shaped, redirected and informed the collection of data throughout

our collective interactions during the fieldwork, this research was *not* co-created with community members throughout all phases of its design.

5. As of 2005, this institution was renamed Nelson Mandela Metropolitan University.

6. This estimate is based upon data from SADSAWU records and the South African Department of Labour. See Chapter Six for a full discussion of union membership.

7. The importance of moving out of the work context became a repeated theme throughout this study among domestic workers, as this interview caption illustrates. While this was seen as an important step to establishing more equitable relationships, it is also bound by geography, economic limitations and a prevailing colonial culture about the "live-in" nature of domestic worker. See Chapter Four for more detail.

8. For the purpose of this study, all employers and workers in the interview sample were women, even though men also employ and work as domestic workers. Importantly, however, two domestic workers were employed by single men.

9. Because the term "feminism" carries wide associations and meanings—particularly in the South African context—in this study, I define feminism as a social movement that seeks to emancipate women from the oppressive circumstances of structural inequality that continue to privilege men. In this regard, feminism carries a strong activist component that similarly aspires to redress other forms of inequality such as racism and xenophobia. Critical to this research, however, I also acknowledge the vast *difference* in women's experiences that leads to diverse perspectives on this term. In the particular South African context, for example, women's priorities include access to safe drinking water, limiting HIV transmission and the alleviation of community-based violence. This locally defined platform represents the lived realities of the majority of women in South Africa. Therefore, feminism as an ideological stance alone, especially in this context, is often seen as an elitist endeavor—much like criticisms of the limited perspectives of second-wave feminism in the United States. As a result, the term "feminist" is not embraced by South African women universally. Rather, its construction is linked to access to economic resources, race, religion and geographic location. Therefore, in this research, when I label participants as "feminists," I am referring to those that self-identify in this way as well as those that espouse gender rights orientations that may not have used this "feminist" term to describe themselves. In this case, "feminists" in this study also illustrated some alignment with the ideological frameworks of political activism as described above. My intent here is not to impose a Western notion of feminism on the sample. Rather, I hope to draw upon the diversity of women's experiences to see how women who align with notions of gender rights deal with their roles as employers of other women—a central component of the intersectional theoretical framework for this study.

10. Not surprisingly, these three women were also feminists with whom I had shared other former interactions. These participants also embodied a

heightened consciousness about the institution of domestic work and the importance of research on the particular exploitation in this sector.

11. This variance speaks to the strong power differentials across the two main informant groups of employers and workers. Related to employers' heightened social positions, they generally shared much less information about their personal lives, allotted shorter time frames for interview appointments and in many instances offered several cues to close the interview between 45 minutes to one hour. Thus, asking the same number of questions to workers and employers was unrealistic. Workers' willingness to extend interviews to sometimes four hours both allowed me to often incorporate 50+ questions and illuminated the pervasive need to 'tell the story' of the multiple vectors of oppression in the institution of domestic work, with an underlying expectation that my capturing these narratives would also facilitate change through the publication of workers' life stories.

12. Each expert interview was designed with specific focus upon the varying experiences of the broad range of participants in this sector. Although every expert was asked to speak about their perceptions of the institution of domestic work and its relationship to social change in South Africa, the remaining questions were highly specific to each individual.

13. I credit my practice of weaving emotions into fieldnotes primarily to Jennifer Rothchild who strongly encouraged me to do so based upon her own fieldwork experiences in rural Nepal. For an integrated account of feminist self-reflexive research practices and daily emotional reflections in fieldwork see Rothchild's (2002) "Moving Beyond Enrollment Numbers: An In-Depth Look at Gender Inequality in Schools in Rural Nepal."

14. I am particularly thankful for the support of the African Gender Institute and the local NGO community for providing a wealth of analytical insights on my initial findings.

15. This objective involves self reflexively locating the researcher within the data in order to understand local meanings rather than imposing outside categories on the data (Emerson, Fretz and Shaw 1998).

16. This process was both inductive and deductive. Many of the codes emerged inductively from unsolicited or emergent interview responses. In other cases, because I was examining five main thematic areas, codes closely matched my initial interview questions.

17. This comment is based upon Ward's valuable contributions to a co-presentation of this chapter with Jennifer Rothchild at the 2002 American Sociological Association Meeting entitled, "Struggling to Put Methods to Practice: Considering Race, Class, Gender and Positionalities in Feminist Fieldwork."

18. This ease of relatedness through shared social positions Cock attributed to the rigidly constructed racial hierarchy of the apartheid stratification system. For further discussion, see Cock's (1990) "Guilt, fear and other difficulties in researching domestic relations" in *Truth Be in the Field*, edited by Pierre Hugo.

19. Amy Biehl was an American Fulbright scholar who was stoned to death in Cape Town's Guguletu township in 1993, while working to support South

Africa's approaching democracy and studying women's roles in processes of citizenship and national transformation. Since her death, the Amy Biehl Foundation was established to model peaceful means of reconciliation and nation-building within South Africa. Lauded by international figures and the South African government, the Foundation works most actively in the community where Biehl was killed to model forgiveness, reconciliation and an ongoing vision of transformation.

20. This "peace of mind" was described by employers in a number of contexts to suggest the comforts of daily life available through the employment of domestic workers.

21. I thank Gay Young for this insight and her supportive reminders of its emergence throughout this project. See also Sjoberg (1968).

NOTES TO CHAPTER FOUR

1. "R" = South African Rand currency. At the time of this study, the rate of exchange was R7=1USD, however, with the further devaluing of the Rand, the rate of exchange for the year 2002 averaged closer to R10=1USD. The 2005 exchange rate averaged closer to R 6.5=1USD. For the sake of consistently, I have chosen to report economic values by applying the exchange rate at the time of this study (R7=1USD).

2. *Ja* is a colloquial South African expression (pronounced "yaw") equivalent to "yeah" in U.S. English.

3. Although, two feminist employers adapted salary schemes that both afforded a living wage and alleviated some of their associated guilt in what was perceived as the collusion in the exploitation of other less privileged woman by employing household labor. Both employed domestic workers three days per week and paid a very fair living wage, which was well above the average monthly wage for full-time work. By doing so, both believed that they lessened the potential of exploitation and created a context that fostered a deeper appreciation for domestic labor because it was shared with other members of the household.

4. The context of these microenterprises was also characterized by a gendered nature, such as developing a childcare center or selling women's clothing.

5. Notably, the first of these two informants held a central leadership role in the national union and voiced aspirations of running for a parliamentary position in the next election period. The second respondent was one of the youngest in the sample.

6. This quote is drawn from a domestic worker interview.

7. I use the terms "family" in this case to refer to the immediate family, namely husbands and children.

8. Importantly, celebrations such as this are highly prioritized in South African culture, particularly among black and coloured populations. The 21st birthday is viewed as a symbolic coming of age ritual, thus heightening the extent to which workers' exclusion from such events represents further inequality and emotional pain.

9. "Separate quarters" is a term commonly used for properties with connected yet physically separate living areas for domestic workers. Real estate listings commonly market this feature or "maid's quarters" to appeal to buyers.

10. These two employers were also strong feminists who felt in conflict with all aspects of the institution.

11. I draw this interpretation from the data based upon insights gained in Linda Carty's "Black Domestic Workers in New York City" graduate course at Syracuse University. For more in-depth analysis of the emotional components demanded of this sector, see Carty's forthcoming book on Caribbean domestic workers in New York City and Toronto.

12. A "long face" is commonly used in the South African context to mean a sad, depressed or dissatisfied facial expression.

13. Similarly, during an interview with an organization representing employers' interests in the context of changing legislation around domestic work, the organization's Director shared that the contracts they sold to employers had built-in provisions for dealing with these negative "attitudes," such as "sulking," in a way that would sanction legal disciplinary action and ultimately dismissal if necessary.

14. This additional expectation indicates another level at which the institutionalized nature of domestic work frees the state from its responsibility to care for the aging population.

15. This forced testing is easily made possible because of the patriarchal colonial culture of domestic service where employers often manage the health care of their employees.

16. This context applies predominantly to full-time live-in domestic workers. Women who work part-time in several different homes are generally not provided healthcare by any of their employers, another distinct disadvantage of the associated (albeit rationed) benefits as this sector moves towards more casual labor.

17. *Char* is a common term used for a part-time domestic worker.

18. This description is drawn from a personal interview with Rita Edwards, Director, Women on Farms Project, February 2001.

19. This reality complicated the methodological approach in this study because assuring that worker participants were protected from psychological harm most often meant instituting strict measures such that employers did not know my identity, association, or relationship to their workers—which added a notable complexity to access and further contact with workers.

20. Romance emerged as a frequent conversational linkage between physical space and workers' dominated circumstances. In particularly powerful acts of agency, some worker informants shared how they confronted the inequality between their own living conditions and that of their female employer in the household by stating, "You have a husband, I also need a boyfriend." Closely related, employers talked about their strong resistance to the "problems" encountered when "maids want to bring their boyfriends around." This emergent romance theme embodies the interrelationship between social power and physical space within the domestic work institution.

21. *Skollie* is a local term for criminal with a particular reference to black and coloured men.
22. This reference is based upon data from my own research of the national democratic transformation process in Cape Town in 1995.
23. This entailed cleaning the brass features throughout a six bedroom house.
24. In this sense, it appeared that employers were responding in ways that would fit their perception of what I would like to hear as the interviewer. In other ways, however, I believe employers reflected particularly positive working relationships to mediate the tension of the asymmetrical power relations central to the job. In this sense, participants were likely verbalizing their own idealized perceptions of their position as an employer.
25. Helen Moffett offered this valuable assessment in a public discussion of this research at the African Gender Institute, University of Cape Town, July 2001.
26. Notably, the one participant who shared that her husband was primarily responsible for most of the housework was one of the youngest in the sample (age 28) and could be categorized as part of the "new black elite" status.
27. In only one worker case were these roles reversed such that the worker constructed the man in the household as "a fighter" and the woman as "far better than him." In the remaining 11 interviews, either both employers were perceived as 'bad' or 'good' overall.
28. Although there are important linkages to be drawn here, I did not collect interview data that directly addressed domestic workers' experience of oppression in their own families. These central connections between institutional oppression in family and work contexts is an important area for future research.

NOTES TO CHAPTER FIVE

1. Although throughout the apartheid era, a minority of the coloured and Indian populations were able to hire domestic workers predominantly on a part-time basis because of their economic privilege.
2. This perception emerged in a personal interview with a 65-year-old labor union activist, based upon his own experience as a coloured person living in Cape Town his entire life.
3. This expression means in the rural areas of Africa, often associated with living either a very primitive underdeveloped lifestyle or amongst game indigenous to the African continent such as lions, elephants and buffalo.
4. In the Western Cape, whites represent 21 percent of the population with the Indian/Asian sector at only 1 percent (Statistics South Africa 2000).
5. This statement came from my interview with Lena, the oldest coloured worker in the sample.
6. Similarly, this connection to Cape Town has been identified as one of the few "cohesive elements" that connects the broader coloured community

and fostered a colloquial reference to the "Cape Coloured" throughout the nation.

7. This is also the community that served as my home for six months of the field research for this study. Because of the particular and highly regional influence of the Muslim coloured community and the dominant discourse about its relationship to domestic work, I wanted to enhance my understanding of the intricate nuances of this particular historical ethnic group in the broader context of social relationships in South Africa.

8. This colloquial expression combines English and Afrikaans as is common to the Western Cape. This expression carries a similar meaning to "that's it" in U.S. English. *Klaar* literally means "finished" in English and its usage in this expression, particularly the repetition of two words with the same meaning, symbolizes the bi-cultural/lingual nature of the "Cape Coloured" community.

9. The assumption about vegetarianism may be related to a more accurate association with the Hindu religious practices of many sectors of the Indian population in South Africa.

10. Notably, one of the two Muslim employers who recognized internal patterns of abuse was also a leading national gender advocate. One Indian employer was interviewed, however she did not make similar references.

11. This discourse presented not only methodological challenges about how to handle overt prejudices within participant groups, but particularly core ethical concerns about how to describe and publicize this sentiment in the context of a global post-September 11th, 2001 culture that is grounded in "othering" Muslim communities through the world.

12. In the context of researching how these local networks operated within coloured communities, I interviewed the following experts: government officials, Department of Labour representatives, national union leaders, women's rights advocates, human rights NGO leaders, feminist academics, two domestic work agency owners, two national news reporters, two employers who utilized agencies and five domestic workers who had been solicited through such agencies. Methodologically, it is important to note that access to employers and workers within these agency structures was extremely difficult because of the substantial isolation, social barriers among employers, and personal safety, as discussed in Chapter Three.

13. Nomhle made this call based upon a gender advocate contact she was given when this office was involved in revealing the abuses of the Spic n' Span agency on the national news and subsequently visited the location where Nomhle was waiting for placement.

14. The Spic n' Span agency was publicized in the national media, therefore its name has not been protected; however, the owner's name is a pseudonym.

15. This creates another serious gender concern because police workers remain predominantly male in South Africa. Thus, in order to access structures of support, particularly for sensitive issues such as these, women must "tell their story" as victims to male gatekeepers who then make decisions on their behalf.

16. A "hiding" is an expression connoting a forceful spanking often associated with the use of a belt or sharp instrument.

17. These standards were outlined by Department of Labour officials at this coalition meeting, June, 2001.

18. When the Spic n' Span agency was publicized extensively by the news media in April, 2001, Department of Labour officials visited its location with the press. During an on-site interview with these officials, I was told that they had not visited the agencies in a few years, indicating that staff resources were minimal and domestic work agencies remained the most difficult to monitor, even though it was a widely acknowledged "problematic area."

19. At the time of this study, black private sector wealth is concentrated in the Johannesburg area, as participants described.

20. This term was used by one informant based upon her analysis of negative views held about both "new employers" and black governance.

21. In this instance, MP participants resided in Cape Town (Legislative Branch) while parliament was in operation, yet other central governance cities include Johannesburg (Executive Branch) and Bloemfontein (Judicial Branch).

22. This contradiction, particularly among women MPs was established in Britton's (1999) research and gender theories on the interlocking nature of family and public structures of oppression (see Chow et al. 1996).

23. I am thankful to Hannah Britton for sharing her further insights about these parliamentary narratives and our ongoing discussions about the central connection between our studies throughout the fieldwork and analysis phases of this research.

NOTES TO CHAPTER SIX

1. The has become a popularized slogan among unionized domestic workers, developed by the South African Domestic Service and Allied Workers' Union. This message was first instituted at the launch of the organization in 2000.

2. The Centre for Conflict Mediation and Arbitration (CCMA) is a national structure established in the new democracy to hear unfair labor dismissal disputes. Domestic workers are now able to bring cases to the CCMA, with variant perceptions of its effectiveness. The CCMA structural process has been analyzed as a critical measure of social transformation and domestic workers' access to rights (see Lazar 2000).

3. This pattern is similarly identified throughout all other global contexts of domestic work, where unionization remains extremely difficult for the same reasons. Contexts where workers migrate outside of their country of origin for domestic work employment present even further challenges to unionization because of heightened elements of isolation, access to rights, and separation from other workers.

4. An extensive historical review of domestic work unionization is beyond the scope of this book and addressed in other sources. For early historical

accounts, see *A Talent for Tomorrow: Life Stories of South African Servants* (Gordon 1985) and "DWEP, How it Grows, A Kind of History" (Gordon 1981). For later accounts of unionization, see Cock's (1980, 1989) *Maids and Madams.* Central to her research on domestic work unionization with a post-apartheid analysis, see Lazar's (2000), "'Ain't I a Citizen?': A Study of Consciousness, Resistance and Identity in the Domestic Service Sector in Post-Apartheid South Africa."

5. As the history of South Africa reveals, religious organizing embodied a protected space where state structures withheld scrutiny and dominance. Collective resistance, therefore, was sometimes masked through religious organization. Similarly, churches themselves served as central spaces for organizing to end apartheid. For an in-depth account of the role of religion and the South African liberation struggle, see Tutu's (1994) *The Rainbow People of God* and Cassidy's (1995) *A Witness Forever.* For analysis of the importance of religious values in national reconciliation processes, see Tutu (1999) and Krog (1998).

6. This shift in orientation toward more political causes resulted in the fracture of leadership. The organization's original founders subsequently split such that the Domestic Workers' Association remained committed to education and ongoing work with employers, while SADWU adopted a heightened political agenda in alignment with the national liberation struggle.

7. These central factors are based upon recollections from former SADWU leaders in my interviews and a more extensive description of this organizational collapse by Roseline Nyman (1997) in "The Death of SADWU: the Birth of New Organisation?"

8. I am grateful to Eunice Tholakele Dhladhla, Myrtle Witbooi, Hester Stephens and Maggie Shongwe for their detailed depiction of this complex history of union organization over the past 32 years.

9. This speech is quoted from Johanna Kehler's documentation of the launch of SADSAWU. See the National Association of Democratic Lawyers' *Rights Now;* Issue 7, June 2000 for a further account of this event.

10. In my research as I established relationships with workers, I was often strongly dissuaded from mentioning any affiliation with the national union when I called workers or met their employers by chance for fear of immediate termination.

11. This narrative exemplifies *quitting* as an act of agency, as found in the research of Rollins (1985), Thornton Dill (1994), and Romero (1992).

12. Also importantly, at the inception of my work with SADSAWU, no membership database had been established. All records of membership were kept in paper files in various offices. This speaks to both the lack of organizational resources and the overextension of leaders, such that record maintenance was impossible because of the overwhelming nature of daily operations. As part of my action research agenda, I found resources to establish a computer database of all membership records for the ongoing development and security of enrollment information. Ironically, the

national government requested enrollment figures from SADSAWU soon
after this database was created.

13. Given these challenges, part of my emergent role with SADSAWU often
involved supporting membership campaigning through the contribution of
transportation for leaders as they recruited women in both township and
work locations. I normally joined leaders who passed out meeting notices
at "taxi ranks" and township markets, adding a complexity to social location issues in the research process itself, particularly noticeable when black
women workers accepted union flyers written in isiXhosa from a white
woman not immediately identified as a foreigner.

14. This sentiment was repeated by several leaders of SADSAWU and domestic
workers.

15. Furthermore, it is already taken up as a central component of South
Africa's political transition by Lazar (2000) and from an internal policy-
oriented legislative perspective by Kehler (2000).

16. This statement was shared by a human rights activist in this study.

17. This was the English name used by this employer to refer to his domestic
worker, rather than her African name.

18. The *1991 Manpower Commission Report on Domestic Workers* investi-
gated the possible measures to protect this sector in five specific areas of
legislation including the Unemployment Insurance Act No. 30 of 1966, The
Labour Relations Act No. 28 of 1956, The Basic Conditions of Employment Act No. 3 of 1983, The Wage Act No. 5 of 1957 and the Workmen's
Compensation Act No. 30 of 1941. This commission endorsed that in principle, domestic workers be included in each of these acts, yet called for further specific investigations into applied mechanisms. In 1993, a
government consultancy group completed thorough investigation (known
as the *Limbrick Report*) into the same case and outlined several specific
means for domestic workers' inclusion in both the Unemployment Insurance Act and the Workmen's Compensation Act. The third investigation
completed by the new governance, *the 1996 Task Team Report* on domestic workers and the UIF, fully endorsed the recommendations of the *Limbrick Report* and clearly validated the inclusion of domestic workers in
unemployment insurance benefits. Yet until the recent SADSAWU campaign, regardless of the extensive amount of resources devoted to this
research, no action has taken place to implement any of the recommendations of these three reports.

19. In the South African parliamentary legislative process, policy drafts are initially written by the relevant government Department. The Portfolio Committee (composed of members of parliament) then reviews and critiques the
bill, holds public hearings to gather input from civil society and eventually
approves the final legislative document along with the National President
and the Minister of Labour.

20. This overarching organizational objective statement is drawn from the an
internal document at the Commission on Gender Equality (2001).

21. I borrowed this title from Shamin Meer's *Women Speak: Reflections on our Struggle 1982–1997,* a collection of accounts of women's agency across several sectors captured in SPEAK, one of the first activist magazines dedicated to "making sure that the struggles of our time would result in liberation for women too" (1998:7).

NOTES TO CHAPTER SEVEN

1. For example, a complete review of *Agenda* the South African feminist journal over the past 20 years revealed only three articles that addressed this sector. Furthermore, the *South African Labour Bulletin,* the key academic labor journal, only included domestic work twice in 1982, after Jacklyn Cock's publication of *Maids and Madams.*
2. This statement emerged from public performance (March 2001) by South Africa's most popular political satire stand-up comedian "Evita."
3. This description was used by a domestic worker regarding her relationship with the children of the family with which she had worked for 20 years.

Bibliography

Acker, Joan, Kate Barry, and Johanna Esseveld. 1983. "Objectivity and Truth: Problems in Doing Feminist Research." in *Beyond Methodology: Feminist Scholarship as Lived Research*, edited by M. M. Forrow and J. Cook. Bloomington: Indiana University Press.

Adler, Glenn and Eddie Webster. 2000. *Trade Unions and Democratization in South Africa, 1985–1997*. New York: St. Martin's Press.

African National Congress. 1994. *The Reconstruction and Development Programme: A Policy Framework*. Johanneburg: Umanyano Publications.

Agar, Michael. 1996. *The Professional Stranger: An Informal Introduction to Ethnography*. San Diego: Academic Press.

Agosin, Marjorie. 2001. *Women, Gender and Human Rights: A Global Perspective*. New Brunswick: Rutgers University Press.

Alexander, M. Jacqui and Chandra Talpade Mohanty. 1997. *Feminist Genealogies, Colonial Legacies, Democratic Futures*. New York: Routledge.

Alrecht, Lisa and Rose M. Brewer. 1990. *Bridges of Power: Women's Multicultural Alliances*. Philadelphia: New Society Publishers.

Andersen, Margaret. 1997. *Thinking about Women: Sociological Perspectives on Sex and Gender*. Boston: Allyn & Bacon.

Andersen, Margaret L. and Patricia Hill Collins. 1992. *Race, Class, and Gender: an Anthology*. Belmont: Wadsworth.

Anderson, Bridget. 2000. *Doing the Dirty Work? The Global Politics of Domestic Labour*. London: Zed Books.

Bailey, Carol. 1996. *A Guide to Field Research*. Thousand Oaks: Pine Forge Press.

Bakan, Abigail and Daiva Stasiulis. 1997. *Not One in the Family: Foreign Domestic Workers in Canada*. Toronto: University of Toronto Press.

Bannerji, Himani, Linda Carty, Kari Dehli, Susan Heald, and Kate McKenna. 1991. *Unsettling Relations: the University as a Site of Feminist Struggles*. Boston: South End Press.

Barrett, Jane, Aneene Dawber, Barbara Klugman, Ingrid Obery, Jennifer Shindler, and Joanne Yawitch. 1985. *South African Women on the Move*. London: Zed Books.

Berg, Bruce Lawrence. 1998. *Qualitative Research Methods for the Social Sciences.* Boston: Allyn and Bacon.

Berger, Iris. 1992. "Gender and Working-Class History: South Africa in Comparative Perspective." in *Expanding the Boundaries of Women's History: Essays on Women in the Third World,* edited by C. Johnson-Odim and M. Strobel. Bloomington: Indiana University Press.

Bernstein, Hilda. 1975. *For Their Triumph & For Their Tears: Women in Apartheid South Africa.* London: International Defence Aid Fund for Southern Africa.

Bhorat, Haroon. 2000. "Are Wage Adjustments an Effective Mechanism for Poverty Alleviation?: Some Simulations for Domestic and Farm Workers." University of Cape Town Development and Policy Research Unit, Cape Town.

Biggs, Michael. 1997. *Getting into GEAR: Government and the Economy.* Cape Town: University of Cape Town Press.

Blee, Kathleen M. and France Winddance Twine. 2001. *Feminism and Antiracism: International Struggles for Justice.* New York: New York University Press.

Boddington, Erica. 1984. "Domestic Service: A Process of Incorporation into Wage Labour and Subordination." University of Cape Town, Cape Town.

Boddington, Erica. 1984. "Domestic Service in Cape Town 1891–1946: An Analysis of Census Reports." in *Economic Development and Racial Domination.* Bellville, South Africa: University of the Western Cape.

———. 1983. "Domestic Service: Changing Relations of Class Domination 1841–1948." Social Science, University of Cape Town, Cape Town.

Bonacich, Edna. 2000. "Intense Challenges, Tentative Possibilities: Organizing Immigrant Garment Workers in Los Angeles." in *Organizing Immigrants: The Challenge for Unions in Contemporary California.* Ithaca: Cornell University Press.

Bond, Patrick. 2000. *Elite Transtion: From Apartheid to Neoliberalism in South Africa.* London: Pluto Press.

Bottomley, Gill, Marie De Lepervanche, and Jeannie Martin. 1991. *Intersextions.* Sydney: Allen & Unwin.

Bozzoli, Belinda with Mmantho Nkotsoe. 1991. *Women of Phokeng: Consciousness, Life Strategy, and Migrancy in South Africa 1900–1983.* Johannesburg: Ravan Press.

Brecher, Jeremy, Tim Costello, and Brendan Smith. 2000. *Globalization from Below: the Power of Solidarity.* Cambridge: South End Press.

Britton, Hannah. 2005. *From Resistance to Governance: Women in South African Parliament.* Urbana: University of Illinois Press.

———. 1999. "From Resistance to Governance: South African Women's Transformation of Parliament." Political Science, Syracuse University, Syracuse.

Brown, Karen and Andre Reynolds. 1994. "New Laws for Domestic Workers." *Agenda:* 76–80.

Budlender, Debbie. 1986. "Domestic Workers." Community Agency for Social Enquiry, Cape Town.

Bunster, Ximena and Elsa Chaney. 1989. *Sellers & Servants: Working Women in Lima, Peru.* Granby: Bergin & Garvey Publishers.

Burawoy, Michael. 1991. *Ethnography Unbound: Power and Resistance in the Modern Metropolis*. Berkeley: University of California Press.

Cannon, Lynn Weber, Elizabeth Higginbotham, and Marianne Leung. 1983. "Race and Class Bias in Qualitative Research on Women." in *Beyond Methodology: Feminist Scholarship as Lived Research,* edited by J. Acker, K. Barry, and J. Esseveld. Bloomington: Indiana University Press.

Carter, Jason. 2002. *Power Lines: Two Years on South Africa's Borders*. Washington, D.C.: National Geographic Society.

Carty, Linda. 1996. "Seeing through the Eyes of Difference: A Reflection on Three Research Journies." in *Feminism and Social Change: Bridging Theory and Practice,* edited by H. Gottfriend. Urbana: University of Illinois Press.

Cassidy, Michael. 1995. *A Witness For Ever: The Dawning of Democracy in South Africa*. London: Hodder & Stoughton.

Chafetz, Janet. 1991. "The Gender Division of Labor and the Reproduction of Female Disadvantage." in *Gender, Family, and Economy: The Triple Overlap,* edited by R. L. Blumberg. Newbury Park: Sage Publications.

Chaney, Elsa M. and Mary Garcia Castro. 1989. *Muchachas No More: Household Workers in Latin America and the Caribbean*. Philadelphia: Temple University Press.

Chang, Grace. 2000. *Disposable Domestics: Immigrant Women Workers in the Global Economy*. Cambridge: South End Press.

Chang, Kimberly and L.H.M. Ling. 2002. "Globalization and its Intimate Other: Filipina Domestic Workers in Hong Kong." in *Gender and Global Restructuring: Sightings, Sites and Resistances,* edited by M. Marchand and A. S. Runyan. 2000. London: Routledge.

Chin, Christine. 1998. *In Service and Servitude: Foreign Female Domestic Workers and the Malaysian "Modernity" Project*. New York: Columbia University Press.

Chodorow, Nancy. 1978. *The Reproduction of Mothering: Psychoanalysis and the Sociology of Gender*. Berkeley: University of California Press.

Chow, Esther Ngan-Ling and Catherine White Berheide. 1994. *Women, the Family, and Policy: A Global Perspective*. Albany: State University of New York Press.

Chow, Esther Ngan-Ling, Doris Wilkinson, and Maxine Baca Zinn. 1996. *Race, Class, and Gender: Common Bonds, Different Voices*. Thousand Oaks: Sage.

Christian, Rucksana. 1998. "An Investigation of Domestic Workers' Perceptions into the Effects of Employer Involvement on Parenting and Parental Autonomy." Clinical Psychology, University of Cape Town, Cape Town.

Clarke, Duncan. 1974. *Domestic Workers in Rhodesia: The Economics of Masters and Servants*. Gwelo: Mambo Press.

Cock, Jackyln. 1980. *Maids & Madams: A Study in the Politics of Exploitation*. Johannesburg: Raven Press.

———. 1988. "Trapped Workers: The Case of Domestic Servants in South Africa." in *Patriarchy and Class: African Women in the Home and the Workforce,* edited by S. S. Parpart. Boulder & London: Westview Press.

———. 1989. *Maids & Madams: Domestic Workers under Apartheid*. London: The Women's Press Limited.

———. 1990. "Guilt, Fear and Other Difficulties in Researching Domestic Relations." in *Truth be in the Field*, edited by P. Hugo. Pretoria: University of South Africa.

———. 1993. *Women and War in South Africa*. Cleveland: The Pilgrim Press.

Cock, Jackyln and Alison Bernstein. 2002. *Melting Pots and Rainbow Nations: Conversations about Difference in the United States and South Africa*. Chicago: University of Illinois Press.

Cock, Jacklyn and Laurie Nathan Eds. 1989. *War and Society: The Militarisation of South Africa*. Cape Town: David Philip.

Collins, Patricia Hill. 1990. *Black Feminist Thought*. Boston: Unwin Hyman.

———. 1991. "Learning from the Outsider Within." in *Beyond Methodology: Feminist Scholarship as Lived Research*, edited by M. M. Fonow and J. A. Cook. Bloomington: Indiana University Press.

———. 1998. "It's All in the Family: Intersections of Gender, Race, and Nation." *Hypatia* 13.

Commission on Gender Equality. 2001. "Vision, Mission and Values Statement." South Africa.

Congress of South African Trade Unions. 1997. "September Commission Report." Johannesburg.

Cowan, Ruth Schwartz. 1987. "Women's Work, Housework, and History: The Historical Roots of Inequality in Work-Force Participation." in *Families and Work*, edited by N. Gerstel and H. E. Gross. Philadelphia: Temple University Press.

Dangor, Zebeda, Lee Ann Hoff, and Renae Scott. 1998. "Woman Abuse in South Africa: An Exploratory Study." *Violence against Women* 4:125–152.

Delphy, Christine and Diana Leonard. 1992. *Familiar Exploitation: a New Analysis of Marriage in Contemporary Western Societies*. Cambridge: Polity Press.

Delphy, Christine. 1993. "Rethinking Sex and Gender." *Women's Studies International Forum* 16:1–9.

Delport, Elize. 1992. "The Legal Position of Domestic Workers: a Comparative Perspective." *Comparative and International Law of Southern Africa* 25:181–201.

Denzin, Norman K, and Yvonna S. Lincoln eds. 1994. *Handbook of Qualitative Research*. Thousand Oaks: Sage.

Department of Labour, South Africa. 2001. "Towards Determining Minimum Wages and Conditions of Employment for Domestic Workers." Pretoria.

DeVault, Marjorie. 1999. *Liberating Method: Feminism and Social Research*. Philadelphia: Temple University Press.

———. 1991. *Feeding the Family: the Social Organization of Caring as Gendered Work*. Chicago: University of Chicago Press.

Dickerson, Bette. 1995. *African American Single Mothers: Understanding their Lives and Families*. Thousand Oaks: Sage Publications.

Dill, Bonnie Thornton. 1994. *Across the Boundaries of Race and Class: An Exploration of Work and Family among Black Female Domestic Servants*. New York: Garland Publishing.

Divinski, Randy; Hubbard, Amy; Kendrick, Richard J. Jr.; and Noll, Jane. 1994. "Social Change as Applied Social Science: Obstacles to Integrating the Roles of Activist and Academic." *Peace and Change* 19.

Donaldson, Shawn Riva. 1997. "'Our Women Keep Our Skies from Falling'": Women's Networks and Survival Imperatives in Tshunyane, South Africa." in *African Feminism: The Politics of Survival in Sub-Saharan Africa,* edited by G. Mikell. Philadelphia: University of Pennsylvania Press.

Eales, Kathy. 1988. "'Jezebels,' Good Girls and Mine Married Quarters: Johannesburg, 1912." University of Witwatersrand, Johannesburg.

Edwards, Rita. 1997. "New Women's Movement: Pap and Bread are Not Enough." *Agenda*:33–36.

Emerson, Robert M., Rachel I. Fretz, and Linda L. Shaw. 1995. *Writing Ethnographic Fieldnotes.* Chicago: University of Chicago Press.

England, Paula. 1993. *Theory on Gender/Feminism on Theory.* New York: Aldine de Gruyter.

Enloe, Cynthia. 1989. *Bananas, Beaches and Bases: Making Feminist Sense of International Politics.* Berkeley: University of California Press.

———. 1993. *The Morning After: Sexual Politics at the End of the Cold War.* Berkeley: University of California Press.

Fanon, Frantz. 1963. *The Wretched of the Earth.* New York: Grove Press.

Farr, Vanessa. 2002. "'A Chanting Foreign and Familiar': The Production and Publishing of Women's Collective Life Writing in South Africa." Women's Studies, York University, Toronto.

Fine, Michelle. 1994. "Working the Hyphens: Reinventing Self and Other in Qualitative Research." in *Handbook of Qualitative Research,* edited by N. K. Denzin and Y. S. Lincoln. Thousand Oaks: Sage.

Flint, Susan. 1988. "The Protection of Domestic Workers in South Africa: A Comparative Study." *Industrial Law Journal* 9:1–15.

Fonow, Mary and Judith Cook. 1991. *Beyond Methodology: Feminist Scholarship as Lived Research.* Bloomington: Indiana University Press.

Forcey, Linda Rennie. 1991. "Women as Peacemakers: Contested Terrain for Feminist Peace Studies." *Peace and Change* 16.

Fortune, Linda. 1996. *The House on Tyne Street: Childhood Memories of District Six.* Cape Town: Kwela Books.

Fouche, Fidela. 1994. "Overcoming the Sisterhood Myth." *Transformation*:79–95.

Francis, S., H. Dugmore, and Rico. 1994. *Madam & Eve: Free at Last.* Cape Town: Penguin Books.

Freire, Paulo. 1970. *Pedagogy of the Oppressed.* New York: Herder & Herder.

Friedman, Michelle. 1999. "Effecting Equality: Translating Commitment into Policy and Practice." *Agenda*:1–19.

Fuller, Abigail. 1992. "Toward an Emancipatory Methodology for Peace Research." *Peace and Change* 17.

Gaitskell, Deborah. 1982. "Housewives, Maids or Mothers: Some Contradictions of Domesticity for Christian Women in Johannesburg." Centre for African Studies, Cape Town.

———. 1986. "Girls' Education in South Africa: Domesticity or Domestic Service?" Pp. 1–10 in *Conference on Culture and Consciousness in Southern Africa*. University of Manchester.

Gaitskell, Deborah, Judy Kimble, Moira Maconachie, and Elaine Unterhalter. 1984. "Class, Race and Gender: Domestic Workers in South Africa." *Review of African Political Economy* 27:86–108.

Galvan, Roshan. 2000. "The Live-In Domestic Workers' Experience of Occupational Engagement." Occupational Therapy, University of Cape Town, Cape Town.

Gamburd, Michele Ruth. 2000. *The Kitchen Spoon's Handle: Transnationalism and Sri Lanka's Migrant Housemaids*. Ithaca: Cornell University Press.

Gerson, Kathleen. 1993. *No Man's Land: Men's Changing Commitments to Family and Work*. New York: Basic Books.

Gibson-Graham, J.K. 1996. *The End of Capitalism (As We Knew It): A Feminist Critique of Political Economy*. Cambridge: Blackwell Publishers.

Gill, Lesley. 1994. *Precarious Dependencies: Gender, Class, and Domestic Service in Bolivia*. New York: Columbia University Press.

Glaser, Barney and Anselm Strauss. 1967. *The Discovery of Grounded Theory: Strategies for Qualitative Research*. Chicago: Aldine.

Glenn, Evelyn Nakano. 1987. *Issei, Nisei, War Bride: Three Generations of Japanese American Women in Domestic Service*. Philadelphia: Temple University Press.

———. 1994. "Social Construction of Mothering: A Thematic Overview." in *Mothering: Ideology, Experience and Agency*, edited by E. N. Glenn. New York: Routledge.

Gobodo-Madikizela, Pumla. 2003. *A Human Being Died That Night: A South African Story of Forgiveness*. Boston: Houghton Mifflin.

Goldbatt, Beth and Sheila Meintjes. 1998. "South African Women Demand the Truth." in *What Women Do in Wartime*, edited by M. Turshen and C. Twagiramariya. London: Zed Books.

Goodman, David. 1999. *Fault Lines: Journeys into the New South Africa*. Berkeley: University of California Press.

Goodwin, June. 1984. "They Want to be Called 'Madam.'" in *Cry Amandla! South African Women and the Question of Power*. New York & London: Africana Publishing Company.

Gordon, Sue. 1981. "DWEP-How it Grows: a Kind of History." Domestic Workers' and Employers' Project, Johannesburg.

———. 1985. *A Talent for Tomorrow: Life Stories of South African Servants*. Johannesburg: Raven Press.

Gorelick, Sherry. 1996. "Contradictions of Feminist Methodology." in *Feminism and Social Change: Bridging Theory and Practice*, edited by H. Gottfried. Urbana: University of Illinois Press.

Gottfried, Heidi. 1996. *Feminism and Social Change: Bridging Theory and Practice*. Urbana: University of Illinois Press.

Grossett, Matthew. 1994. *Your Domestic Worker and the Law*. Pretoria: Southern Book Publishers.

Grossman, Jonathon. 2001. "Submission on the Protection of Domestic Workers' Rights." edited by T. C. R. Committee. Cape Town.

Hansen, Karen Tranberg. 1989. *Distant Companions: Servants and Employers in Zambia, 1900–1985.* Ithaca: Cornell University Press.

Harlow, Barbara. 2001. "'What Was She Doing There?' Women as 'Legitimate Targets.'" in *Women, Gender and Human Rights: A Global Perspective*, edited by M. Agosin. New Brunswick: Rutgers University Press.

Hartmann, Betsy. 1993. "A Womb of One's Own." in *Feminist Frameworks: Alternative Theoretical Accounts of the Relation Between Women and Men*, edited by A. M. Jaggar and P. Rothenberg. New York: McGraw Hill.

Hartmann, Heidi. 1976. "Capitalism, Patriarchy and Job Segregation by Sex." *Signs* 1:137–168.

Hassim, Shireen. 1991. "Gender, Social Location and Feminist Politics in South Africa." *Transformation*: 65–82.

———. 1999. "From Presence to Power: Women's Citizenship in a New Democracy." *Agenda.*

Held, David, Anthony McGrew, David Goldbatt, and Jonathon Perraton. 1999. *Global Transformations : Politics, Economics and Culture.* Cambridge: Polity Press.

Heyzer, Noeleen, Geertje Lycklama à Nijeholt, and Nedra Weerakoon. 1994. *The Trade in Domestic Workers: Causes, Mechanisms and Consequences of International Migration.* London: Zed Books.

Heyzer, Noeleen and Vivienne Wee. 1994. "Domestic Workers in Transient Overseas Employment: Who Benefits, Who Profits?" in *The Trade in Domestic Workers: Causes, Mechanisms and Consequences of International Migration.* London: Zed Books.

Higginbotham, Elizabeth and Mary Romero. 1997. *Women and Work: Exploring Race, Ethnicity, and Class.* Thousand Oaks: Sage.

Higginbotham, Elizabeth and Lynn Weber. 1992. "Moving Up with Kin and Community: Upward Social Mobility for Black and White Women." *Gender and Society* 6:416–440.

Hirschmann, David. 1998. "Civil Society in South Africa: Learning from Gender Themes." *World Development* 26.

Hochschild, Arlie. 1983. *The Managed Heart.* Berkeley: University of California Press.

Hondagneu-Sotelo, Pierette. 1996. "Immigrant Women and Paid Domestic Work: Research, Theory, and Activism." in *Feminism and Social Change: Bridging Theory and Practice*, edited by H. Gottfried. Urbana: University of Illinois Press.

———. 1998. "Latina Immigrant Women and Paid Domestic Work: Upgrading the Occupation." in *Community Activism and Feminist Politics: Organizing Across Race, Class and Gender*, edited by N. Naples. New York: Routledge.

———. 2001. *Doméstica: Immigrant Workers Cleaning and Caring in the Shadows of Affluence.* Berkeley: University of California Press.

hooks, bell. 1989. *Talking Back: Thinking Feminist, Thinking Black.* Boston: South End Press.

———. 1994. *Teaching to Transgress: Education as the Practice of Freedom.* New York: Routledge.

hooks, bell. 2000. *Where We Stand: Class Matters.* New York: Routledge.

Hsiung, Ping-Chun. 1996. "Between Bosses and Workers: The Dilemma of a Keen Observer and a Vocal Feminist." in *Feminist Dilemmas in Fieldwork,* edited by D. Wolf. Boulder: Westview Press.

James, Wilmot, Daria Caliguire, and Kerry Cullinan. 1996. "Now That We are Free: Coloured Communities in a Democratic South Africa." Cape Town: IDASA.

Jones, Jacqueline. 1985. *Labor of Love, Labor of Sorrow: Black Women, Work, and the Family from Slavery to Present.* New York: Random House.

Karides, Marina. 2002. "Linking Local Efforts with Global Struggle: Trinidad's National Union of Domestic Employees." in *Women's Activism and Globalization: Linking Local Struggles and Transnational Politics,* edited by N. Naples and M. Desai. New York: Routledge.

Katzman, David. 1978. *Seven Days a Week: Women and Domestic Service in Industrializing America.* Chicago: University of Chicago Press.

Kedijang, Mmatshilo. 1990. "The Best Kept Secret: Violence against Domestic Workers." University of the Witwatersrand.

Kehler, Johanna. 2000. "Women Will Not be Free Until Domestic Workers are Free!" *Rights Now:*10–11.

———. 2000. "Maternity Benefits: Do They Reflect the Needs of Working Women? Evaluating the Adequacy and Accessiblity of Maternity Benefits in Various Sectors of Employment." National Association of Democratic Lawyers, Human Rights Research and Advocacy Project, Cape Town.

Kemp, Amanda, Nozizwe Madlala, Asha Moodley, and Elaine Salo. 1995. "The Dawn of a New Day: Redefining South African Feminism." in *The Challenge of Local Feminism: Women's Movement in a Global Perspective,* edited by A. Basu. Boulder: Westview Press.

Khan, Zohra. 2002. "A Local Solution for a Local Problem." in *Mail & Guardian.* Johannesburg.

King, Elizabeth M. and Anne M. Hill. 1993. *Women's Education in Developing Countries: Barriers, Benefits, and Policies.* Baltimore: The Johns Hopkins University Press.

Kleinman, Sherryl and Martha Copp. 1993. *Emotions and Fieldwork.* Newbury Park: Sage Publications.

Korton, David. 1995. *When Corporations Rule the World.* West Hartford: Kumarian Press.

Krog, Antjie. 1998. *Country of my Skull: Guilt, Sorrow, and the Limits of Forgiveness in the New South Africa.* New York: Three Rivers Press.

Lan, Pei-Chia. 2000. "Global Divisions, Local Identities: Filipina Migrant Domestic Workers and Taiwanese Employers." Sociology, Northwestern University, Evanston.

Lazar, Eva. 2000. "'Ain't I a Citizen?': A Study of Consciousness, Resistance and Identity in the Domestic Service Sector in Post-Apartheid South Africa." Political Studies, Queen's University, Kingston.

Lengermann, Patricia and Jill Niebrugge. 1996. "Contemporary Feminist Theory." in *Modern Sociological Theory*, edited by G. Ritzer. New York: McGraw-Hill.

Lerner, Gerda. 1972. "Black Women in White American: A Documentary History." New York: Vintage Books.

Liebenberg, Sandra. 1995. *The Constitution of South Africa from a Gender Perspective*. Claremont: Community Law Centre.

Ling, L.H.M. 2002. *Postcolonial International Relations: Conquest and Desire between Asia and the West*. London: Palgrave.

Lofland, John and Lyn H. Lofland. 1995. *Analyzing Social Settings : a Guide to Qualitative Observation and Analysis*. Belmont: Wadsworth.

Lorber, Judith. 1994. *Paradoxes of Gender*. New Haven: Yale University Press.

———. 1998. *Gender Inequality: Feminist Theories and Politics*. Los Angeles: Roxbury Publishing Company.

Lorde, Audre. 1984. *Sister Outsider: Essays and Speeches by Audre Lorde*. Freedom: The Crossing Press.

Lycklama à Nijeholt, Geertje. 1994. "The Changing International Division of Labour and Domestic Workers: A Macro Overview." in *The Trade in Domestic Workers: Causes, Mechanisms and Consequences of International Migration*. London: Zed Books.

Magona, Sindiwe. 1991. *Living, Loving, and Lying Awake at Night*. Claremont, South Africa: David Philip.

———. 1999. *Mother to Mother*. Boston: Beacon Press.

Mainardi, Pat. 1993. "The Politics of Housework." in *Feminist Frameworks: Alternative Theoretical Accounts of the Relation Between Women and Men*, edited by A. Jaggar and P. S. Rothenberg. New York: McGraw Hill.

Makosana, Isobel Zola. 1989. "The Working Conditions of African Domestic Workers in Cape Town in the 1980s." Sociology, University of Cape Town, Cape Town.

Mama, Amina. 1995. *Beyond the Masks: Race, Gender and Subjectivity*. London: Routledge.

Mandela, Nelson. 1994. *Long Walk to Freedom*. Boston: Little, Brown and Company.

Mange, Nondwe. 1995. "Experiences African Domestic Workers Undergo as a Result of Sending Their Children to Predominantly White Schools." Clinical Psychology, University of Cape Town, Cape Town.

Marchand, Marianne H. and Anne Sisson Runyan. 2000. *Gender and Global Restructuring: Sightings, Sites and Resistances*. London: Routledge.

Mathabane, Mark. 1994. *African Women, Three Generations*. New York: Harper Collins.

Mathews, Shanaaz, Naeemah Abrahams, Lorna J. Martin, Lisa Vetten, Lize van der Merwe, and Rachel Jewkes. "'Every Six Hours a Woman Is Killed by Her Intimate Partner': A National Study of Female Homicide in South Africa." Tygerberg: Medical Research Council, 2004.

Meagher, Gabrielle. 2000. "A Struggle for Recognition: Work Life Reform in the Domestic Services Industry." *Economic and Industrial Democracy* 21:9–37.

McCord, Margaret. 1997. *The Calling of Katie Makanya: Abridged Edition*. Cape Town: David Philip.

Meer, Shamim Ed. 1998. *Women Speak: Reflections on our Struggles 1982–1997.* Cape Town: Kwela Books.

Mendez, Jennifer Bickham. 1998. "Of Mops and Maids: Contradictions and Continuities in Bureaucratized Domestic Work." *Social Problems* 45:114–135.

Michelman, Cherry. 1975. *The Black Sash of South Africa: A Case of Liberalism.* Cape Town: Oxford University Press.

Mies, Maria. 1994. "'Gender' and Global Capitalism." in *Capitalism and Development,* edited by L. Skair. London: Routledge.

Mikell, Gwendolyn. 1997. *African Feminism: The Politics of Survival in Sub-Saharan Africa.* Philadelphia: University of Pennsylvania Press.

Milkman, Ruth. 2000. *Organizing Immigrants: The Challenge for Unions in Contemporary California.* Ithaca: Cornell University Press.

Milkman, Ruth, Ellen Reese, and Benita Roth. 1998. "The Macrosociology of Paid Domestic Labor." *Work and Occupations* 25:483–510.

Mohanty, Chandra Talpade. 1991. "Under Western Eyes: Feminist Scholarship and the Colonial Discourses." in *Third World Women and the Politics of Feminism,* edited by Ann Russo and Chandra Talpade Mohanty, Lourdes Torres. Bloomington: Indiana University Press.

Mohanty, Chandra Talpade, Ann Russo, and Lourdes Torres. 1991. *Third World Women and the Politics of Feminism.* Bloomington: Indiana University Press.

Moller, Valerie. 1984. "Images of Retirement: An Exploratory Study Among Black Domestic and Service Workers." Centre for Applied Social Sciences, Natal.

Morrell, Robert. 2001. *Changing Men in Southern Africa.* Pietermaritzburg: University of Natal Press.

Moser, Caroline. 1998. "Violence and Poverty in South Africa: Its Impact on Household Relations and Social Capital as Assets of the Poor." The World Bank, Washington.

———., Caroline O.N. 1993. *Gender Planning and Development: Theory, Practice, and Training.* New York: Routledge.

Mwiya, Charity. 1995. "Domestic Workers: Partners in Housekeeping or Simply Exploited?" *Namibia Review* 4:27–29.

Naples, Nancy. 1998. *Community Activism and Feminist Politics: Organizing Across Race, Class and Gender.* New York: Routledge.

Naples, Nancy and Manisha Desai. 2002. *Women's Activism and Globalization: Linking Local Struggles and Transnational Politics.* New York: Routledge.

Needham, Anaradha Dingwaney. 1992. "At the Receiving End: Reading 'Third' World Texts in a 'First' World Context." in *Turning the Century: Feminist Theory in the 1990's,* edited by G. Carr. London: Bucknell University Press.

Neely, Barbara. 1992. *Blanche on the Lam.* New York: Penguin Books.

Non-European Affairs Department. 1962. "Your Bantu Servant and You: A Few Suggestions to Facilitate Happier Relations Between Employer and Employee." The Non-European Affairs Department, Johannesburg.

Ngqakayi, Nomsa. 1991. "Subjectivity in the 'Maid'/'Madam' Relationship and its Effects on the Occupational Child Care-Giving Functions of the Domestic Worker." Clinical Psychology, University of Cape Town, Cape Town.

Ntombi. 1987. *Thula Baba.* Johannesburg: Ravan Press.

Nuttall, Sarah and Carli Coetzee. 1998. *Negotiating the Past: The Making of Memory in South Africa.* Cape Town: Oxford University Press Southern Africa.

Nyman, Roseline. 1996. "An Organisational Challenge-The Unionisation of Domestic Workers." National Labour & Economic Development Institute, Johannesburg.

————. 1997. "The Death of SADWU: the Birth of a New Organisation?" *South African Labour Bulletin.*

Oakley, Ann. 1981. "Interviewing Women: A Contradiction in Terms." in *Doing Feminist Research,* edited by H. Roberts. London: Routledge.

Okihiro, Gary. 1994. "Is Yellow Black or White?" in *Margins and Mainstreams: Asians in American History and Culture,* edited by G. Okihiro. Seattle: University of Washington Press.

Olesen, Virginia. 1994. "Feminisms and Models of Qualitative Research." in *Handbook of Qualitative Research,* edited by N. Denzin and Y. Lincoln. Thousand Oaks: Sage Publications.

Orr, Liesl. 1998. "Maternity Benefits: Proposed Amendments to the UIF." National Labour & Economic Development Institute, Johannesburg.

Ostreng, Dorte. 1997. "Domestic Workers' Daily Lives in Post-Apartheid Namibia." The Namibian Economic Policy Research Unit, Windhoek.

Pape, John. 1993. "Still Serving the Tea: Domestic Workers in Zimbabwe 1980–90." *Journal of Southern African Studies* 19:387–404.

Parreñas, Rhacel Salazar. 2001. *Servants of Globalization: Women, Migration and Domestic Work.* Stanford: Stanford University Press.

Pateman, Carole. 1988. *The Sexual Contract.* Stanford: Stanford University Press.

Peterson, V. Spike and Anne Sisson Runyan. 1993. *Global Gender Issues.* Boulder: Westview Press.

Pettman, Jan Jindy. 1996. *Worlding Women: A Feminist International Politics.* London: Routledge.

Preston-Whyte, Eleanor. 1976. "Race Attitudes and Behaviour: The Case of Domestic Employment in White South African Homes." *African Studies* 35.

Ramphele, Mamphela. 1993. *A Bed Called Home: Life in the Migrant Labour Hostels of Cape Town.* Cape Town: David Philip.

Reason, Peter. 1994. "Three Approaches to Participative Inquiry." in *Handbook of Qualitative Research,* edited by N. Denzin and Y. Lincoln. Thousand Oaks: Sage.

Redding, Sean. 1996. "South African Women and Migration in Umtata, Transkei, 1880–1935." Pp. 31–46 in *Courtyards, Markets, City Streets,* edited by K. Sheldon. Boulder: Westview Press.

Rees, Rob. 1997. "'If the Union is Not There, Nothing is Caring for the Domestic Workers': the Feasibility of Advice Offices for Domestic Workers." National Labour & Economic Development Institute, Johannesburg.

Reid, Frances and Deborah Hoffmann. 2000. "Long Night's Journey into Day." New York.

Reinharz, Shulamit and Lynn Davidman. 1992. *Feminist Methods in Social Research.* New York: Oxford University Press.

Republic of South Africa. 1996. "The Constitution of the Republic of South Africa, 1996."

Rey, Cheryl De La. 1997. "South African Feminism, Race and Racism." *Agenda*:6–10.

Rive, Richard. 1986. *'Buckingham Palace' District Six*. Cape Town: David Philip.

Rollins, Judith. 1985. *Between Women: Domestics and Their Employers*. Philadelphia: Temple University Press.

Romero, Mary. 1992. *Maid in the U.S.A*. New York: Routledge.

Romero, Patricia. 1998. *Profiles in Diversity: Women in the New South Africa*. East Lansing: Michigan State University Press.

Rothchild, Jennifer. 2002. "Moving Beyond Enrollment Numbers: An In-Depth Look at Gender Inequality in Schools in Rural Nepal." Sociology, American University, Washington D.C.

Roux, Tessa le. 1995. "'We Have Families Too.' Live-in Domestics Talk about their Lives." Co-operative Research Programme on Marriage and Family Life, Human Sciences Research Council, Pretoria.

Rubin, Herbert J. and Irene S. Rubin. 1995. *Qualitative Interviewing: The Art of Hearing Data*. Thousand Oaks: Sage.

Rupert Taylor, Jackyln Cock, and Adam Habib. 1999. "Projecting Peace in Apartheid South Africa." *Peace and Change* 24.

Russell, Diana. 1989. *Lives of Courage: Women for a New South Africa*. New York: Basic Books.

Russell, Kathy, Midge Wilson, and Ronald Hall. 1992. *The Color Complex: The Politics of Skin Color among African Americans*. New York: Doubleday.

Salzinger, Leslie. 1991. "A Maid by Any Other Name: The Transformation of 'Dirty Work' by Central American Immigrants." in *Ethnography Unbound: Power and Resistance in the Modern Metropolis*, edited by M. Burawoy. Berkeley: University of California Press.

Samela, Monde Ishmael. 1993. "The Law and the Disadvantaged, Exploited Workers with Special Focus on South African Domestic Workers." Faculty of Law, The University of the Witwatersrand, Johannesburg.

Sanjek, Roger and Shellee Colen. 1990. "At Work in Homes: Household Workers in World Perspective." American Anthropological Association, Washington DC.

Sassen, Saskia. 1998. *Globalization and Its Discontents*. New York: The New Press.

Scott, Joan W. 1989. "Gender: A Useful Category of Historical Analysis." in *Coming to Terms: Feminism, Theory, Politics*, edited by E. Ward. New York: Routledge.

Seidman, Gay. 1999. "Gendered Citizenship: South Africa's Democratic Transition and the Construction of a Gendered State." *Gender and Society* 13:287–307.

Sharoni, Simona. 1995. *Gender and the Israeli-Palestinian Conflict: the Politics of Women's Resistance*, Syracuse: Syracuse University Press.

Sheper-Hughes, Nancy. 1992. *Death Without Weeping: The Violence of Everyday Life in Brazil*. Berkeley: University of California Press.

Siltanen, Janet. 1994. *Locating Gender: Occupational Segregation, Wages and Domestic Responsibilities*, Edited by U. Press. London.

Sjoberg, Gideon and Roger Nett. 1968. *A Methodology for Social Research*. Prospect Heights: Waveland Press.

Smith, Dorothy. 1987. *The Everyday World as Problematic: A Feminist Sociology.* Boston: Northeastern University Press.

Smith, Gail. 1996. "Madam and Eve: A Caricature of Black Women's Subjectivity?" *Agenda*:33–39.

Smut, Jan and Corle Grobler. 1998. *Domestic Labour Practice: A Guide to Fair Employment at Home.* Goodwood: Zebra Press.

Sparks, Allister. 1990. *The Mind of South Africa.* New York: Ballantine Books.

Sprague, Joey and Mary Zimmerman. 1993. "Overcoming Dualisms: A Feminist Agenda for Sociological Methodology." in *Theory on Gender/Feminism on Theory,* edited by P. England. New York: Aldine de Gruyter.

Stack, Carol. 1996. "Writing Ethnography: Feminist Critical Practice." in *Feminist Dilemmas in Fieldwork,* edited by D. Wolf. Boulder: Westview Press.

Statistics South Africa. 2000. "October Household Survey." South African National Government, Pretoria.

Staudt, Kathleen. 1990. *Women, International Development, and Politics.* Philadelphia: Temple University Press.

———. 1998. *Policy, Politics, and Gender: Women Gaining Ground.* West Hartford: Kumarian.

Stichter, Sharon and Jane Parpart. 1988. *Patriarchy and Class: African Women in the Home and the Workforce.* Boulder: Westview Press.

———. 1990. *Women, Employment, and the Family in International Division of Labor.* Philadelphia: Temple University Press.

Stivers, Camilla. 1993. "Reflections on the Role of Personal Narrative in Social Science." *Signs* 18:408–425.

Streek, F.E. 1974. "Domestic Servants: A Study of the Service Conditions of Domestic Servants Employed by Border Members of the Black Sash and South African Institute on Race Relations." The Black Sash, Cape Town.

Stromquist, Nelly. 1992. *Women and Education in Latin America: Knowledge, Power, and Change.* Boulder: Lynne Rienner Publishers.

Sweetman, Caroline Ed. 1998. *Gender and Migration.* Oxford: Oxfam.

Taylor, Viviene. 1997. "Economic Gender Injustice: the MACRO Picture." *Agenda.*

Thompson, Leonard. 1990. *A History of South Africa.* New Haven: Yale University Press.

Thorne, Barrie and Yalom, Marilyn. 1992. *Rethinking the Family: Some Feminist Questions.* Boston: Northeastern University Press.

Tinker, Irene. 1990. *Persistent Inequality: Women and World Development.* New York: Oxford University Press.

Tutu, Desmond. 1994. *The Rainbow People of God.* New York: Doubleday.

———. 1999. *No Future without Forgiveness.* New York: Doubleday.

van Niekerk, Philip and Barbara Ludman Eds. 1999. *A-Z of South African Politics 1999: The Essential Handbook.* London: Penguin Group.

van Onselen, Charles. 1982. *Studies in the Social and Economic History of the Witwatersrand 1886–1914.* Johannesburg: Raven Press.

Vetten, Lisa. "Man Shoots Wife: Intimate Femicide in Gauteng South Africa." Crime and Conflict 6 (1996): 1–4.

Vollenhoven, Sylvia 1993. "South Africa Through Women's Eyes." *Ms.,* pp. 11–15.

von Kotze, Astrid. 1991. "English is the Umbrella of all Languages in South Africa: Domestic Workers' Englishes." Pp. 1–18 in *Women & Gender in Southern Africa*, vol. Paper No. 31. University of Natal, Durban.

Walker, Cherryl. 1991. *Women and Resistance in South Africa*. Claremont: David Philip Publishers.

————. 1995. "Conceptualising Motherhood in Twentieth Century South Africa." *Journal of Southern African Studies* 21:417–437.

————. 1990. *Women and Gender in Southern Africa to 1945*. Cape Town: David Philip.

Walker, Liz, Graeme Reid and Morna Cornell. 2004. *Waiting to Happen: HIV/AIDS in South Africa*. Boulder: Lynne Reinner.

Ward, Kathryn. 1990. *Women Workers and Global Restructuring*. Ithaca: Cornell University Press.

Weaver, James H., Michael T. Rock, and Kenneth Kusterer. 1997. *Achieving Broad-Based Sustainable Development: Governance, Environment, and Growth with Equity*. West Hartford: Kumarian Press.

Weinert, Patricia. 1991. "Foreign Female Domestic Workers: Help Wanted!" International Labour Office, Geneva.

————. 1994. "Future Interventions and Action: An International Organization's Perspective." in *The Trade in Domestic Workers: Causes, Mechanisms and Consequences of International Migration*. London: Zed Books.

Wells, Julia. 1993. *We Now Demand! The History of Women's Resistance to Pass Laws in South Africa*. Johannesburg: Witwatersrand University Press.

West, Candace and Sarah Fenstermaker. 1995. "Doing Difference." *Gender and Society* 9:8–37.

West, Candace and Don Zimmerman. 1987. "Doing Gender." *Gender and Society* 1:125–151.

Western, John. 1996. *Outcast Cape Town*. Berkeley: University of California Press.

Whisson, Michael and William Weil. 1971. "Domestic Servants: A Microcosm of 'The Race Problem.'" South African Institute of Race Relations, Johannesburg.

Wolf, Diane. 1996. *Feminist Dilemmas in Fieldwork*. Boulder: Westview Press.

Wong, Sau-ling C. 1994. "Diverted Mothering: Representations of Caregivers of Color in the Age of 'Multiculturalism.'"in *Mothering: Ideology, Experience and Agency*, edited by Glenn. New York: Routledge.

Young, Gay and Bette Dickerson. 1994. *Color, Class, and Country: Experiences of Gender*. London: Zed Books.

Young, Gay, Vidyamali Samarasinghe and Kenneth C. Kusterer. 1993. *Women at the Center: Development Issues and Practices for the 1990s*. West Hartford: Kumarian Press.

Zinn, Maxine Baca and Bonnie Thornton Dill. 1994. *Women of Color in U.S. Society*. Philadelphia: Temple University Press.

Zulu, Lindiwe. 1988. "Role of Women in the Reconstruction and Development of the New Democratic South Africa." *Feminist Studies* 24:147–157.

Index

www.ingramcontent.com/pod-product-compliance
Ingram Content Group UK Ltd.
Pitfield, Milton Keynes, MK11 3LW, UK
UKHW020433010325
455677UK00029B/1135